FIFTY ACRES *and a* POODLE

also by Jeanne Marie Laskas

THE BALLOON LADY
AND OTHER PEOPLE I KNOW

WE REMEMBER

Women Born at the Turn of the Century Tell the
Stories of Their Lives in Words and Pictures

Bantam Books

NEW YORK   TORONTO   LONDON
SYDNEY   AUCKLAND

FIFTY ACRES

and a

POODLE

A Story of Love, Livestock, and
Finding Myself on a Farm

by

JEANNE MARIE

LASKAS

FIFTY ACRES AND A POODLE
A Story of Love, Livestock, and Finding Myself on a Farm

A Bantam Book / October 2000
All rights reserved.
Copyright © 2000 by Jeanne Marie Laskas.

Book design by Laurie Jewell.

Library of Congress Cataloging-in-Publication Data
Laskas, Jeanne Marie, 1958–
Fifty acres and a poodle : a story of love, livestock, and
finding myself on a farm /   Jeanne Marie Laskas.
p. cm.
ISBN 0-553-10904-9
1. Laskas, Jeanne Marie, 1958– 2. Journalists—United States—
Biography. I. Title: 50 acres and a poodle. II. Title.

PN4874.L258 A3 2000
070'.92—dc21
[B]   00-036075
Published simultaneously in the United States and Canada

Bantam Books are published by Bantam Books, a division of Random
House, Inc. Its trademark, consisting of the words "Bantam Books" and
the portrayal of a rooster, is Registered in U.S. Patent and Trademark
Office and in other countries. Marca Registrada. Bantam Books,
1540 Broadway, New York, New York 10036.

PRINTED IN THE UNITED STATES OF AMERICA
BVG   10   9   8   7   6   5   4   3   2   1

FOR MY HUSBAND

CONTENTS

*The names and other identifying details
of some characters have been changed to
protect individual privacy.*

The Farm Dream

IT'S HARD TO SAY HOW A DREAM FORMS. ESPECIALLY one like mine, which at first seemed so utterly random. It could have been a sailing-a-boat-to-Tahiti dream, a quit-your-job-and-hitchhike-to-Alaska dream. It was a fill-in-the-blank dream, born of an urge, not content. An urge for something new.

I was thirty-seven years old. I lived on Eleventh Street, the last house on the right, in South Side, a gentrified old mill town on the banks of the Monongahela River. I rented an office in downtown Pittsburgh, a fifteen-minute bike ride away, which is where I spent my days writing stories and magazine articles. I had a garden. I had a cat. I had a dog.

And I had a farm dream, a fantasy swirling around in my head about moving to the country. Where in the world was this coming from? That's what I wondered. It might have made sense if I was a miserable person, sick of my life. But I was not. I had a good life; it had taken me a long time to get it that way.

A farm dream would have made sense, I supposed, if I was at least the farm dream *type*. A person with some deep personal longing to churn butter. A person who had had city life forced upon her and now was determined to go be true to herself and live among the haystacks. A person who wore her hair in long braids, used Ivory soap, and liked to stencil her walls with pictures of little chickens and cows. A person who, at a minimum, had a compost pile in her yard where she diligently threw lawn clippings and coffee grounds and eggshells and earned the right to use the word *organic* a lot.

But I was not that person. I was not even sure what hay was, or why anyone would stack it. And if I composted anything, it was only by mistake.

In fact, I was a person who liked to go to the mall. I was a person who had no conflict about liking to go to the mall. I wore my hair in a bob courtesy of Christine, who also touched up my roots every six weeks with bleach. I used Clinique products on my skin, mainly because I was a sucker for the free stuff you could get during Clinique Bonus Time. I had a formidable tower of Stouffer's Lean Cuisine in my freezer, and I harbored little or no fear of processed foods. I believed very deeply in the power of air conditioning, microwave ovens, and very many things you plug in.

And I had a farm dream. The real source of this dream was something I was able to admit only after a lot of torment, as I'm sure plenty of people can understand: My farm dream had its roots in *Green Acres*. Which was never even my favorite show. But to grow up in the suburbs of the 1960s is to have TV, glorious TV, as your reference point. And I had always been one to side with Eddie Albert. "Farm livin' is the life for me." And I knew every single word of that song—"Darling, I love you, but give me Park Avenue"—and suddenly, after decades of not singing that song at all, I couldn't get it out of my head. *Ba-da-de-dum-dum. Dum dum.*

It's funny how the urge for something new can really be an urge for something old. Something you let go of a long time ago.

·   ·   ·

I GREW UP IN THE SUBURBS OF PHILADELPHIA, ON a happy little street called Lorraine Drive, which featured a row of tidy ranch houses and a most excellent hill for riding bikes down. That's what you saw when you looked out our front windows. You saw: suburbs. But if you looked out our back windows, you saw a farm. A working dairy farm that once encompassed the land that became Lorraine Drive. That farm was the backdrop of my life. It was the scenery I emerged from. That was the way I saw it, back when I understood everything.

I was eight years old. I understood exactly how the world was organized. Everyone was either this or that. Everyone was either Italian or Irish on their mother's side. Everyone was either Lithuanian or German on their father's side. Everyone was either Catholic or Jewish. Everyone was either a country-person or a city-person. And everyone had a willow tree in the backyard.

That these categories overlapped, or consisted of subcategories, or didn't exist for some people at all, was a realization that would continually shock me. For instance, I remember the horror I felt when I visited Laureen Hampton, my very first city-person friend. I went from window to window, room to room, pulling back curtains and pushing up blinds in a most desperate way.

"What is the matter, dear?" her mother finally said.

"Where is your willow tree?" I asked.

I did not understand her explanation, not for a long time. How could you not *have* a willow tree?

In my family, we were Irish and we were Lithuanian and we were Catholic and we had our willow tree, and some of us were country-people and some of us were city-people. No, you couldn't just be a "suburb-person." That didn't mean anything. The suburbs were an in-between place, a place you were headed into or out of, depending on your country/city orientation.

I was a country-person, at my core, in my heart. Because I loved that farm in our backyard. I would play there, in those woods and in those fields and in that barn. "Oh yeah, I live on a farm," I would practice saying, loving the sound of those words. When I was upset, I would run there. I would pack a pretend suitcase and move into a shed near the barn. A little red shed, with benches and rusted old tools and bags of chicken feed to prop your feet on. I would sit there. I would say, "Well, I'm home. Thank goodness I'm home." There was a secret passageway in that shed, a board that swung left that I could squeeze behind. I had my stuff there. I had my paints and my sketch pads. I had my secret scrolls. I had things I would say to God. I had stories I would write about my life on the farm back in the olden times when there weren't even any toilets.

Perhaps most important, there were animals on that farm. There were horses and goats and rabbits and all those cows. These were my friends. My most trusted friends. In the real world, I had siblings, John and Kristin, a distant twelve and eight years older than me, and Claire, just two years older. Claire was my friend, but she was better than me at every single solitary thing I ever tried to do, so this friendship had its limitations. This friendship so often was seen through a wall of tears. I was a painfully shy kid; I would cry if you tried to talk to me. The grade school teachers would send notes home to my mother saying, "We can't get her to stop crying." I remember how hard it was to make it through a whole day of school without at least once bursting into tears, how I would congratulate myself if I actually accomplished this. I would leap off the school bus and run past our house and head down to the farm, and I would tell the goats. I would tell the horses. I would say, "Hey everybody. I did it. *I did it!*" And I swear to you, those goats would applaud. The rabbits would run in circles with glee. The horses would sing.

I felt safe, like I belonged, on that farm.

One day at the farm, God spoke to me (which, to tell you the truth, I half-expected). He said, "Okay, I am getting a headache from all these prayers coming at me for me to take care of people. People, people, people. What about animals? Somebody down there has to take charge of praying for the animals." So He anointed me. It wasn't a big deal. It wasn't like He promised that I'd one day show up on a stained-glass window or anything. It was more like "Hey, could you do this for me? Could you pray for the animals?" And I said, "Sure." So I began looking out for the welfare of turtles. I became an activist for chipmunks. I had meetings with many neighborhood cats on a bill of rights I was drawing up on behalf of the sparrows. Eventually, I became a crusader for the eternal life of all animals. I would bless myself, in the name of the Father, and of the Son, and of the Holy Spirit, every time I saw a dead animal on the road. This act would send the animal to heaven. This was my job. I took pride in my job.

As I got older, I never quite abandoned my animal friends, but by the time I reached junior high school, I was done being shy. I turned into a loudmouth. I won the award for Wittiest and Peppiest in the Eighth Grade. I had discovered, rather late, that there was more to being a person than just having an inner life. And the outer life was a blast. I was having so much fun in the outer life that I stopped doing homework and played hooky and took up bowling and smoking and almost flunked out of school. My mother yanked me out of that school, dressed me in a uniform, and whisked me away for ninth grade to a private all-girls school. My siblings had all gone to private schools. I was my mother's public school experiment, which she saw as a failure.

I didn't see it that way. Leaving public school was the worst tragedy of my entire life.

I turned shy again. I couldn't quite figure out how to have both an inner and an outer life at the same time. The inner life was safe. The inner life, which I had come to equate with the farm, the animals. The farm, the animals, they brought me toward God. Toward prayer. Toward an urge to step back, really far back, and try to understand what was going on in the giant universe. It was strange how the inward would catapult you upward. I turned inward and inward and inward. By the time I got to college, I felt like the only place I really belonged was in my own head. I discovered writing. Thank God for writing. It was a way of getting all the inward stuff out. It was like installing a ventilation system, a link of fans blowing through ductwork, releasing emotion and thought to the wind.

Right after graduation, all my college friends got married, settled quickly. They had clear paths set out for them. They were turning into accountants and middle managers, and soon they all got Subarus.

I had no clear path set out for me. There was no set path toward becoming a writer. I moved to Pittsburgh to go to graduate school because I didn't know how else to become a writer.

Pittsburgh opened my eyes. In Pittsburgh I understood how someone could actually be a city-person. I loved the neighborhoods, each one its own minisociety tucked in the fold of a hill. I loved the huge sycamore trees. I loved all that energy, which wasn't the same as the collision of energy in the East Coast cities. In Pittsburgh there was collaboration, participation, a weird but contagious spirit of civic pride. I loved the way drivers wouldn't cut you off when you were trying to merge. In Pittsburgh they waved you in.

I took to exploring the city neighborhoods on my bike. One day I crossed the bridge into South Side, and I was hooked. That neighborhood captured me. I loved the abandoned steel mills, huge hunks of orange and brown, bent this way and that, stretched across the sky. I loved the hilly, cobblestone streets. Some of the streets were so steep, they weren't streets at all, but stairs with street signs. I loved the flower gardens in patches of dirt surrounded by little plastic picket fences. Tiny flower gardens adorned with aqua blue Virgin Mary statues and yellow and purple pinwheels. I loved the red brick houses that leaned into each other, held each other up. I loved the utter absence of straight lines. I loved the way everything was so old and hobbled and slumped.

Soon South Side became my every-Sunday destination. I would go to the Lithuanian church there and sit in the wooden pews darkened by generations of prayer, of hope, of thanksgiving, and I would bask in the whispers of my ancestors. One day I rode my bike down Eleventh Street and there it was: 136 South Eleventh Street. A house for sale. It was like a lot of them: It needed help. Paint, new windows, pointing, chimney repair; it needed a lot of help. I loved it instantly and without reservation. "This is where I belong," I thought, and soon I was a homeowner. Soon I was an urban dweller. I had a newsstand four blocks from my front door, a corner market, a dry cleaner, and shoe-repair place within skipping distance. I felt as though I had entered a storybook, and I half-expected to bump into Gepetto walking Pinocchio to school.

I was twenty-six years old. My house became my coming-of-age house: I renovated it, and it renovated me. I tore down walls, opened up rooms, added windows and skylights, spent three months chipping plaster, inch by inch, reclaiming a wobbly brick fireplace. In this house I learned how to handle a hammer, a socket wrench, a leaky faucet, a frozen downspout, a trowel, and many, many bags of tulip bulbs. In this house I acquired a community of friends who came to represent family: Beth up the street, B.K. and Kit over the hill, Nancy and Lynn and Sally across the river, and the rest of the so-called babes, a group of single women who en-courage one another's dreams.

It was while living in this house that I discovered my love of gardening. In that most wonderful garden. By the standards of the neighborhood, my yard was large: an L-shaped piece of land, about a quarter acre, going alongside of and behind the house, separating me from the Conrail tracks. Freight trains would come moseying by a few times a day. I came to depend on the clatter, and I liked waving to the engineers when I was out there pulling weeds. This was an urban garden, a little oasis, a miniparadise surrounded by the noise and smells and warmth of the city.

It was while living in this house that I became a writer. I wrote essays for *The Washington Post Magazine,* traveled the world and wrote about the collapse of the Soviet Union for *Life* magazine, and for *GQ* I traipsed around after a cult of very happy people who be-lieved they would live forever. I wrote about rock stars and preach-ers and old ladies I met, as well as plenty of characters I stumbled across in my own head.

But the writing life, it turned out, was difficult. It wasn't like you could sit down and flip a switch and crank on the ventilation system. Sometimes it didn't work, and sometimes you couldn't even find the switch. The truth about writing was, writing made you nuts. It made you adopt weird napping habits. It made you overly sensitive to smell, touch, sound. It made you eat nothing but popcorn for thirty straight days, and then nothing but carrots, and then nothing but Pop-Tarts. It made you not belong anywhere. And there were all those old college friends trading in their Subarus for even better Subarus, and they got condos and then one of them had a baby, so then they all did. Then they traded in their Subarus for minivans and started driving through the Taco Bell Drive-Thru. And South Side didn't even have a Taco Bell. I was way, way, way off track. Married? Kids? Minivan? Hell, I didn't even have a boyfriend. And as anyone knew, first you had to get a boyfriend to get the ball rolling. But really, the only men worth any time at all, I found, were men you met in foreign countries and brought home to show your friends. I brought home a man from Israel, a man from Switzerland, a man from Russia. Funny how these men revealed their tragic flaws only when on American soil. These were relationships that could exist only when I was in another place, another time zone, another planet.

I was terrified of love. Love was so chaotic. Love was freedom and passion and Wittiest and Peppiest in the Eighth Grade. Freedom and passion meant you flunked. Freedom and passion called for intervention. Freedom and passion meant you should wear a uniform. You should stop having freedom and passion and start having a structured environment. Well, you had a choice. You could have an intellectual and spiritual life. Or you could have love.

You couldn't have both. You couldn't have inward and outward. It was impossible. Inward was order and outward was chaos. How could you have both?

I chose order. Of course I did. We always choose the familiar path first.

And so this is how I ended up, at thirty-seven years old, at 136 South Eleventh Street, the last house on the right. I spent my days writing stories and magazine articles. I had a garden, a cat, a dog, a good life.

And I had a farm dream, a song I couldn't get out of my head.

FARM
SHOPPING

ONE

ONCE AGAIN THE AIR CONDITIONER IN MY LIVING room is not keeping up. I should have gotten the 12,000 BTU. Obviously. Because these are high ceilings. And this is a brick house. And it's so hot out. It's the hottest summer in Pittsburgh's history. Well, not really, but it might as well be. I feel like a loaf of bread. I feel like a bloated loaf of bread in an oven experiencing a teeny, tiny draft. A pathetic little breeze. My God, with all the clunking and clanking and complaining this air conditioner is doing, you'd think it would have more to offer.

And now look. Now Bob is coughing. Bob is my cat, sitting beside me here on the couch. Okay, why is he coughing? The vet did not say anything about coughing. *It's all right, Bob. Calm down. That's right. . . . God, you shed. One thing I am not going to miss is the way you shed. All right. You can stay here a few minutes longer. But stop staring at me. Go on, now. Go to sleep, Bob. You are a . . . cat. Take a nap, Bob.*

He's okay. And don't worry; I am not a person who has long, complicated cat conversations. Technically speaking, I am not a person who even talks to cats. Because I never say the words out loud. And Bob does not talk back with any cat telepathy or anything. We're normal, me and Bob. We are not the kind of overinvolved cat and cat owner you see in photographs on bags of premium cat food or anything. But we are a unit, me and Bob.

Bob is a big orange cat, like the one in that movie *Thomasina* I saw as a kid. I always wanted an orange cat like that. I remember nothing about that movie except it was about a girl who had a deep love for her cat. So of course I related.

But Bob isn't just a big cat. Bob is a *huge* cat, a very tall cat. I tell people Bob used to play basketball in college. Bob has a very luxuriant tail, a thick tail, a tail like a raccoon's with stripes that go in circles, orange, white, orange, white, all the way up. It's a tail I think any cat would be proud to own, although I cannot verify that. The only other particularly noteworthy feature about Bob is his love for me. Bob drools with pleasure at the very sight of me. I can't let Bob in my bedroom at night because he will sleep on my head and slobber with happiness. Sometimes when I'm holding Bob, he'll purr so loud, I'll feel it in my teeth. You'll never meet a happier cat than Bob when he is in the presence of me. And I'm not saying this to brag. In fact, I don't know why I'm saying this, except to say that sometimes saying is easier than feeling. And when it comes to Bob, I am sick of feeling.

A few months ago, the vet said, "I'm sorry." He said, "Bob is dying." That was a blow. Because for eleven years I've had Bob. For eleven years he's been Bob, the wonder cat, the mighty cat; he's been Ram-Bob, defender of my universe, or at least of my yard, or at least of my heart, and now he is dying. Only no, he doesn't look like he's dying. He doesn't look like some pathetic, skinny, scrawny, icky thing you are afraid to touch. He looks . . . normal. So it's hard to remember that he's dying. But the vet says he is. The vet says the combination of feline leukemia and feline HIV is a one-two punch, leaving Bob with a lethal disease and no immune system to fight it. In fact, the vet was awfully surprised that I got Bob past that last infection. But I did. Because I will do anything for Bob. Because for so long—for so, so long—it was just me and Bob. Bob was all the love I could handle, all the love I wanted. And I know, there is something pathetic about that, woman-with-cat. Young-writer-and-her-cat. There's something so cartoonish about that. You could imagine, if you were a lesser person, me and Bob appearing as a silhouette on a bath towel or something. But it really was the truth, my truth, for a decade. And yes, things are a lot more complicated now, but don't think there aren't days when I don't yearn for just me and Bob, the unit. And now Bob isn't allowed outside, because there is no way he could survive another fight, or even a little scratch—and really, I am doing fine. I am totally finished feeling anything about this. I am done being hysterical. I cried for three straight hours the day the test results came back, wailing like an infant in the living room, having no idea that Lois, the cleaning lady, was upstairs listening, or trying not to. That will cut into your crying. That will bring reality back into your gut with a thud. Hey, it's a cat. A stinkin' cat. And Lois, jeezus, the life that lady has lived? With all those divorces and kids being born and a few dying and those men beating her up? Lois has lived fourteen lives in the time that I've lived just a third of one puny one, just me and Bob. And I know, Bob is dying. That is a fact I do not need to be reminded of. In fact, I would really prefer if we not discuss it at all.

Well, then.

· Okay, then.

I just wish this air conditioner had more oomph. And to tell you the truth, I'm starting to hate the way I have to have an air conditioner going in order to concentrate, in order to sleep at night. In order to live. Isn't it a bad thing when you need a giant air compressor plugged into your life in order to survive?

That can't be right. That's not right.

I have to get out of here, away from this clunking noise. I should go farm shopping. This is my current favorite escape. No, I have no intention of actually buying a farm. Of course not. This is a fantasy, a game. Farm shopping is a reason to get away, a reason to sit in my swanky new VW Passat with the sunroof, leather seats, and most excellent air-cooling system.

All right, Bob. Excuse me. I am standing up. I am not going to waste this Sunday sitting around whining about . . . air. I'm going to go down and get a paper so I can look at the ads.

I open the back door, slam through the wall of heat, and step outside to find Betty, my dog, chewing a large piece of garden vegetation formerly known as a variegated hosta.

"Oh, come on, Betty. Give me that." Betty, a mutt of unknown lineage, has made a complete mess of this little garden. She dug up my petunias. She trampled my dahlias. Now she's working on my hosta, making little dog beds where the plants used to thrive. My poor hosta. My poor garden.

Ugh. I know; I'm starting to sound like Mr. Wilson on *Dennis the Menace* or something. What a whiner. Who cared about his stupid flowerbeds?

Actually, now that I look at her, Betty does have a Dennis the Menace quality to her. She is blond. She is short. She is a rascal. But in order to really capture the essence of Betty, you'd have to cross Dennis with, say, Ginger, on *Gilligan's Island*. Betty is a beauty queen. A mischievous, privileged princess.

"Betty, sit. No, girl, down!"

Betty is a jumper. I really have to work on that. Betty has dainty paws that belie their digging and scratching potential. Also, Betty has extremely beautiful brown eyes. Everyone comments on her eyes, which seem to be encircled in eyeliner. Some people say Betty would make a very convincing canine Marilyn Monroe. These are the people who haven't seen her with a variegated hosta in her mouth.

My poor garden. Before Betty came along, I had a perfect garden. Well, not perfect, but definitely on the way. Gardening is all about the urge for excellence, which a gardener never achieves, which is what keeps the gardener hooked. Gardening is about power. You are the master of that world. You are the king and the queen and the duke and the duchess. You see what happens when you can tame a four-by-six slice of nature, and pretty soon you think: What about ten by twenty? You tame, and you tame, and you tame, and all you can see is what is not tamed.

Taming the land. Controlling nature. This was one of the ways in which, up until recently, I was able to keep my life extremely tidy. Writing was another way. The control! The characters in your stories did what you wanted them to do. The people cried when you wanted them to. Love happened exactly on the page number set by you. I have only very recently discovered that this was all a ruse. I mean, I certainly was not conscious of the fact that my ordered life, my near-perfect garden, my carefully structured stories, my rigid exercise schedule, my first-this, then-that way of life was a protective cover for my heart.

Well, it doesn't matter. Because Betty came along and ruined everything. Well, not everything, but she might as well have. And, ouch. If she would just stop this jumping. "Down girl! Yee-ouch! Betty, you either have to cut your nails, or I am going to have to stop wearing shorts."

I got Betty two years ago at the pound. Just walked in one day and saw her, an eight-week-old puppy curled up in a cage. The tiniest little angel puppy. Who knows how it happens? I fell instantly and thoroughly in love. I plunked down thirty-five dollars and took her home and loved her. God, how I loved her. But not quite like I loved Bob. This was not a replacement love for Bob. This wasn't some kind of insurance-policy love. I don't know exactly what kind of love it was, but it was something entirely new.

I couldn't stop staring at her. For weeks I sat there staring at the little angel mutt with the bedroom eyes. Then one day, when we were in the garden and I was staring at her, she got stung by a bee. Her neck started to inflate. Inflate like a balloon. It kept getting bigger and bigger. Jeezus! Soon it was as big as a beefsteak tomato. It was the most horrifying sight. I stood there with my mouth dropped open, paralyzed.

To make matters worse, I had a date. Some handsome young

man I hardly knew was due to pick me up within the hour. I didn't want to have a date. I didn't like dates. I didn't even like the word. I would say "fig" instead. I would tell the babes, "I have a fig tonight," and they would say, "Good for you!" It was, they said, good to have a fig. A single woman in her thirties was supposed to have figs. Whatever.

So, panicked over the sight of my little love puppy with the neck the size of a beefsteak tomato, I called the guy. I told him there was an emergency, that I would have to cancel. I thought perhaps he would hear the terror in my voice and offer to help.

He said: "So what am I supposed to do with these theater tickets?"

I gave him another chance.

"My puppy," I said. "Something is terribly wrong. Her neck is blowing up!"

He said: "See, this is why I don't have pets. Pets are so much trouble—"

I hung up on him. Hung the hell up on him. Because now Betty was throwing up, over and over again, violently.

I called Alex. He was a friend, a friend for some six years. He's who I would always call. He said, "I'll be right there." He dropped everything and zoomed over and whisked me and Betty to the vet's. And Betty lost consciousness, right there in the waiting room. She suddenly and completely went limp. The nurse grabbed her, yelled something to another nurse, everybody started running. They stuck an IV in her little leg. I stood there horrified, seeing my puppy lying limp on a shiny silver table, looking most definitely dead.

Then . . . a twitch of her paw. Then another paw. Then . . . eyes. The most beautiful eyes! A resurrection! I was crying my eyes out, watching this, feeling this intersection of fear and longing and hope and elation. And Alex was there. Just as Alex was always there. And he was holding me. He was assuring me, he was saying, no, this isn't stupid. It's never stupid to cry your eyes out. Go ahead and wail. Alex was always there. And maybe deep down, I always knew. Maybe he knew, too. But neither of us had ever said it. It all seemed so impossible. He was so much older than me, fifteen years older than me. We'd come from such different worlds, traveled such different paths.

I stood in that vet's office for a long time, a blubbering fool.

Over a dog.

But not just over a dog. Because I was cracking up. Or maybe cracking open? Crack, crack, crack. The cracks were doing me good. It's only when you crack, really crack open, that someone else can get in.

I hugged Alex. I mean, he'd been holding me all along, but I turned to hug him, to thank him. We'd hugged a million times before. Hugged when we said hello. Hugged when we said good-bye. We were friends who hugged. But this hug was different. This hug was important. Not so much like two friends expressing affection as in the past, but more like two people holding on to an awakening and undeniable future.

A few months later, I confessed to Alex, and he confessed to me. Because it was the truth, and the truth was so simple. The truth is never hard to explain. Lies are what take up all your time.

NO, BETTY, YOU WAIT HERE. I'M JUST GOING TO RUN down and get a paper. You wait here for Alex, and I'll be right back." Alex is on his way over, due any minute. I'm sure he'll be up for a Sunday drive; any excuse to get out of this heat. I hope he has Marley with him, though, because then we can leave Marley in the yard with Betty, and we won't have to hurry home to do dog duties.

Marley is Alex's poodle.

Yes, well. A poodle. "My boyfriend has a poodle." Sometimes I have to practice saying that. Because I come from a long line of mutt people (i.e., people who laugh at poodle people). Alex is a psychologist. Yes, I know. I practice saying that, too: "My boyfriend is a shrink." When I am feeling very courageous, I practice saying the whole thing: "I am in love with a shrink with a pet poodle." Whew. You never know where you're going to end up.

Alex's grandfather and my grandfather were born in the same tiny town in Lithuania. Alex doesn't have any Irish in him, though. Not even a drop. His mother was pure Russian. As Jews living in Eastern Europe, his parents fled to America early in World War II, with a baby daughter, Marina, in their arms. When the war was over, they got word that nearly the entire rest of the family had perished in the Holocaust. Then they had Alex, their only son.

Alex has no willow tree in his yard. He is fifty-two years old, and he calls himself a city-person, but I don't think categories like that matter as much to him.

Okay, the newspaper. I'm heading down to Mabel's newsstand for the paper. I feel the heat bounce from the concrete as far up as my knees. It's amazing how concrete radiates heat. It's way too amazing. They should have more grass in South Side, that's what I'm thinking. Lately I find myself drawn to the weeds growing between the cracks of the concrete. Lately I find myself *identifying* with the weeds growing between the cracks. Misplaced, choking, *what am I doing here?*

A blast of exhaust from the neighbor's air conditioner hits me in the face. Oh, that was nice. Then the stench from an overflowing Dumpster, baking in the sun, slugs me in the throat. And now, oh, great. Now here comes that neighbor brat with the crazy eyes who, for lack of a more interesting hobby, has taken up terrorizing Helen, the old lady who lives across the street from me. Poor Helen. I love Helen. Helen has lived in that green insulbrick house her whole life. She was born in that house. She is eighty-five years old, and she is probably going to die in that house. She doesn't even have an air conditioner. I should buy her an air conditioner.

I don't want to die at 136 South Eleventh Street. I don't. If I wanted to die in my house, I would have put in hardwood floors. But I just put down carpeting. I said it's not worth investing a lot in a house you're not going to own for long. I never intended to live in this house for ten whole years.

And now here's the neighbor brat. Oh, God. I'm not even going to look at him. I'm going to avoid those crazy eyes. How can an eleven-year-old boy have so much power over my life? The other day he decided to play hockey with raw potatoes, using Helen's front stoop as his goal.

"Stop it!" I said out my front door. "What are you *doing*? Leave Helen alone."

He gave me a look. A look of "Well now, this is getting fun." And then he stuck his tongue out. He swirled his tongue up and down, wagging it, shutting his eyes, then opening them, shutting them, opening them, like that toy monkey banging cymbals. His point was well taken: "I am a lunatic."

So then he switched the direction of play. He started firing potatoes at my front stoop. I got even more upset. I stepped out of the house, dodging the potatoes, and went to speak to the boy's mother. I knocked on her door. The boy's teenage sister answered. She knew why I was there.

"He won't take his medication!" she said. "I can't get him to take it!" She told me her mother was at work. She said this had happened before. She said the only thing she knew to do when her brother was going bonkers like this was to lock herself in her room and hide. She suggested I do the same.

Great. Just great. I was being terrorized by an eleven-year-old boy, and all I could do was surrender. Hide. Shield myself from the wrath of his crazy potatoes. So this is what I did. I went back to my house and shut the door and tried to ignore, through dusk and into nightfall, the *thunk, thunk, thunk* on my front stoop.

And now here he is again. Whatever. What*ever*. I step off the sidewalk, onto the street, and move to the other side, over here where that nice-old-man violin maker lives.

Lately, in this city I love, this neighborhood I love, all I seem to notice are the intrusions. Hot air. Reeking garbage. Lunatic neighbors. Bus fumes. I am inventing filters. Air filters. Stinky-garbage filters. Lunatic-neighbor filters. Noxious-bus-fume filters. Sometimes I imagine plugging a big air conditioner into the front of my head so I can block the rest of the world right the hell out.

That's not right.

That can't be right.

Okay, a dollar fifty for the paper. Thank you very much. Yes, a bag. Thank you, Mabel.

As I approach the house, I can see Alex waiting in the yard. That's a breath of fresh air. He's sitting under the spruce tree, introducing the dogs to a Frisbee. He looks so cute sitting there. I know; men don't like being called cute. But he is cute. He's cute the way, say, a beagle is cute. Smart and tough and silly and innocent all at once. His body is strong and sturdy and densely muscled. He has an intelligent face, a professor type with pushed-back black hair, and little intellectual glasses surrounding the softest brown eyes.

He's trying to engage Marley in a game of Frisbee. Oh, this should be good. I stand by the fence and watch. He tosses the bright pink disk, sends it sailing toward the lilac bushes. "Go get it, boy!" he says. Marley looks in the direction of the Frisbee. Marley looks at Alex. Looks at him like "Why are you throwing stuff?"

Betty zooms in, a flash of yellow light. Betty zooms and grabs that Frisbee. "Well, good girl!" Alex says. "Now, bring it here! Bring it here!" Betty runs toward Alex. This is great! A dog that can actually fetch! Alex stands, eager to receive the prize. But Betty keeps on zooming, right past Alex, up the hill, where she sits in the shade and commences shredding the Frisbee.

"All right," Alex says, sighing. "Never mind."

"Hey!" I say.

"There you are!" he says, flashing an easy grin.

"I went to get a paper," I say.

"I was trying to teach the dogs to play Frisbee," he says.

"I saw."

"Yeah, well."

"Maybe it's too hot for fetching," I say. "It's so stinkin' hot."

"It's not the heat," he says.

"I know . . ."

"It's the *hu-man-ity*," he says.

"Right." But I don't laugh. Because he always says this. And we are past the part of a relationship where you have to laugh at every little thing. Plus, he's a repeater. He's one of those people who says the same joke over and over and over again, so pretty soon the humor is in the repetition, not the joke.

"Did I ever tell you about the time I walked into the store and saw a sign that said 'All men's pants half off'?" he'll say.

"Oh, please," I'll say, rather than suffer yet again through the punchline, which, for the record, is something about him pulling down his pants and taking one leg out because that's what the sign said to do. Something like that. It was worth a snicker or two—the first time.

"So what do you think about this patio?" he asks me, tracing his toe along the edge of the brick he has put down to indicate a border. "Do you think it should be bigger? Wider? But if it's too wide, it might look, I don't know, *bulky*."

I never actually asked him to build this patio; he just decided one day that I needed a patio. He loves building stuff.

"I think we shouldn't think about the patio today," I say. "It's too hot."

"Too hot to think about a patio?"

"Exactly."

"You want to go farm shopping, don't you," he says.

"Well, I did get the paper. And we haven't checked the ads in a while."

"But I really thought I could get this all dug out today," he says, slumping as if in defeat in a big white Adirondack chair under the tree.

"Ugh," I say, plopping myself into the other one. "If you work on the patio, then that means I'll work in the garden. Because I'll feel like a slug sitting here. And I can't bear to work in the garden. I can't. It's too hot. And look at this place. I don't even know where to begin."

"All right. You're right."

"What?"

"I said, 'You are right, dear.'"

"Thank you very much."

It is always worth stopping and noticing when one of us says the other is right. Because being right is something we each love. It's a routine we have.

"You were funnier than I was tonight," I'll say, after a night out with friends.

"No, *you* were funnier," he'll say.

"No, you were!"

It will go on like this, until one of us gives in. "You're right. I was funnier."

"What?"

"I said, '*You're right,* dear.'"

"Thank you very much."

Who plays which role in these conversations is completely interchangeable.

It's fun. Being in love is so much fun. I'm surprised how quickly I took to being a "girlfriend." To having a "boyfriend." I'm surprised how well I am still doing with continual loss of order. Which is not to say it isn't difficult for me sometimes. I don't get nearly as much work done as I once did. My rigid running and exercise regimen, my sleep schedule, my *patterns* are thoroughly disrupted. I eat things I would never eat before. I eat Miracle Whip and ham on Wonder Bread. So many of my rituals—doing my nails, say, every week while watching *60 Minutes*—are completely kerflooey.

But kerflooey feels surprisingly good. It feels wonderful to think: *It doesn't matter.* Life will go on if I don't get my nails filed by eight o'clock on Sunday nights, if I don't have the laundry folded by nine. And of course, kerflooey feels predictably horrible. My garden is the very symbol of kerflooey. I can't even bear to look at it.

Maybe this is how you integrate the inward and the outward life. Maybe you learn not to look too hard at either one. Or you learn to periodically shut your eyes.

Anyway, we're definitely not doing yard work today. Thank God. We're sitting here under the spruce tree reading the paper.

There aren't too many ads for farms for sale. Not that it matters. Because I really have no intention of buying a farm. Alex, a lifelong city dweller, has even less intention of buying a farm than I do. Plus, I mean, it's not like we live together or anything. He has his house in East Liberty, about ten minutes away, and I have my house here. Couples who don't live together don't go off and buy farms together.

Farm shopping is just something we do. Like all happy little lovebirds, we enjoy a day in the country. We'll pack a picnic, put our bikes in the car, and look at land. We might go to the Youghiogheny River, dip our toes in the water, and bike the trails. On the way home we'll stop at some cozy country inn and sip sherry by the fire.

And of course, we talk. We talk the dreamy talk all lovers talk. "Let's stay in this moment forever." And "Let's run away and live like this forever." And "Wouldn't it be wonderful to live in this place forever?"

It's the way you're supposed to talk. But that's all it's supposed to be: talk. I can't say for sure why the talk hasn't stayed talk for me, why it seems to have oozed inside me, like a slurp of water feeding a wilted zinnia. I can only say that lately I have been thinking "Hmm." And "Why not?" And "Surely it must be possible."

TWO

HEY, HERE'S ONE," I SAY TO ALEX, AS I CIRCLE
one of the ads. " 'Fifty acres. Four-bedroom farmhouse, new addition with skylights. Cedar barn circa 1880. Lily pond. Natural gas
well. Open house today between two and four.' "

"Where is it?" he says.

"You're not going to believe it," I say.

"Where?"

"Scenery Hill."

Scenery Hill is smack dab in the middle of our favorite farm-
shopping place—Washington County, about an hour south of
Pittsburgh. Suburban sprawl hasn't touched that area, so it's not like
you find yourself winding through farms that used to be farms but
now are developments with farmy-sounding names. We love the
hills of Washington County, rolling hills, brown and purple and
vermilion hills you expect to see depicted on canvases in museums.
We love the history of Washington County. An ancient village in
the area, known as Meadowcroft Rockshelter, dates back to at least
12,000 B.C. and is the earliest known human settlement in the

whole western hemisphere. There is something quite seductive about going to a place where time seems to have begun.

And we think it's interesting—no, amazing—that about five years ago, way before we fell in love, when we were both off leading entirely separate lives, different friends, different worlds, when we were just buddies sitting around one day over coffee, we talked about buying property in Washington County. We said, let's split it. I'd take it one weekend, for my friends. And he'd take it the next weekend, for his friends. We sometimes wonder if, even back then, five years ago, we knew that our time was beginning.

"Well?" I say. "Should we go?" I must have that look in my eye.

"It appears the train has already left the station," he says, folding up the comics.

The train leaving the station is what Alex says when he knows I've got my mind made up about something. Because when my mind gets made up, it is hard for me to unmake it. He loves this train metaphor. He'll tell my mother it's the secret to our relationship success. "When the train leaves the station, you can either go for the ride or get out of the way," he'll say. "But you cannot stop the train."

My mom will laugh. My mom loves the train metaphor, too.

I am not particularly impressed one way or the other by it.

"Should we take the dogs with us?" Alex says.

"You're kidding, right? Marley would be dead."

"True."

Marley gets carsick. Yes, well. ("I am dating a shrink with a carsick poodle.") Yes, well.

P ROBABLY I SHOULD PAUSE HERE AND EXPLAIN the history of this poodle. Because it is important to note that Alex did not *have* this poodle when I fell in love with him. I did not know that Alex was a poodle person when I fell in love with him. Repeat: *did not know.*

Alex dropped the poodle bomb about a year into the relationship. He said it so casually at dinner one night; he said it as if it were the most inconsequential piece of information for a man to impart to a woman.

"Poodles," he said. "Poodles are my favorite dogs."

"Poodles?" I said.

"Standard poodles," he said. "Not those little yappy things."

"Uh-huh." But it was a blow. I'm telling you it was a terrible, terrible blow. Because, as I said, I come from mutt people. People who believe in normal dogs. Dogs that slobber and scratch and sleep all day. Dogs that aren't suffering from doggie nerve disorders due to an estrangement from their own inner dogs. Dogs that don't spend their days posing for pastel artists who have set up easels at the mall.

Not that I am a stranger to poodle people. When I was nine, my very good friend Bridgette Davidson had poodles. She lived in a pink house. Her mother, who skated in the Ice Capades, had an entire room full of blond wigs, which we were not allowed to play with. Which we did. Which was why we got yelled at—which was when her mother's teeth fell out. Well, not *on the floor,* just all the way off the gums, which was horrifying enough.

Poodle people.

So imagine my shock when I discovered I was dating one.

"Poodles," he said. "Poodles are my favorite dogs."

"Poodles?" I said.

"Standard poodles," he said. "Not those little yappy things."

"Uh-huh."

"Standard poodles are really smart," he said. "Did you know they were used as sentry dogs in Vietnam?"

No, I did not. But even if poodles could pilot helicopters, I didn't think my stance on them was likely to budge. He got a little huffy with that remark.

We agreed to disagree on the poodle issue, while I secretly planned, as anyone would, to convert him.

A few months later: The Big Dilemma. I was at my friend Marge's. She runs a small kennel out of her home, where I leave

Betty when I go out of town. We were sitting in her kitchen next to that giant parrot thing she has in a cage that goes *raaaaaack raaaaaack* at Betty all the time. Betty is terrified of this bird. But she has learned to put up with it because putting up with it means she gets to be upstairs with Marge (who adores Betty) instead of downstairs in some cage with all those mangy mutts Marge cares for. (Betty doesn't actually know she is a mutt.)

Anyway, one day I was leaving Marge's and the bird was going *raaaaaack raaaaaack* and Marge happened to mention that she was looking to find a home for a nine-month-old puppy that some family had abandoned because their spoiled teenager had decided she wanted a horse instead. The dog, a purebred, had cost more than a thousand dollars but was now free to a good home.

"It's a standard poodle," Marge said, "a really great dog."

"A poodle?" I said. "Marge—you like poodles?"

"Oh, poodles are my favorite dogs," she said. "You know, standard poodles."

I was feeling surrounded.

The more Marge told me about the dog, the more I realized it was probably Alex's dream dog.

So what was a girlfriend to do? Tell the boyfriend and run the risk of becoming a woman who is dating a man with a . . . poodle? Or not tell him and live with the guilt?

I told him. "Let's just go see it," I said. "You may not like it."

"Okay, let's go see it," he said, but not with his Mister Enthusiasm voice. And this was because of what was going on in his life. For months Alex seemed to have been living in some sort of fog. Some days he seemed on the verge of getting swallowed up by it. Maybe it was a midlife thing. He had raised two children as a single dad. His daughter, Amy, had just graduated college, and his son, Peter, was about to. His house was empty. And his work, well, it didn't seem to give him quite the joy it once did. He was feeling burned out, as probably any shrink feels, after sitting in people's misery for twenty-five years.

I thought: *This guy needs a dog.*

So that's how it happened. That's how we came to show up at Marge's that day to look at a standard poodle that was free to a good home. Marge showed us into a room with a couch and a TV, and she went to get the dog. A few minutes later, into the room came charging sixty pounds of jet black curls. I had no idea poodles could be so big. The dog came bounding straight for Alex, as if he knew, somehow knew, that this guy was his ticket out of the place. He jumped into Alex's lap, threw his paws on his shoulders, and began licking his face, his glasses, his ears, his entire head.

Alex was laughing. Giggling like a little boy. Rolling over, a child again.

Then the dog came over and tackled me. "Whoa," I said, and "Oh" and "Ugh." The dog was all over me, bombarding me with love. I forgot, for an instant, that it even was a poodle. I forgot, for an instant, all about the pink house and the wigs and the Ice Capades and those teeth. Because this was not some nervous little froufrou thing. This was a handsome, slobbery, shaggy creature with real dog breath. My God! (You can go your whole life not knowing how closed-minded you are until the object of your own bigotry is suddenly in your lap.)

The hair on top of the dog's head was long and had grown over its eyes in dreadlocks.

"Marley," Alex said, naming the dog after Bob Marley.

Or so I thought. "Lively up yourself," I said.

Alex laughed. "No, not Bob," he said. "Jacob."

"Jacob Marley?"

"This dog is my warning to pay more attention to what is going on in my life," he said.

It must be hard going through life as a shrink.

The dog sat in the front seat of Alex's car on the ride home. I was in the back, watching. Marley sat there looking at Alex. Just sat there studying his new owner. And the drool coming out of that dog was, well, wow. A lot of drool. But Alex didn't care. It was his dog. *His dog!* I could see Alex's eyes in the mirror, the proudest, smiling eyes.

I felt so good playing a role in cheering this man up. It had been so long since I felt that good. Had I ever felt that good? I felt like doing something for Alex again. Again and again. I felt like a starving person ready to gorge. Gorge on the act of giving. I felt like going out and buying Alex a whole set of plates with poodles on them. I felt like buying him a tie with poodles on it. I felt like decorating his living room with pink-and-green poodle art.

But—my God! The drool coming out of that dog's mouth. Soon it was long strands of drool, like heavy rubber bands hanging from his mouth. This wasn't happiness drool. Oh, no. This was something else entirely.

Alex pulled up to his house, opened the car door. Marley got out, heaved, and threw up.

"Oh, dear," Alex said. "Oh, my . . ."

Well, that's basically how we got Marley. Something about that carsick poodle cemented our relationship. It may sound strange to say. But looking back, I can see that it did. Because already I was saying "we" got Marley. I was becoming a part of a "we." How I loved adding that word to my vocabulary. It had been so long since I was part of a "we." Was I ever really part of a "we"?

S₀, IT'S A FARM-SHOPPING DAY. ALEX IS AT THE wheel of the Passat, and we are headed down to Scenery Hill on a stinking hot Sunday in June. I am telling Alex my thoughts on processed air. On my need for filters. "That's what it is," I say. "That is the whole problem with living in the city. You can't be happy unless you block most of your awareness out."

"But . . . ," he says.

"Why live in a place where you are forced to shut down your senses?" I say. I am gesticulating wildly, for emphasis. "I want to be in a place that encourages my eyes to open wider! My ears to hear an increasingly wider range! My nose and taste buds to go to new extremes! Not a place where I am forced to go numb in order to stay sane."

"Well . . . ," he says. He's getting sick of hearing about the filters; I can tell. This filter bit is sort of my summer theme song.

"Okay, what exit am I supposed to take?" he says.

"Nine," I say. "Right here. Turn here."

The hills of Washington County are rolling toward us. That's how it seems. Like they're in motion and we're sitting still. Like we're at the movies and this is just a film about hills. Hills that remind me of the Cotswolds in England, or the countryside in southern Switzerland. Hills dotted with sheep, and tiny villages nestled in the folds. The road winds like a tunnel through the woods, and then suddenly there is a clearing, and here you are, high on a ridge, overlooking the world, but not overlooking the world like you overlook the world on a mountaintop, where everything is overwhelming, everything is vast, everything is *everything*. Here, the world you overlook is cozy, quaint.

"Wooo!" I say. And "Ahhh." It's a great adventure in sightseeing. We have been doing this for months, driving into gorgeous scenery, saying *Woo* and *Oooh* and *Ahhh*. We say we won't buy a farm unless it has one of these vistas. But I'm telling you, we have no intention of buying a farm at all. We have no intention, at least not a stated one, of even moving in together. Yes, we are in a serious relationship, but we are certainly not serious about these gorgeous hills. We have not even once discussed logistics: time, distance, money. Could either of us afford a place with a yard measured in acres? Could Alex afford the time commuting to the city? Would he want to? Could I take the isolation if I moved my office out to the boonies? We have not talked about these things because they would just get in the way.

Dreams are matters of the heart, things that pull you along as if they have hooked you someplace deep inside. Dreams should not become matters of the head until, well, you're ready for them to come true.

"Hey, this place is right near the Century Inn," I say, looking at the map. "I've been to the Century Inn. I had the pork chops. Did you know pork chops have been served continuously at the Century Inn since the late seventeen-hundreds?"

"God," he says. "Weren't they a little tough?"

"Ha," I say.

"Maybe we should have dinner at the Century Inn on the way home," he says.

"Yes, yes, yes," I say. "I love it down here. I love this road. Isn't this a great road?"

I once wrote about this road. One of my first assignments, years ago, was an article recommending day trips people could take from the city, and I wrote about the Century Inn, and about Route 40, the "National Pike" on which it sits. It started as a buffalo and Indian trail. General Braddock and Colonel Washington traveled it while fighting the French and Indian Wars. Then, when the birth of a new nation called for an actual "smooth way" to link the eastern seaboard to the western frontier, George Washington chose to pave the National Pike, making it the nation's first federally funded road, connecting Cumberland, Maryland, to the shores of the Mississippi. Thousands of families followed this route, eager to settle the fertile land of the Ohio Valley. Small towns sprang up. Blacksmith shops and livery stables and hundreds of roadside taverns. Whiskey, dancing, the thrill of a new life in the new frontier, it was all here. This onetime little buffalo trail became known as the "cement of the nation," celebrated in song, story, painting, and poetry.

The heyday ended in the 1850s, when, thanks to the invention of the steam locomotive, road travel began to fade. Soon the Pennsylvania Railroad reached Pittsburgh, and the B&O rolled into Wheeling.

"We hear no more the clanking hoof and the stagecoach rattling by," wrote a forgotten poet, "for the steamking ruleth the travel world, and the Old Pike's left to die."

So now, at least in this part of the country, the National Pike is a gentle highway wandering through small villages, including the aptly named Scenery Hill.

We pull into town. The Century Inn is definitely the biggest thing going. There is also a post office and a hardware store, plus a bunch of antique stores for city-folk like us who like to dress up in rugged Lands' End and Eddie Bauer clothing and take day trips and fantasize about country living.

"Turn right here," I say. "Spring Valley Road." Spring Valley Road drops along the base of the valley, so on either side green and brown and yellow fields stretch above us, like patches on a quilt. For a mile we drop down and then climb up hills that make your stomach sink, sink from the motion and sink from the spectacle. Corn stretches into the horizon in a swirling pattern. In front of the corn, cows. In front of the cows, sheep. There are four short donkeys grazing beside a mailbox.

"Here it is," I say to Alex. "Wilson Road. Turn here."

Wilson is a dirt road winding back into a forest, tunneling into a cathedral of trees. We see a driveway. We see a pond, blooming with lilies à la Monet. We see a barn, a crooked old thing baking in the sun à la Wyeth. I sit here hoping this is the place, thinking: This can't be the place, this is too beautiful, this is too perfect. I look down at the directions, up at the place, down at the directions, up again.

"Oh, my God," I say. "This is the place."

"This is the place?" he says.

"This is the place," I say. My eyes are bugged out. "Okay, don't get too excited," I tell Alex. "Do-not-show-any-enthusiasm-to-the-sellers," I say, stepping out of the car, at which point I do twirls like Marlo Thomas in *That Girl*. I look up and around and around and around. Then I breathe. I take the hugest gulp of fresh air.

A woman comes out of the house, approaches.

"Is this your place!" I say. "Jeeeeezus! It's like *heaven!*"

"Welcome," she says, extending her hand. "Fran," she says. She is tall, lanky, really tan. In her mid-forties, I'd guess. Kind of dainty for a farm wife, if you ask me. I was imagining someone a little more . . . substantial.

She tells a few things about the property. The barn was built in 1887 by the Amish, and it is an authentic Pennsylvania "bank barn," a two-story structure built into the side of the slope. She tells us that the huge gray bird with skinny legs standing in the pond is a resident blue heron, and it likes to eat frogs. The pond is fed by several freshwater springs, as well as a stream zigzagging beneath a towering chestnut grove, which we are welcome to go look at later.

Then she leads us toward the house, a funky house, a strange-looking excuse for a house. We enter through a door into the basement, where there are four other people who have also recently arrived. We can hear more people upstairs and soon realize that there are other tours ahead of ours. There must be ten families here to take a look. I had no idea there were so many other people sharing my dream. This panics me. I think these tourists should go back to the antique stores and buy some stuff and take it home, like they're supposed to.

We stay in the basement a long time looking at pipes and tanks and other basement things. Fran is awful proud of these pipes and tanks and is talking on and on about them, but I don't process a word she is saying. I am busy jumping for joy inside. It's hard to tell if it's this place, or if it's me. Do you feel wonderful inside because of your beautiful surroundings? Or do your surroundings look beautiful because you feel wonderful inside? Which comes first? It is becoming increasingly difficult for me to separate the inward from the outward.

Fran eventually leads us upstairs. The rooms meander, and as I meander along with them, I find that I am unusually forgiving. I am not usually this open to fake paneling and dropped ceilings with water stains and kitchens with indoor-outdoor carpeting. This is hardly the grand old stone farmhouse I had envisioned in my dream. But there is something lovable about this house, sort of like the South Side house. It's a lovable house in that it is a house that needs love.

We continue our tour and head toward the new addition that has been recently completed.

"This is my studio," Fran says. "Sorry if there's fumes."

She opens the door.

"Wow," I say.

"Whoa," Alex says.

The room is vast, with a cathedral ceiling, skylights, and giant windows opening to the pond and barn. It's the kind of room I dreamed about when I was a kid, sitting in that old shed. I would sit there and imagine my life as a grown-up: I would have a big renovated barn that would fit all my favorite things: my paints, a potter's wheel, a pinball machine, a pool table, my record collection, a basketball court, and maybe a stable of horses.

All of these things, and more, would fit in this room.

Fran paints huge canvases and says she needs a room this big. Her husband built the studio for her as a separate building. Then later he put on a small connecting addition, so the old farmhouse and the new giant room are one.

Which is to say the house makes absolutely no cohesive design sense—modern on one end, fake paneling and dropped ceilings on the other. The net effect is something like a chalet stuck onto a trailer. It's a house with an identity crisis, all right. "Poor house." This house needs me. This house needs Bob, snoozing on a windowsill. This house needs Betty prancing around, and a good dose of Marley entertainment, too.

"Okay, let's get out of here," I say to Alex. We'd really better get out of here. I didn't feel this way about any of the other farms we've seen on our farm-shopping trips. I did not feel even close to this way. We'd better get out of here.

"You want to take a hike out back?" Alex asks. As long as we're here. As long as we've got our brand-new Eddie Bauer trail-blazer hiking boots on. We don't even say good-bye to Fran; we slip out while she's talking to some architect who's saying the giant room sure would make a great drafting room, while his kid is saying no, Dad, this is a room for a big-screen TV, a huge TV, and an air hockey table.

The land behind the house features a most inviting path through the brush. Alex and I walk, and we don't say much. The silence is strange. Not strange between us, but strange because I am unaccustomed to country silence which is so very . . . thick.

"Can you imagine being able to take this walk every day?" Alex says finally.

"I would take it every single day," I say.

Our voices sound as if they are stabbing the silence, and still it doesn't puncture. And there are all kinds of colors around us. I mean, there is every shade of green, and tall blue wildflowers with yellow buttons, and jagged purple weeds, bright purple, the brightest purple, and then there is the silky sky and, in the distance, the velvety hills. All kinds of colors and all kinds of textures. And I feel, I just feel *oxygen* everywhere. Like, thank God. Thank God the concrete is gone. I am finally able to breathe.

We reach the crest of the hill and turn left, past a grove of craggy apple trees that look exactly like those trees in *The Wizard of Oz*. I'm half-expecting a branch to start moving, turn into an arm, and start pummeling us with apples. But no. These are friendlier trees. Or these trees are busy. These trees are buzzing with the loudest bees. These trees must have a headache from all these bees.

We walk along the ridge above the property and can see the house and barn below. It's a nice view. But not one of *those views*. Not one of the Scenery Hill views. Thank God. Because we said we would consider a property only if it had the view—not that we are considering buying property at all. But that *vista*. If you were going to live in Scenery Hill, you should definitely have the Scenery Hill view.

We continue following the trail, the farm down the hill to our left, the woods to our right. I wonder what's in the woods, wonder where the property line is. So we make our way into them, searching. It isn't a very deep woods, just some towering maples and a thin wall of very nasty briars to tiptoe through. Soon we reach the edge of the woods.

"Oh, my God," Alex says.

The woods open to a valley, a giant valley, a valley like you'd see on the label of a salad dressing or something. The view. The *vista*. Miles and miles of hills. The hills are round, like the beer bellies of men, belly after belly, huge, fat, laughing. The hills are dotted with tiny sheep, and lonely barns, and swirling crops.

"Uh-oh," Alex says.

The view.

"Okay, the first thing we would do," he says, stomping his foot, "is put a gazebo right here."

"Right here," I say.

I look at him. Does he mean this? I can't tell if he means this. I really want him to mean this, to be here, to be in this dream with me. This dream that suddenly feels like it is coming true. Is it coming true? I don't want it to come true without him.

Because it's here. Everything is here. The view is here. The privacy, here. The woods, here. The . . . air. This is it. This spot under my toes is where my future begins. I know this. I hope he's with me. I really hope he's with me.

Because the train has left the station. The train has left the station big-time. I know; usually I'm chugging toward something a little more manageable. A set of All-Clad professional cookware, say, factory fresh, with only a few dings, and for sale at half price. Or a huge clump of Christmas fern growing wild on the side of the road behind some blackberry bushes, which I know is the perfect fern for my garden back home if only I could—ouch—get to it.

"I love this place," I say, spinning around and around, my head tilted back, watching the lacy treetops twirl against the bluest sky.

"I love you," he says.

"I love you, too," I say, stopping my spin. "But you know, *I love this place.*"

He doesn't say anything.

"Let's move here," I say tentatively. Tenderly. Holding steady in the silence that follows.

"That's what I was thinking," he says.

"Really?"

"It was," he says.

"Me, too!"

And then we don't say anything, not for a long time. We just stand here looking at the view.

THREE

BETTY, COME!" I SHOUT, AS I DASH THROUGH THE South Side yard. "Come on, girly. We're going to visit your cousin Marley." Oh, jeez. Now what is her problem? Why is she just standing there on the deck? She loves to ride in the car. I'm late. I told Alex I would be over at his house an hour ago. "Betty, *come!*"

Betty?

Oh. The invisible fence. "Sorry about that," I say. I forgot to take her little receiver collar off. I had this fence put in only a few days ago, which means I now have an intricate pattern of wires running underneath the flowerbeds. Betty wears the receiver collar, which means if she goes in any of the beds, she gets . . . zapped. Poor Betty. Her first zap was, oh, my heart sank. She screeched her highest screech and went tearing inside. She hid under the coffee table. I could not get her out. She stayed there all day and all night, peering out with the saddest Marilyn Monroe eyes.

It worked, though. And I'm sure my flowers, at least those remaining, appreciate it. But then again, maybe it was stupid to get the fence, seeing as I'm probably about to buy an entire farm. But I had already ordered it, and, well, maybe I'll keep this house. I don't know. Do I sound confused? Do I sound nervous? Transitions. This is what it is to be in transition.

"Here you go, good girl," I say, removing her collar. I open the back door to drop the collar in the kitchen, where Bob is lying, stretched out in the sun. *Well, here goes nothing, Bob. Wish me luck. Alex and I are going to put a bid on the farm today. You're going to love it there, Bob. There are probably thousands of mice in that house. Or maybe not—maybe just one or two. All right. 'Bye, Bob. Be back in a few hours. Enjoy your cottage cheese.*

Betty and I hurry out to the car, and as I head over to East Liberty, I think about that moment on that hill just two weeks ago.

I love this place.

I love you.

Let's move here.

That's what I was thinking.

This is what we said. But this is not all we've said. Ever since, it seems, everything has gotten so complicated. What he wants, what I want, where he came from, where I came from, what baggage he's lugging, what baggage I'm lugging, what we better watch out for, what it would *mean* to do this or that, what the implications, the ramifications, the reverberations would likely be.

And the truth is never complicated.

We keep "processing," as shrinks like to say, the decision to buy the farm. He seems to need to process this a lot more than I do.

"We don't know the first thing about farming," he said last night at City Grill, a South Side restaurant with excellent grilled shrimp.

"True," I said. Then I said, "How hard can it be?" That was all the processing I was really able to do on that point.

"It's kind of far away," he said.

"True," I said, refilling his wineglass.

Scenery Hill is exactly forty miles from Pittsburgh. But it's straight highway, with only one traffic light to get through. I can make the trip in forty-five minutes without traffic, and sixty minutes with. Well, that's not bad at all.

"If this were New York or Atlanta, that would be an average commute," I said.

"True," he said.

"If this were Washington or Los Angeles, Scenery Hill would already be suburbs," I said. "The farms would be chopped up into plots with big houses and perfect landscaping out front. There would be the Scenery Hill Mall with a fourteen-screen movie theater, and there would be a Taco Bell Drive-Thru."

"True," he said. "But you love the Taco Bell Drive-Thru."

"True," I said.

We talked about money.

"Where in the hell are we going to get the money?" he said.

"Well, I don't know," I said.

We are, neither of us, moneybags. We are normal working stiffs. But hey, we have good credit ratings. And we both have some investments we can cash in. Not only that, but we both have equity in our houses. We'll pool our resources, make it work. Whatever. I mean, if I have learned anything about money in my thirty-seven years of living, it is to ignore it. It just scares you. Never, ever add numbers up. It just makes the numbers bigger and scarier. It's like, what if you had to add up all the meals you would need to eat to keep yourself alive for the next forty years? What if you had to sit and calculate all those sandwiches and all those potatoes and all those pounds of broccoli and all the trips to the store to buy all that stuff and all the time it would take to cook it? Well, you'd be too exhausted to eat. You'd be too worried about how in the world you were going to accumulate nineteen thousand pounds of chicken.

Same way with worry, in general. You take it one meal at a time, and you put your faith in digestion.

That's what I was telling him, bouncing my fork in the direction of his plate of shrimp.

"Okay," he said. "So where are we going to get the money?"

"I have no idea."

Then I changed the subject. Because, well, that's another way of dealing with money. And really, the bigger worry in this whole scheme is: We're going to buy a farm *together*? We have, neither of us, ever really expressed an interest in living together. He has his space, I have mine. Maybe that's weird. Maybe after two years of dating, we should be further along than this. We spend all our time together, either in his space or mine. And why mess with a good thing? We both know where this relationship is headed. We both know that, one way or the other, we'll grow old together. Don't we know that? I think we know that. All the babes seem to know that. My family seems to know that. His kids seem to know that. But no, we don't actually discuss the details of the growing-old-together arrangement. I can't say why Alex hasn't brought up marriage. For me, it's just that I am really not the bride type. I am just not. I don't know what type I am. I mean, I was thinking about this last night as we sat together. I was thinking maybe we could just elope so I wouldn't have to do the whole bride thing. I was having an entire let's-elope fantasy in my head. I had us there in Vegas, at some seedy purple altar with a fat guy in a pink tux as our witness and a big-haired lady with skinny legs playing the organ. I was going to tell Alex about this Vegas fantasy. I really was. I almost did. I almost said, "So, um—are we going to get married or something? Seeing as we're thinking of pooling our finances together and plunking down a bundle on fifty acres?" I was going to say, "How's the weather in Vegas this time of year?" But I don't know. I looked at him. He had his Mister Exhausted face on. He seemed so stressed out by the whole farm scheme. He seemed in no mood for a whole new scheme. Plus, he hates Vegas. Plus, I hate Vegas. I may not be the bride type, but I am really not the Vegas type, and then, poof, the fantasy was gone.

So instead I said, "Hey, *there's a gas well on the property!*" I don't know where that little brain blip came from. But that was a good move.

"True," he said, looking up.

He loves that gas well. It seems to appeal to his handyman side.

And I have to admit, the gas well has captured my imagination, too. An enormous pool of natural gas sits beneath Washington County. The first well was discovered quite by accident in 1882 when the Niagara Oil Company was drilling on the old McGugin farm, and at 2,247 feet they struck gas. The force was so great that it sent tools flying a hundred feet into the air. It was the largest flow of natural gas in the world. By accident, or mischief, the gas flow caught fire. The well burned for two years. Thousands of people came from miles away to picnic by the light of the "Mighty McGugin." Eventually, they got the fire out, the gas was piped to Pittsburgh, and the great oil and gas boom of southwestern Pennsylvania was on, breathing new life into the region after the faded glory of the National Pike.

The gas well at the farm in Scenery Hill is nothing to look at. Just a thin little pipe sticking out of the ground with a valve on top. But out of that pipe comes all the gas for the farm, heating the house, the barn, even a giant greenhouse if we built one.

"Free gas!" I said to Alex. "Think about it!"

"I'm thinking," he said, looking down, and then he started smashing a tomato under his fork. Not a good sign. Things went downhill from there. He agreed that we would place a bid on the property, but he sure didn't seem happy about it.

He didn't sound much better today when I called to say I was coming over so we could make the call. He was sort of quiet. I didn't know what to say. I mean, I'm so used to making my own decisions, following my own dreams, making my own plans. The truth is, I wanted to scream. I wanted to say, "Dude. Let's make this work! Let's take control." I wanted to say, "My train has left the station—what the hell is the matter with yours?"

But I didn't.

So, now I'm here. At his house. "Come on, Betty," I say, opening the car door, and when I get up to his porch, I shout, "Yoo-hoo!" and step inside. This is a great old house, a remodeled Victorian with wonderful mahogany woodwork throughout. Marley comes bounding out. Betty tears toward him. They tumble all over each other, gleeful and carefree.

Alex comes out of the kitchen, holding the cordless phone.

"Oh, I know, sugar," he says into the receiver, and that's how I know he's talking to Amy. He's been helping her with her résumé. She's recently moved to New York City, joining Peter there, the two of them trying to find their way. Amy wants to do something in publishing, and Peter, well, Peter is a brilliant engineer who could do anything he wanted but has no idea what he wants. "Okay, why don't you read that last part to me again?" Alex says to Amy.

Amy and her dad are close. Amy and Peter and their dad. This is a unit. A more complex unit than me and Bob, but a unit. Amy and Peter have welcomed me in. To tell you the truth, I think it was a little easier for them to accept me than Marley. "Dad, *a poodle*?" Peter said.

"A *standard* poodle," Alex said. "Not one of those little yappy things."

"Uh-huh." Amy and Peter didn't know their dad was a poodle person either. I think that poodle issue helped me bond with Alex's kids.

I sit on the couch, waiting for Alex to get off the phone. Marley is done tumbling with Betty and has commenced leaning on my leg. He's a leaner, that dog. He'll lean into you and then roll his neck back, his snout up in the air, as he tries to eye you upside down.

"Okay, Marley," I say, petting him. "What's this? More burrs here? Oh, jeez." I head over to the drawer to get the poodle comb.

"Yep," Alex is saying. "Fax me this version, and I'll be able to read it all the way through. Okay? I think it's good, though. I think it sounds really good. All right. Okay. Bye-bye, sugar. I love you."

He turns to me.

"Is she okay?" I say.

"Oh, God, yeah," he says. "She's just about got it done."

"Well, I got about five burrs out," I say, fluffing the hair on Marley's head.

"More burrs," he says. "Aw, Mar. You're a mess, buddy."

Enough small talk. "So let's make the call," I say bluntly. No sense stalling. And he does have the phone in his hand.

"You want to do it?" he says, holding it in my direction.

"Yeah, right," I say. "You know I'm too shy."

He hates when I say this.

"You are not shy," he says.

"Well, I used to be," I say. "Did I ever tell you I wet my pants every single day in kindergarten?"

"If you tell me that again, I'm going to have to excuse myself and commit suicide."

"Ha! Listen to Mister Redundant Face! That's the kettle calling the, or, the cook spoiling the—"

"The kettle spoiling the broth."

"Right."

"All right, I'm going to make the call," he says.

"Good."

"But I'm going to bid low."

"Not too low," I say.

"*Low*," he says.

Oh, dear.

I sit on the floor. I hold Marley. Betty is over by the radiator destroying Marley's stuffed frog. Marley is so much better than Betty for calming people down. Something about his thick poodle curls. There is tension in those curls that you can pull, stretch out, then let go and watch them spring back. He's got thousands of these little tension-relievers all over his body.

"Hello?" Alex says. "Is this Fran?"

Oh, jeezus. It's her. I feel like we're calling the Queen of England.

"Yes, we came down to see your place a few weeks ago?" he says. "Uh-huh."

"ASK HER IF THE FARM IS STILL FOR SALE!" I shout. "DID SOMEONE ELSE BUY IT?!"

He is waving his hand at me, silencing me. Fine. I clutch Marley tighter. Afro-dog. We should have named him Fro.

"That's right," Alex says. "It's a beautiful place. Uh-huh. Oh, I know. That's exactly what we said."

"WHAT? WHAT DID WE SAY? WHAT IS SHE SAYING?"

"Uh-huh. Yes, well, Fran. Fran, we'd like to make an offer on the farm. Yes. And if you'd like us to come down there and we could talk face-to-face, or . . . Now? Right now? Over the phone?"

Oh, jeezus. This is like having your best friend ask the cutest boy in school to the prom for you.

"Oh, okay. Sure. We can, I mean, what I'd like to do is, well, actually, start the bidding, you know, lower than, well—"

Oh, my God. JUST SAY A NUMBER!

He says a number. Oh-my-God. He says a number that is a full twenty-five percent lower than their asking price. Oh, my God. He said he was going to bid low, but jeezus, that is way, way, way, way low. Oh, my God. She's going to laugh in his face. I can't believe this. Poor Marley. I'm twisting this dog's ear off.

Why did he say that low? He doesn't *mean* that low. He means let's get down lower to a place where we can negotiate. So why didn't he *say that*? You don't bid below the whole damn chart, forgodsakes.

Unless, of course, you're not serious with your bid. . . .

I should have done the bidding. Damn it.

"Hello?" he is saying. "Hello?"

Apparently, Fran is not saying anything.

"Hello?"

I am on the floor, curled up in a ball.

"Uh-huh," he says. "Okay, then. Well, good-bye."

He hangs up.

I look at him. "That was really low," I say.

"Well, she said she'd have to call us back."

"Well, that was really low," I say. I feel like crying. He can see it. "You don't want the farm, do you?" I say.

"I thought we should start the bidding low, so we have lots of room to negotiate," he says.

"Well, there's low, and then there's *low*," I say.

"Look," he says, "she's going to call back in the morning with a counteroffer. I gave her your number in South Side."

"All right."

THE NEXT MORNING I SIT BY THE PHONE. I SIT there waiting for that phone to ring. It doesn't.

I sit by the phone all day. I lie on that couch with Bob on my stomach, waiting for her call.

Nothing.

The day after that I live from pay phone to pay phone, checking my machine from the mall, the grocery store, the movie theater. Nothing. All weekend. Nothing.

For an entire week. Nothing. Well, that's weird. Is she going to call back or what?

I sit in this limbo for two hideous weeks, three hideous weeks . . . *six hideous weeks*.

Six weeks. Time seems to have stopped, but time hasn't stopped at all. It's now August. Mid-*August*! We are now heading toward my birthday. On September 22, I am going to be thirty-eight years old. Thirty-eight! That is a serious number. And my life, what is my life? Same old life. I check the paper and see the ad has been pulled.

Apparently, the farm has been sold to someone else.

I can't believe this.

I just can't believe it.

This couplehood thing sucks. I hate it. If I were alone, I would have made the call myself. I would have negotiated a fair price. By now I'd be moving to the country.

But, well. Fine.

It's over.

Done.

Draw the curtain or roll the credits or whatever.

She didn't even have the courtesy to call us and tell us that she sold the farm to someone else. And Alex, he shouldn't have bid so low. He didn't mean that low, so why did he say that low? It's his fault. For six weeks, I've been so furious at him I could cry. He blew it. Because he didn't want it like I wanted it. His train hadn't left the station. I should have taken care of my own stinkin' train.

Forget it. It's time to say good-bye to Scenery Hill.

Draw the curtain or roll the credits or whatever.

FOUR

O H, B O B, W H Y A R E Y O U C O U G H I N G A G A I N ? D A M N
*it, the vet did not say anything about coughing. Do not die now, Bob. No, I
mean it. I am absolutely too upset for you to die now. I need you to hang on
a little longer, Bob. That better just be a hairball. . . .*

It's September, mid-September. About a month after I gave up
on Scenery Hill. Exactly ten days before I make the leap to thirty-
eight. I am here at my house, and it's still hot out, still hot enough to
challenge this poor air conditioner. I'm here with Bob. My beloved
Bob. He certainly looks healthy enough. I don't know; maybe I
should get another cat. Maybe I should get an insurance-policy cat.
Because I don't know how long Bob is going to last. I should call
that vet. I should say, "Hey, how long is he going to last?"

I don't remember asking that. I don't remember asking anything on that day last spring when that vet used the D-word. I
thought: *Dying?* Dying? My God! I had sort of forgotten about
dying. I hadn't experienced a death since my Pop Pop Pete died
when I was fifteen. "Dying." I had so little experience with dying. I
thought: When it comes to dying, I am a baby.

So of course I wailed like an infant in my living room that day. Because I was an infant. And say what you will about pets just being pets, I say loss is loss and grief is grief.

Well, that was Alex's point. That's what he managed to communicate to me through my heaving sorrow way back then, when Bob was diagnosed. It was a comfort. Sometimes you just need permission to feel as awful as you feel.

I'm trying to apply that same simple lesson to the farm. Loss is loss and grief is grief. I am trying to drum up some entitlement here. Some permission for feeling as sad as I do about losing my dream. Even though it was just a stupid *Green Acres* dream. Barely even a dream at all.

It was just a song I couldn't get out of my head, Bob. Just a stupid, idiotic song.

Bob seems to have finished with his coughing. Now he is bathing. He's licking his paw, stretching his prickly tongue with all his might, then rubbing his paw over his eyes. He seems perfectly healthy. It's not right. If he's dying, he should look sick.

Alex is outside. Through the kitchen window, I can see him working on the patio, beads of sweat dripping off his head. He's laying the brick in a checkerboard pattern. I should go outside and marvel.

"Wow!" I say, stepping out into the heat. "I love the way the bricks go! You want some iced tea?"

"No thanks," he says. "Not yet, anyway."

"Well, this looks great," I say. "I mean, really great."

He smiles. We're doing better. We are done being angry. Well, I'm done being angry at him, so he's doing better.

My dreams are my dreams, not his. That's one thing I've discovered. You don't stop loving someone because your dreams don't exactly align, or because your train schedules don't match.

I mean, I guess that's the way it works. I don't know. I am new at love. I need to get a love book. I need to get a boyfriend book. I need to get a dream book.

Because the weird thing, the truly weird thing, is that Alex is having some kind of delayed reaction to the lady never calling back. I'm here trying to finish up with my grieving, and he's just getting started. I don't understand this at all. Sometime during these weeks of waiting to hear from her, he decided, yes, the farm. I was right. ("Thank you very much.") We should do it. We should go. And if we can't have that farm, we should start farm shopping again.

I don't know; maybe that's the way he works. Maybe he needs things to be taken away from him to realize he wants them.

No, I don't think so. I don't think that's the way Alex works. I think maybe he isn't much for planning, for big pictures, for schemes like I am. I mean, look at the way he's building this patio. I would have sketched it out first on paper. I would have at least measured. I would have said, here's the square footage, and here's how much brick we'll need.

Not him. He just . . . starts. He just digs. And then he digs some more. And then he steps back and looks. And then he lays a few bricks, then a few more. He doesn't *see* what he's doing. He *feels* it. He intuits it. He applies these same problem-solving skills to many areas of his life. For instance, his East Liberty house. I mean, here we are, without the farm, with no clear future direction, and here's Alex *putting his house on the market*. He up and did it last week. I couldn't believe it.

"But where are you going to live?" I said. Was he trying to say he wanted to move into South Side with me? No, it didn't seem so. He didn't seem to be that far along in his thinking.

"Well, the house isn't sold yet," he said.

"True."

Suddenly he felt it was time to sell his house. I mean, he has a good point. His once-delightful neighborhood of huge old homes is slowly deteriorating into a crowded neighborhood of rental properties. If he doesn't sell soon, he may end up being an absentee landlord, like so many of the rest of his old neighbors. And anyway, he figures it will take a long time for the place to sell, so there's no reason to panic about living arrangements.

See, I wouldn't do it this way. I would plan. I would say, "Where am I heading?" before I actually took off.

"OUT OF THERE, BETTY!" I shout, seeing her go near the daylily bed. "Girly girl, GET OUT!" I don't know why I have to tell her this. Does she want to get zapped?

"Betttttyyyy," Alex growls, in a deep bass voice. Betty hears this. She knows this is the sound of trouble. *"Betty, you'll be sorry. . . ."* She lowers her head, comes slinking over to us. She sits at my feet.

"Poor Betty," I say. "My angel mutt with the bedroom eyes. How is this collar?"

"Fine, if you don't mind electroshock therapy," Alex says. "Huh, girl."

"I'm sorry, girl," I say. "I know. This is no life for a dog."

"Oh, please," Alex says. "This is one privileged dog."

"Well, she is a *celebrity,*" I say.

The phone rings. I run inside to get it before the machine picks up.

"Hello?"

I recognize the voice. I recognize it, but I don't recognize it. It takes me a minute to catch on.

It's . . . *her.* It's her?

"Fran," she says.

It's *her*? It's the lady with the farm. What? *What?* Why is she calling? We put our bid in over two months ago, for heaven's sake. I'm done with her. I'm done feeling angry at her for leaving me hanging like that and flicking my dream into the gutter like a piece of trash. But, what? What is she saying? I run outside, start waving my arms at Alex.

What? *What? Farm not sold after all. Oh, dear. Dream still alive.*

Oh, dear.

She says they took the farm off the market for a time because they got sick of showing it, sick of meeting people who didn't appreciate it the way they appreciated it. And the truth is, they were somewhat ambivalent about the whole thing. Transplants from

New York City, they loved the place, too. They'd followed this dream for a decade and now wanted to go live by the sea somewhere. So yes, they were leaving. They were definitely leaving. And would we still like to buy their farm? Would we like to start negotiating?

I am waving my arms at Alex, trying to communicate all of this, but he is looking blank. What? *What?*

"Well, okay. Okay. Okay. I'll have to call you back," I say to Fran. I hang up. I am exploding inside. Oh God, I'm going to start singing something really stupid.

"It's not sold!" I shout. "The-farm-is-not-sold!"

"What? *What!*"

He turns to the dogs. "Marley! Did you hear that! Betty! *It's not sold!*"

We pace around the garden. Oh, dear. Dream alive. Dream within reach. Oh, dear. It becomes a question of integrity, of squaring up with the gods. Do you really want the thing you say you want? Do you have the courage to accept it?

"I need to see the place again," I say.

"I don't think we should wait," he says. "I think we should snap it up. I should call her back and give her a new number."

"No!"

We seem to be having something of a role reversal here. Now he's Mister Go Get It. So what's my problem? What happened to Miss Train Left The Station?

What happened, perhaps, is that now I've got to take charge of my own brakes. When you are in a relationship and someone else has the brakes, you are free to be a runaway train. Of course you are. Because you know, deep down, that the other person is going to keep you safe.

But when your partner lets go of the brakes, that's when you really come face-to-face with what you're made of.

It's strange how much you get to learn about yourself when you are not just *of* yourself.

"Let's go down one more time," I say. "Please."

"All right. But call her and tell her. Make sure she knows we're serious. You want me to call her?"

"No!"

"All right."

I make the call. Fran says not to worry; they're headed out of town for a few days, but if we want to come down to take another look, she'll leave the door open.

"Open?"

"Oh, we never lock," she says.

Wow. I love the country.

T WO DAYS LATER ALEX AND I ARE MAKING A BAGEL- and-cream-cheese picnic while watching footage of Hurricane Fran on the kitchen TV. It's interesting to have a hurricane with the same name as the lady who owns your dream. Alex says maybe this isn't the ideal day to go farm shopping, what with the hail and the floods. I point out that we are technically only in the *outskirts* of a hurricane.

"Right," he says.

I have to go, have to see, have to know.

We pile ourselves and our Eddie Bauer boots and our Lands' End Gore-Tex rain gear in the car. We head on out through the wall of water. I feel like we're Gilligan and the Skipper negotiating that storm.

When we get down to the farm, the rain is even heavier. We pull up to the barn, duck inside, and put our rain gear on. It's so creepy in here. So creepy and crawly and musty and perfect. Above our heads the rain is making quite a clickety-clack on the metal roof. There are daddy longlegs running by. There is all manner of junk everywhere, gas cans and raccoon traps and empty fertilizer bags and bicycles missing various parts. We find some trash cans to sit on, and a car fender to prop our feet on.

"Let's wait until the rain holds up a little," Alex says, flicking a slow, nearly dead hornet off his knee. "Then we'll walk up the hill."

"Right."

We look around. We tap our feet.

"Hey, did I ever tell you what the difference between a tavern and an elephant's flatulence is?" he says.

"Oh, God."

"A tavern is a bar room," he says, starting to laugh. "And an elephant's flatulence is a *barrooom!*"

He doubles over laughing. He slaps his foot on the floor. I can't believe he finds this to be a major knee-slapper after the four hundred and ninety-seventh time. He's probably been telling this joke since he was in the eighth grade. Well, I would probably have laughed when I was in the eighth grade. Seeing as I was Wittiest and Peppiest and all. I wish I'd known Alex back then. We would have been such pals. But then, wait a minute, when I was in the eighth grade, he would have been . . . twenty-eight. Yikes. Well, never mind.

In most areas of life, it really is never good to do the math.

We stay in the barn waiting for the rain to stop, which it doesn't, so we head on out anyway. We climb the slippery hill, feel the hail bouncing off our heads. I can't believe we are doing this. We pass the apple trees. Poor trees. All wet and miserable. But no bees. We make our way to the woods lining the ridge.

"Was it here?" he says. "Is this where we went in?"

"I can't tell, honey!" I say, yelling through the rain noise.

"I think it was here!" he yells.

There is a crack of thunder.

Oh, jeezus. Now I feel like we're Lucy and Ethel.

Eventually, we find the break in the woods and make our way through it. This is so stupid. Was this my idea?

And there it is. The view. This is why we are doing this. It's as if we needed to make sure this picture was really here, was true.

"The view," I say. Kind of foggy. But the view. I see the hills, the bellies still laughing, as if mocking the storm. We trace the spot for the gazebo with our toes. We stand here a long time. The picture is here. The picture is true.

"We should get a willow tree," I say to him.

"Definitely."

THE NEGOTIATIONS BEGIN ON MONDAY, MY BIRTH-day, and conclude on Friday. I am officially thirty-eight years old, and our final bid on the farm has been officially accepted—contingent on financing and inspection. To sweeten the deal, Fran and her husband, Bob, threw in their 1984 Chevy pickup and their 1958 International Harvester 350 utility tractor with three-point hitch, blade, lift bar, tire chains, and brush hog.

"What's a brush hog?" Alex asks.

"Actually, I think it's *bush* hog," I say.

"Well, what's a bush hog?" he says.

I have no idea.

No longer is the talk of sheep-covered hillocks. For weeks, and through much of October, it's jabber jabber about down payments, portfolio liquidation, interest rates, inspection riders, hand money, survey, title search, barn doors, wood-boring-insect infestation, water tables, agricultural zoning implications, farm insurance, algae control, beefy engineers injecting green dye into the septic system, and other things you never knew you knew how to talk about.

Everything is happening so fast, tumbling and tumbling. We're working on the farm deal, and just like that, Alex gets a bid on his house. It's weird the way his life all comes together. I'm telling you it's truly weird.

We're closing on the farm in a few weeks, and he couldn't be happier. He's walking around like a little kid, sort of as he was on the day Marley jumped into his arms. And so naturally, I'm having second thoughts. Third thoughts. Fiftieth thoughts. I guess that's how it works with couples. You polarize.

The babes are backing the farm idea a hundred percent. In fact, when I brought them out to see the place, Nancy and B.K. rushed up to the second floor and picked the rooms they intended to spend the weekends in. Ellen said, "I don't think you realize how serious we are about making this our country place."

My mother, on the other hand, thinks I'm out of my mind. (She is a city-person.) She thinks I'll be isolated out there in the middle of nowhere. She thinks I'm going to stop brushing my teeth like all those other toothless country-folk. (Not her exact words.) My father is polarizing my mother, saying, well, it sure sounds like an adventure. My sister Kristin likewise loves the idea. My sister Claire thinks, "Ew." But she doesn't even understand why I would want a dog. "Dogs," she says, "smell."

"Stink," I say. "Noses smell."

"Whatever."

My brother John, a physician with a thirty-acre gentleman's farm near Philadelphia, thinks I'm finally doing something truly wonderful with my life, and he keeps sending me sheep magazines in the mail.

I have decided not to sell the South Side house, in case I need an escape. In case the country gets too . . . well, whatever too it might get. And I hardly owe anything on it, so it's probably a good investment to keep it. Or so I tell myself. The truth is, I love that house and can't let go.

I've been calling Fran at least once a day with questions. "Um. Does Federal Express deliver out there?" I asked this morning. She laughed. Of course it does. And so does UPS. I asked her about the dirt road. Who maintains it? Are we expected to maintain it? Of course not. It's a township road. And what about that field across the road? How often do you have to mow it? And, um, *how* do you mow it? How does the tractor work? How do you turn it *on*? And how does the well work? How does the septic system work? Where does the drainage off the barn roof go?

"Why don't you guys come down here," she said, "and Bob and I will give you farm lessons. We'll go over everything."

"Great idea," I said, hanging up the phone, feeling much relieved.

So here we are again, heading back to the farm, this time in Alex's Mazda. This time we have the dogs with us. We figure it's time to introduce them to the property. We stop several times to give Marley and Alex's upholstery a break. Marley is never going to be a commuter dog; there is no way.

A commuter dog. I have some vague notion that Alex and I are going to use this farm as a weekend place. Or a place for me to come and write. Alex says no. He says he's moving. He's now Mister Get Going. Well, he's also Mister No Longer Has A House. He says if he could live anywhere in the world, it would be on those fifty acres in Scenery Hill. He's gotten the bug, gotten it bad. Apparently, his train was on a different schedule. Or his train doesn't have a schedule. His is a much more magical train.

"Well, I mean, you're right," I say to Alex.

We have been driving in silence, until this point.

"What?" he says.

"I said, '*You're right,* dear.' "

"Well, thank you very much," he says. "But what am I right about?"

"About moving to the country," I say. "Because I mean, think about it. Why live in a place where you are forced to shut down your senses?"

"Oh, no," he says. "Not the filter bit."

"*It's all about filters,*" I say. "Isn't it? Right? I mean, wasn't I right? It's about doing away with the need for filters." I begin gesticulating wildly, for emphasis.

"Please, honey," he says.

"I want to be in a place that encourages my eyes to *open wider*! My ears to hear an increasingly wider range! My nose and taste buds to go to new extremes! Not a place where I am forced to go numb in order to stay sane."

I look at him. I want validation. I want him to say, "Yes! Dear! We are going to live the filterless life, happily ever after!"

But he has a distracted look on his face. Arched eyebrows. He's letting out a long sigh.

"Did I ever tell you about the time I walked into the men's store and the sign said 'All men's pants half off'?"

"Forget it," I say.

When we get to the farm, we open the car door. Marley throws up.

"Oh, dear," Alex says.

Betty hops out of the car, looks around, and immediately starts zooming. She zooms up the hill, and then back again toward us, head low, legs moving so fast they blur. Her tongue is hanging out one side, flapping up and down in the wind. My God! And I've been trying to leash-train this dog? Electrify the boundaries of her life? I had no idea there was such fire in Betty's muscles. Maybe this is the source of her jumping and scratching and chewing and digging and garden destroying. She wanted to zoom. A dog, I think, needs fifty acres.

Marley is no less enthusiastic. He gains his digestive composure, then trots after Betty. Soon his trot gives way to a prance. He looks like a slow-motion dog in a dog food commercial. He is beautiful. He is so beautiful, you half-expect someone to yell "Cut!" and to lead him back to his trailer and powder his nose.

I hope Betty isn't jealous. No, Betty would never do a dog food commercial. Betty is more the foreign film type.

When we get up to the house, Fran and Bob invite us in. Well, not the dogs. They are definitely not the dog type. In fact, they don't have a single pet on this entire farm. This is hard for me to comprehend. We sit at the kitchen table, sip lemonade, and share a laugh about Fran having a hurricane named after her. We listen to their plans for a dream house by the sea. We slurp our last slurps, and Fran and Bob begin their farm lessons. Interestingly, the first thing they do is take us into the basement, where they show us . . . filters.

Filters. Okay. Soon we are standing before a well-water filtration system that occupies an entire room. "Wow. A lot of filters," I say. The filters have replacement dates written on them. The chlorinator has a bucket of chlorine pellets next to it, and a scoop.

"I guess I went a little overboard when I bought this system," Fran says. "But you never can be too sure about well water." She talks giardia and cryptosporidium. She talks reverse osmosis and gastrointestinal distress while Bob untwists a four-foot-long casing and shows us how to change a Pall Ultipor N66 membrane. Alex says he needs a pen. He starts taking notes as Fran talks about imparting a positive zeta potential and Bob explains the life span of a chlorinator.

They get off the subject for a moment as they show us how to prime the pump, how to use the backup generator, the backup kerosene heater, the battery charger for the tractor. They ask us if we want to buy their leaf blower, their snow blower, their 28.0 cc gas Bushwhacker, their sixteen-inch gas chain saw. They ask us if we want to buy their rifle.

"Rifle?" I say.

"Oh, we never thought we could shoot anything either," Fran says.

It is, apparently, a jungle out here. And among the enemy is an army of raccoons. In the beginning Fran and Bob would catch the varmints in have-a-heart traps, drive them miles away, and release them. But the raccoons would come back. They tell stories about the three-legged raccoon that traveled thirty miles to get back here to home sweet home.

"So finally we did what everyone else around here does," Fran says.

"Kill 'em," Bob says, shrugging.

This reminds Fran of a story. "Oh, Bob, tell them about the rat," she says.

"Oh, the rat," Bob says, laughing. The rat, he says, had found passage into the house via the oven.

"The oven," I say.

"There was a hole," Fran says. "And I just had had it with that rat. And then one night I heard it. I said to Bob, I said, I know that rat is in that oven. He didn't believe me. But he gets up, opens the oven, and there it is."

"In the oven," I say.

Alex has his jaw dropped real low.

"And so I get this little pistol we had," says Bob, "and I open the oven and aim."

"In the oven," I say.

"Well, I missed," he says. "But I must have stunned it. Because it just sat there frozen."

"And so he grabs it by the tail," Fran says, "and he goes running for the toilet to drown it."

"And I have it there by the tail," he says, "and it's like waking up or something."

"And then the tail," says Fran. "The tail came off."

"Excuse me?" Alex says.

"The tail came off," she says. "I guess rats can shed their tails for protection or something."

"Rat in the oven," I say. I have registered nothing past this plot point.

"So I go running for something to keep the rat down with," says Fran. "And I grab the fireplace shovel, and Bob, he holds the rat in the toilet with the fireplace shovel, until it drowns."

"And it died," he says.

"Died," I say.

"Oh, it was just a fluke-type thing," Bob says.

"Oh, we have such stories about this place," Fran says.

I say I'd like to take a walk outside.

"But what about these filters?" she says. They're not finished with the filter lecture. I am sick of filters, an image that has officially backfired.

"And what about the gun?" Bob says.

Alex says we're not really gun people, but we'll look at it. We head outside. Bob brings out the gun. Betty and Marley are romping. They are trying on their new personae as farm dogs. It is taking some getting used to. Marley, with his thick curly poodle fur, is a walking Velcro dog. An impressive sampling of weeds from the back field is now stuck to him. Betty, a very clean city-dog, has discovered an inner passion for dead things. She has discovered that she likes to roll on dead animals, swiping the stench of decay upon her fur. Her shoulders are covered in black goo. She reeks. Which is only part of the problem, as I see it. The other is: Where is she finding all these dead things? How many dead things are out there?

Alex agrees to try the gun one time, pointing out once again that he is really not the gun type. Bob puts a brick in the grass about fifty yards away, says aim for that. Alex holds the rifle up, peers through the scope, and slowly squeezes the trigger. BOOM! Betty dives under a porch chair. Marley ducks into the barn. The brick vaporizes. The brick is no longer. It is one hell of a gun. I am imagining what it would do to a poor raccoon.

Bob is saying, "Nice shot!" We are all staring off at the spot where the brick was.

"My eye," Alex says. "My eye." We turn and see him doubled over, holding his right eye. The gun is on the ground. Blood is coming from between his fingers.

I think for a moment that there is a hole in his head. I think that Alex has shot himself in the head.

I think this farm idea may not have been such a good one after all.

It turns out that Alex, who is not—did I mention?—the gun type, held his face too close to the scope. The rifle's recoil slammed the scope back, slicing him in an arc around his eye socket.

"Oh," Bob is saying. "Oh, dear."

We decide not to buy the gun. We say thanks for the farm lessons. Good-bye. Good luck. We gotta go. I drive us back to the city so Alex can keep the ice bag on his face. We have two extremely stinky dogs in the backseat. We have dozens of owner's manuals for dozens of pieces of farm equipment on the floor at Alex's feet. We have a notebook full of information about filters, continuous filament polypropylene media with absolute rate downstream sections and continuously profiled pore size upstream sections. We have dead rat stories in our heads.

We are opening our senses. We are in hot pursuit of our increasingly commingled dream. We are moving to the country.

Green acres, here we come.

COLD AIR

FIVE

IT'S A SNOWY NOVEMBER MONDAY, BRISK AND COLD. We just spent the long Thanksgiving weekend packing up my office, the contents of which are now rolling along behind us in a big white truck.

Wilson Road is transformed by the cold. The cathedral of trees has lost its color and now forms the most intricate lace pattern overhead. A thin layer of snow softens the look of everything, like powder smoothing out an old lady's cheek.

The driveway, "our" driveway, is about an eighth of a mile long and unpaved. The surface is a bed of small rocks, like most country driveways. I wonder if the layer should be thicker than this, though. Is this why the surface is so slick? An inch of snow should not be this treacherous.

"Whoa," I say to Alex, as the Mazda skids. I unbuckle my seat belt, turn around, and make sure that Betty and Marley are safe in the backseat. "Okay," I say. "I think we should make a pact with each other right now that we will not wear our seat belts when we drive past this pond."

He looks at me.

"Because if the car slides in, we'll have a better chance of not drowning if we aren't strapped in," I say.

"Well . . . ," he says.

All right. Stupid, I know. "I'm scared," I say. I've been unnerved for weeks now, ever since we closed on the property. Everywhere I look, I see problems. And if I don't see problems, I feel them. "I'm itchy," I say. "I feel like I've got head lice. You know how when you get scared, you just itch?"

"Not really," he says.

"Well, it's fear," I say. "I'm walking around scared all the time."

"Or else you have head lice," he says.

Thanks.

The movers make it up the driveway and jump out of their truck. Alex and I get out of the car and open the back door for the dogs. Betty zooms over to sniff the movers, while Marley staggers, rights himself, then throws up. "Okay, no problem," I say, trying to normalize this.

The movers have long hair and thin faces. "Wow," one says, looking around. "This reminds me of that Chevy Chase movie. You know, the one where he moved to the country?"

No, I don't know. And I don't want to know. I'm in no mood for comedy. I'm a nervous wreck. I am having chaos anxiety. Well, I guess you're supposed to have chaos anxiety when you move, but . . .

BOOM!

I jump into the stratosphere. What the hell was that? Everything that happens just reminds me that I have no idea what is going on.

BOOM! BOOM!

The booms sound like the ones created by Alex's rifle experience, except farther away, more drawn out, more like CRACK! followed by FWOOOM!

"I guess somebody else out there is trying to decide whether or not to buy a gun," Alex says, rubbing his eye as if he can still feel the punch.

Well, maybe. But jeezus. This is not my idea of the sound of welcome.

Alex talks to the movers, explaining which doors to use. I am standing here looking at the truck. Inside that truck is the entire contents of 1701 Benedum Trees Building, 222 Fourth Avenue, Pittsburgh, PA 15222. This is stage one of our move. Because this is how we've decided to do it. First, I bring my office here. Next, Alex will move down here. He accepted the bid on his house and will need to be out of there in about six weeks. Then, and gradually, I'll move much of the contents of my South Side house to the farm. I'm still committed to keeping the South Side place, though. And I'm really in no hurry to set up house here at the farm. In fact, I'm needing to slow things down. I feel like a person who has done a very impressive dive off the diving board and is in the pool but now is doing a slow crawl over to the side, trying to catch her breath.

I am having chaos anxiety. Or maybe it's relationship anxiety. Commitment anxiety? Hmm. There's no question that Alex and I are committed to each other. But will there be order, a structure to this commitment? Will we put the stamp of approval on it? Will we institutionalize it? Will we do the M-thing? *Marry?* Is that really what I want? I can't even say the word out loud.

It's funny how chaos anxiety just creates order anxiety.

Which only leads to endless loop anxiety.

Because really anxiety is just anxiety, no matter what you call it. Making sense out of anxiety is just an intellectual exercise that does nothing, absolutely nothing for this itching.

I'm here scratching my head, out by the barn, looking at the house that really makes no sense, a chalet stuck onto a trailer, but not really a trailer and not really a chalet. Just a long, funny house, cheap white aluminum siding and tiny windows on one end, dark cedar siding and huge, extravagant windows on the other. In between, lots of doors. An awful lot of doors. Why are there so many doors on this house? This house is like a story, a novel. One of those stories in which a different person is invited to add the next chapter, and the next. There is no central vision to this house, no one mood or one theme or one emotion.

I scan the fields beyond the house, the vast hills reaching toward the sky. Okay, fifty acres, that's what I'm thinking. Fifty acres. And let me get this straight. I mean, let's review:

I couldn't keep up with my one-quarter-acre garden in the city. So I bought . . . fifty acres.

Okay, fifty acres. Alex and I have been talking a lot about what to do with fifty acres. How, for instance, do you mow fifty acres? We learned that you mow fifty acres with the brush hog, which turns out to be the low flat thing that you attach to the back of the tractor. It's the mower attachment. See, now, I never knew tractors even *had* attachments. I mean, I never really thought about it. To me, a farm tractor is a thing you see in the distance when you are on the Turnpike going somewhere, and it is out there on those fields doing very important farm things. That the farm tractor is made up of parts—attachments and levers and hydraulic-powered thises and thats—was not in my consciousness. Why should it have been in my consciousness?

This is one example of a much larger principle I am dealing with, ever since we closed on the farm.

Because, fifty acres. Fifty acres in a place called Scenery Hill. Fifty acres of gorgeous scenery. *Scenery.* We bought scenery. We bought a postcard. We bought green hills and a pond blooming with lilies *à la* Monet. We bought a creaky old barn leaning in the wind *à la* Wyeth. We bought the most beautiful picture we could possibly find.

We bought 2-D. Not 3-D. It did not enter my consciousness that the three-dimensional version of this thing was included with the package. Because how could it be in my consciousness? When would it have had the opportunity to get in? Chaos never announces itself, never advertises. Who would buy chaos?

It's getting in. It's creeping in. Slowly, slowly, we are entering the picture, poking our fingers and our toes through some kind of protective film like you might see in a futuristic movie featuring awesome special effects.

This is what it is to enter the future, a future you imagined as simple and perfect and new and . . . what? What's all this green? Well, it's grass, of course. But the grass is what? The grass isn't just grass? The grass is hay? What, actually, is hay? And what do you mean you're not supposed to mow it, you're supposed to bale it? Use it? Consume it? A what? A hay baler? What does a hay baler look like? Another tractor attachment? How much does that tractor attachment cost? Exactly how many tractor attachments are there? A catalog of tractor attachments? Hundreds of tractor attachments? Hundreds of tractor attachments costing thousands of dollars each.

I never knew. How would I ever have known? *Why* would I ever have known?

Alex and I have been talking a lot about sheep and other animals that might eat fifty acres of green for us and do away with the need for all those tractor attachments. So far, we believe sheep are the answer. They're easy, according to the sheep magazines. You fence the sheep in. They eat the grass. (Hay?) You provide them with a little hut for the winter and some water. In exchange, you get mowed fields, free wool, and stink-free fertilizer in convenient pellet form.

But I am beginning to suspect that the idea of sheep is another two-dimensional picture. Idyllic sheep grazing on a field doing your yard work is really just another postcard. There are a lot of sheep details I can't even conceive of, not until I crawl into that picture.

Of course, I'm glad I'm crawling into this picture. The truth is, I'm glad I'm here. Because I know I will be able to breathe here. It feels like there is enough air here to fill all of outer space. I'm glad I'm here because there are trees, glorious trees here. Trees that tower over me and rock gently in the breeze, as if holding me on a swing. I'm glad I'm here because it is peaceful here. I think working here will be good for me, good for the writing life. I will have the solitude that all writers crave. I will have Betty here, curled up at my feet. I will have Bob here, at least for a time, drooling with pleasure as he watches me diligently meet my deadlines. I won't have those investment brokerage people in the Benedum Trees Building looking at me on the elevator and making me feel like I should wear pantyhose.

Solitude. Solitude is what I'm ultimately after. Or at least, this is what I am telling myself. I have a somewhat complicated relationship with solitude, having spent much of my life alternately loathing and longing for it. You don't grow up a kid hiding in a shed in a neighbor's farm and not know something about solitude. You don't go inward, inward, inward and avoid splashing around in the murky water of solitude. When I was nineteen, I was a sucker for Emerson and Thoreau and the Transcendentalists who made solitude sound so romantic. As soon as I learned about Thoreau, I knew I wanted to be Thoreau, walking around that pond. I was clearly cut out for that job. I arrived at adulthood having embraced some of the tenets of the Transcendentalist philosophy quite on my own accord—as perhaps many children do. The Transcendentalists just gave it language, form, organization. I already believed in a monistic universe, one in which God was in nature, of nature; I learned that way back when God gave me that animal-soul-rescue job. I already believed, really believed, in a mystical world in which God is present in all things, and that thinking of the people/God connection as the only real connection, the only holy connection, is just plain silly—is merely a symptom of the basic truth about the human condition, which, as far as the rest of the universe is concerned, is narcissism.

The Transcendentalists gave me a reason for being the way I was. I was part of a pantheistic world, one in which the objects of nature, cats and bugs and trees and people, are equally holy. A world in which you could experience God during a walk in the woods, or through contemplation of a salamander. I was part of a world in which all events could be both material and spiritual, just as Emerson described: "The man who has seen the rising moon break out of the clouds at midnight has been present like an archangel at the creation of light and of the world."

I loved that. In college I would take my watercolors into the woods and paint pictures that said that. At least to me. The Transcendentalists had given validation to the inward life I knew so well as a kid and had crawled out of, then back into, then out of, like a turtle sticking its neck in and out of a shell.

I miss solitude.

I sometimes fear that I've lost my capacity for it, lost it in the elevator of the Benedum Trees Building, lost it while standing there thinking I should be wearing pantyhose. Hell, I was a grown-up now; I was supposed to be part of the outside world. A functioning member of society. Not some kid hiding in a shed on a neighbor's farm.

I miss that kid.

I am longing for solitude again. Solitude is surely here, on these fifty acres, along with the gas well, the birds, the trees, and all this air.

At the moment, however, I am forced to wonder if solitude itself is another two-dimensional picture. Just a postcard of a place I want to return to.

There is, of course, a bigger problem emerging: How in the world can solitude coexist with love?

AFTER MUCH DISCUSSION AND SEVERAL SWITCH-ings of drivers, each man trying his skill in maneuvering a van full of office furniture on an ice-covered lawn, the truck is successfully backed up to the door of the giant room. The room with the skylights, the room that overlooks the pond and barn, the room that will be my office. Talk about a writer's retreat. I imagine a pinball machine in here. I imagine a Ping-Pong table. I imagine my paints and a potter's wheel and all of my favorite things. I imagine writing stories galore, the best stories I've ever written. The movers put the ramp down, drink a lot of iced tea, get psyched up. They are having a good time.

BOOM!

They look at each other.

CRACK—FWOOOM!

"Uh, what's with the fireworks?" one guy says.

"Maybe it's the Hatfields and the McCoys going at it," another guy says. "Heh heh."

"Heh heh," I say.

They joke about the snow, about the truck sliding off the ice and into the pond. They joke about calling their boss and telling him the truck is at the bottom of the pond. They drink more iced tea and imagine, heh heh, losing their jobs. They look at the snow, now coming straight down with official force.

BOOM!

"We better hurry and get outa here," the short guy says. And so with a great burst of energy, they start unloading the truck. I tell them to dump everything in the middle of the room, because I have no idea where anything will go. I like figuring that stuff out when I am alone. I have all week to get my new working life in order. Then next Monday it will be business as usual. This is so exciting.

BOOM!

Alex walks into the room, carrying a box of telephone stuff from his car.

BOOM!

He looks at me. He shrugs. "Well, I have no idea," he says.

"Well, you're awfully calm," I say.

"Actually," he says, "I'm hungry. I'm about to keel over."

"All right." We decide to head out to find some take-out food. I take orders from the movers. They specifically request french fries. All right. But I don't promise anything, because I have no idea if we are really going to find fast food out here in the middle of nowhere.

I put the dogs in the basement, to keep them safe while we're gone, and Alex and I hop in the car. And I don't care what he says— I don't put my seat belt on until we are safely on Wilson Road. We go east on 40 for about fifteen minutes, finding nothing except a big stone monument on the side of the road, a lone statue of a woman.

"Hey, pull over," I say. I want to have a look. The woman is holding a baby, and there's a child tugging at her dress. Underneath her it says "The Madonna of the Trail." It says "To the pioneer mothers of the covered wagon days." It's a monument to the women who traveled the National Pike in search of a lot more than take-out food.

"Aw, she's pretty," I say to Alex, as I lean out the window.

"Ask her if there's a place around here to get something to eat," he says.

I give a long, audible sigh. "Aw, she looks cold," I say. "Don't you think they should have given her a heavier coat?"

"But then in the summer she would look hot," he says.

"True."

I get out of the car, take a quick walk around.

"She's so tall!" I say.

"Well, ask her if there's a Pizza Hut or anything around here," he says.

I roll my eyes. "Men!" I say to her.

But she doesn't reply. She just stands there looking . . . soft. I look at her face. How do they make such soft features out of stone? She is so young. God, when I was her age, I still smoked. She is so innocent. I stand next to her and look out, wondering what she stares at all day long. I think of all she has seen driving by on this road. I think of her seeing me, and instantly I feel embarrassed. She probably thinks this Eddie Bauer down vest looks stupid. She probably thinks I'll never know the hardships she has endured in the name of adventure, of a new life, of survival. She probably thinks I have no right to be scared in my adventure. My God! My anxiety is the anxiety of privilege. This woman, now this woman really knows itching. Probably she had head lice for real.

It occurs to me that I really should stop referring to this countryside as "the middle of nowhere." Because as this stone woman knows, it was once the center of everywhere, it was the thread, it was the link, it was the "cement of the nation." It was once the path to a new frontier, and for me it still is. I wonder why it has taken me so long to come to respect my own dream.

"Um," Alex says, "remember how I said I was keeling over? Well, I've keeled."

"All right." I touch the stone woman. "Well, good-bye," I say to her. "Good-bye, Madonna of the Trail. It has been very nice meeting you."

We go west on 40 and finally spot a restaurant announcing "home cookin' and beer" with a sign featuring a cartoon turtle holding a hamburger and a mug of beer.

"Well, that looks good," Alex says.

"It does?"

"It *does*," he says. "There is food in there." The sign says "Tradesmen's Inn," which doesn't really have anything to do with a turtle. But then again, what does a hamburger have to do with a clown, when you think about it. Anyway, we go rolling into the gravel parking lot, feeling short.

"Do you feel short?" I say.

"Extremely short," Alex says.

Our little sedan is the only vehicle here that is not actually a pickup truck.

We walk past all the pickup trucks and marvel at how many different styles of pickup trucks there are. Huge pickups, tiny pickups. Pickups with giant tires, pickups with tops, and topless pickups. Pickups with lots of extra lights and pickups with little backseats and pickups with mud flaps adorned with shiny, silver naked girls.

Most of the pickups appear to be hauling nothing, leading me to wonder why, exactly, people have pickups.

We open the door to Tradesmen's Inn, and in one gigantic blinding moment—I mean, one intergalactic explosion—we step into a sea of orange. Orange everywhere. I mean, the brightest damn orange. My eyes take a moment to calm down, to stop pulsating, and soon I see that orange is the color of the men, of which there are many, occupying the barstools of Tradesmen's Inn. Every barstool, a man. A man dressed in orange sitting next to another man dressed in orange, next to another. All of these men have on orange hats. The hats turn in unison, perhaps fifty of them. They look at us, the only two hatless people in the place, the only two nonorange people in the place. They look at us as if to say, "Who *are* you?"

Or maybe that's the way we are looking at them.

Hunters. Now there's one thing I hadn't figured on. I sort of forgot about the fact that country equals wildlife equals hunters. This is part of the 3-D that looked so much better as 2-D. This explains all those booms in the distance. But what are the chances? I mean, what are the chances that we would decide to begin our move down to the farm on opening day of buck season?

One out of 365, that's what the chances are. And here we are. We learn about opening day from a guy at the bar downing some chili. He says, "You guys gotta try the chili." He's a bulky man with a wiry beard, a generous neck, and deep-set eyes that smile even when he isn't smiling. He says he bagged a buck two hours after sunrise this morning. He says the snow helped. Because as anyone knows—or as we now know—you can track a deer very easily in the snow. Especially a deer like that six pointer he hit this morning but didn't kill, and so of course that deer started running, bleeding to death, because he shot him in the "brisket," and with the snow you can track a blood trail with no problem, a child could do it, an idiot could do it, until you find that rascal curled up in a ball, dead.

He seems to be waiting for us to say something.

"Um," I say.

"Well," Alex says.

"Six points," the hunter says. "Ain't nothin' to brag about. But I'll take it." He says the only problem with getting a buck within two hours of buck season starting is now you have nothing to do, because you can bag only one buck during all of buck season.

"Yep," I say.

"Well, then," Alex says.

"Lucy!" the man calls to the waitress. "How about two bowls of chili over here for these people. Put it on my tab!"

"But—" I say.

"He looks hungry," the man says, motioning toward Alex with his left hand, which I now notice is missing two fingers.

"Well, thanks," Alex says. "But listen, you don't have to, buddy. . . ."

Buddy? Oh, dear.

"Don't mention it," the hunter says.

And in no time Lucy, a large blond woman with a high forehead, brings over two bowls with puffs of steam swirling out. She gives us each a spoon and a napkin with a picture of a turtle on it.

"Thank you," I say to the man.

"That was mighty neighborly of you," Alex says, blowing on the chili, slurping it.

Mighty neighborly? Oh, dear.

"It sure is beefy chili!" Alex says to the hunter. "*I love beef.* I'm a meat eater, you know. Oh yeah, I've always been a meat eater."

Oh, *dear.*

I've never really tested Alex out on how good he is at faking being a country-person.

I wonder what this hunter thinks of us. I look at Alex, me. I've got Eddie Bauer labels all the hell over me. Alex has Lands' End labels all over him. We're both done up in Polartec fleece gear with only the finest-quality lining designed to radiate body heat. Oh, God. This is embarrassing. We believed these were the clothes of country-people.

But no. Of course not. These are not the clothes of country-people. These are the clothes of country-wannabes.

Because *these* are the clothes of country-people: blaze orange numbers that may very well be doing a lot of damage to a lot of optic nerves.

"Hey, that stuff will keep you warm," the hunter says, smiling, taking a swig of his beer. "Lucy makes that chili herself. *By hand.*"

"Super!" Alex says, rubbing his belly. Alex is enjoying the hell out of this hunter. I half-expect him to ask to try on his orange coat.

"We have to go," I say.

"We do?"

"French fries?" I say. "The movers?"

"Oh," Alex says. And then he calls Lucy over. Calls her over like he's been coming here all his life. "Lucy, can you get us three orders of fries to go?"

"Coming right up, Alex!" she says.

Oh, brother. One big happy family here. I miss the Madonna of the Trail. I liked her better. When Lucy comes back with the fries, Alex stands and says good-bye to his new friend. "And hey," he says, earnestly, "congratulations on your . . . dead deer."

Congratulations on your dead deer? Oh, God.

We make our way out the door, past the pickups to our car. "A hunter!" Alex says excitedly as we get in the car.

"Congratulations on your dead deer?" I say.

"He was proud of it."

I don't even know where to begin.

"Well, wasn't he a nice guy, though?" Alex says.

"He murders helpless little animals," I say bluntly, forcefully.

"Well, that's what people do in the country," he says.

"Well, that doesn't mean we have to *endorse* it," I say.

"But we're country-people now!"

"Country-people," I say. I don't even know where to begin. Number one, no. We are not country-people. And if we were to become country-people, we would not be the kind that murder helpless little animals. And if we were to lose our minds and all our teeth and a few fingers and actually become the kind that murder helpless little animals, we would not say "Congratulations on your dead deer" to anyone. I'm trying to explain this to Alex.

"Uh-huh," he says. But he is distracted. He is probably wondering if he should have asked that three-fingered man over for dinner some night.

I am feeling very much alone.

·   ·   ·

WhEN WE GET BACK TO THE FARM, THE MOVERS are finished, and no, they don't want to hang around for chili. But sure, they'll take the fries with them. They're worried about this snow, which is starting to pile up. There's already maybe three inches out there. Alex sees this as an opportunity.

"I can plow!" he says. He's been dying to drive the tractor. He used to fly small airplanes. He loves machines. He's good at mastering complicated equipment. You don't think of a middle-aged shrink with little intellectual glasses as being good at such things. But he really is.

We let the dogs out of the basement, and they come bounding out into the snow as if it is some amazing gift. We go down to the barn and approach the tractor. It's a beauty, all right. I loved this tractor the first moment I saw it. It looks so . . . farmy. It looks like something you'd see in a coffee table book about farms of yesteryear. The body is red and skinny and almost delicate. It looks like a giant rooster standing there. And on the side it says "Farmall" in white letters that have slipped and become crooked over the years. The tires are huge, almost as tall as my five-foot-six frame. The stuffing is long gone from the seat.

I think this tractor is going to be very good for my inner tomboy. I think of how I would have loved something like this when I was a kid. I am hoping that this farm adventure—minus the dead animal part—reawakens the tomboy I once was, have gotten away from, have abandoned in favor of, well, the mall.

I hop on, pretend I'm driving. I push the many pedals, some of which go down together if you push one lever, or by twos if you push a different lever. The pedals require every ounce of my leg strength. They must have made farmers stronger back in the 1950s, when this thing was built. But then again, they didn't make tractors for farm wives. But then again, I'm not a farm wife.

"Okay, start 'er up," I say to Alex, as I hop off and give the beast over to him.

"I love this!" he says, turning the key.

Nothing.

He turns it the other way.

Nothing.

Betty and Marley are sitting before us, like, "Hello?"

Alex pushes pedals and turns dials, does everything he can think of before concluding, "Battery must be dead."

So we hook up the electric battery charger that came with the tractor that came with the farm. But it quickly becomes apparent that there is no electricity in the barn. So we hook up the many, many extension cords that came with the battery charger that came with the tractor that came with the barn. We run the extension cords through the branches of the trees all the way up to the house and plug it in. We figure we better give it overnight to charge.

"You know, I wonder if the Elly May Clampett truck actually works," Alex says. Good question. We refer to the pickup that came with the farm, a light blue '84 Chevy, as our "Elly May Clampett truck" not only because it looks like something you'd see on *The Beverly Hillbillies* but also because the tailgate doesn't stay up, so you have to use a C-clamp to "clamp it" closed. We never did think to ask why the hood has all those bullet holes in it.

Alex hops in the truck, and lo and behold, it turns over. This cheers us up. The truck even has a valid state inspection sticker on it.

"Which expires . . . tomorrow," I point out, on further examination.

"Oh," he says, sighing.

"We'll take it in tomorrow morning," I say.

"Yeah," he says.

We are getting tired. One thing I'm noticing about life in the country is, it makes you very, very tired. The snow continues to fall. The sun is beginning to set. The movers are long gone. The wind starts to whip the falling flakes and whistles through the bare branches of the maple tree near the barn door.

We go up to the house, choosing the second door from the left to enter. We make a fire in the fireplace, and Betty and Marley curl up in front of it. We don't have any sherry to sip, as we used to do back when a day in the country was just a fantasy trip to some romantic country inn.

Let's stay in this moment forever. That's what we should be saying. We should be sipping sherry and saying "Let's stay in this moment forever."

But then again, we are in this moment forever.

SIX

J OE CROWLEY'S GARAGE IS A FEW MILES DOWN THE
road. When I called to make a truck appointment, Joe said we
didn't need an appointment. He said we should knock on the
kitchen door and he'll come on out.

"A kitchen door at a garage?" Alex asks.

"That's what he said."

When we pull up to Joe's, we see that his garage is, well, a two-
car garage attached to a house. "Hey, the wife made pancakes," Joe
says, emerging, wiping his mouth on his sleeve. He is a short,
balding man in a T-shirt, his arms documenting at least part of his
love life in tattoos.

"You ever had pancakes with *pineapple?*" he says, shaking his
head back and forth, like, she did it again, that wife, she did it again.

"*Pineapple?*" Alex says. "Can't say's I have."

Oh, dear. Now he's doing *Mayberry RFD* talk.

We show Joe the truck, saying we want an estimate on the cost
of inspecting it. Privately, we've already agreed that if he wants more
than two hundred dollars, we'll say forget it. That is our cutoff price.

Because the truck probably isn't even worth two hundred dollars. It's an old truck that probably needs all kinds of repairs. But we've heard prices are cheaper in the country than they are in the city.

Joe says, "Wait here."

He pulls the truck into the garage, while we wait in the front yard. There are a lot of kids running around. There are dogs and there are chickens. We stand here looking at the kids and the dogs and the chickens. Warm air has moved into the valley, and already the snow is melting. The booms in the distance, which neither the kids nor the dogs nor the chickens seem to notice, continue sporadically.

In ten minutes, Joe is back, rubbing his hands on a rag.

"Well, I'm done," he says.

Done?

"Sixteen dollars," he says.

We look at him, incredulous.

"It runs good," he says. "I checked everything. I put the sticker on."

We look at him. In Pittsburgh a state inspection on even a brand-new car will run you at least fifty dollars. In the city they fix things that may not even have been broken before they put the sticker on.

"Sixteen dollars?" Alex says.

He looks at us, wondering what the problem is. "You don't have to pay me now if you can't," he says.

I hand him a twenty. He puts it in his boot, pulls out four ones.

"Hey, thank you for your business," he says. "Outa there, Mandy," he says to his dog, who has climbed into our truck. "Mandy!"

"It's okay," I say. "We have dogs."

"A poodle," Alex says. "We have a poodle."

Now why in the name of the good Lord in heaven did he have to bring that up? I'm sorry, but having a poodle is a private matter. (I have a poodle in my closet.)

"A *standard* poodle," I say. "Not one of those little yappy things."

"Is that right?" Joe says, clearly unsure of what he is supposed to say here. Mandy, a German shepherd mix, is now at his feet. Joe introduces us to his children. We talk about hunting. I ask him if he knows where we can buy a load of rocks.

"Rocks?" he says.

"For our driveway. You know, like, to pave it?"

"Oh, stone," he says. "Limestone. Or red dog?"

"Limestone," Alex says, seeming more confident about his choice than I know him to be.

"Joe Crowley," he says.

"Excuse me?"

"Joe Crowley can deliver you some," he says.

I look up at the sign on top of his garage, which definitely has "Joe Crowley" on it. He can see my confusion.

"Oh no, not me. A different Joe Crowley," he says. "No relation. You want his number?"

"Sure."

He writes it down, hands it to me. "Now make sure you ask for Joe the son," he says. "Because his pap is Joe Crowley, too. . . . Oh hell, I'll just call him for you."

There are *two* more Joe Crowleys?

We follow him as he ducks into the garage, dials the phone. "Hey, Joe?" he says. "Joe. Joe around? What? Nah, I didn't get your papers this time. I got my own papers. Well, I don't know, Joe. Did you check your mailbox? Yeah, they're my papers, because I checked. Yeah, I'll hold."

He looks at us. "Me and Joe got our divorces at the same time, so we'll get each other's support papers in the mail sometimes."

"Ah," Alex says.

"Well, then," I say.

"Joe?" he says into the phone. "Hey, I got a customer for you. The new people. Yeah, I got the new people right here."

The new people? We have a reputation already?

Joe schedules a time later in the day for Joe to come over to look at our driveway and see what we need.

We thank Joe for the inspection, and for the other Joe, and we head back to the farm, thinking about all we have learned.

BOOM!

This, again, is what greets us as we return to the farm. As we get out of the truck, we note that the booms here sound a lot louder than Joe Crowley's booms.

BOOM!

I jump. Alex jumps. Betty dives under the pickup, and Marley runs over to Alex and leans on his leg.

"That one was close," I say.

"I feel like we're in Europe during the air raids," he says.

We wonder how long the shootings will go on. We wonder how long it takes to get used to it like those kids and those dogs and those chickens.

Alex says, let's install phone lines. He loves doing stuff like this. I love that he loves doing stuff like this. I say I'd rather go get the mail.

"How many phone lines did we order?" he asks.

"Four," I say. That sounds like a lot of phone lines, I know. But I have my reasons: one for the business, one for personal, one for the fax, one for the Internet. I think: Connect me. If I'm going to be working out here in a place that at least *feels* like the middle of nowhere, I'm going to need access to the outside world. It's important to have access. Solitude is one thing, but you could turn into the Unabomber if you don't have some connection to people.

And, anyway, when I get anxious, I buy electronics. Stereos or speakers or computers or little hand-held gizmos that store phone numbers. Electronics calm me down. The more complicated, the better. When the world feels like too much, when friends are betraying you or family is all worked up over who should be doing what, or what it means if what happens to whom, there's nothing like installing a new hard drive in your computer to calm you down. There's nothing like A plugging into B and making C happen. It works! Something works. Something you can understand and touch. Electronic things offer the most concrete opportunity I know of taming chaos.

So of course, as this whole farm dream started gathering steam,

I went on an electronics binge. I got a new two-line telephone with dual keypad and caller ID and a digital answering machine built in. I got a personal photocopier. I got a new color printer. I got a color scanner. I got a new electronic personal postal system and an Iomega Jaz drive capable of storing one gigabyte per each removable cartridge. I've convinced myself that these are things that will make my home office a more productive place. I will get more writing done if I have these things. Well, maybe not the scanner. Why exactly do I need a color scanner? Um. Well, I can take pictures of Bob and scan them and then e-mail them to people! Yeah, that's it. And who exactly will I e-mail pictures of Bob to? Well, I don't know. In any case, it will be nice to have pictures of Bob in my computer. I can have Bob wallpaper on my Windows 95 desktop! I can have little Bob icons everywhere, and I can print out Bob greeting cards and Bob thank-you notes.

See, there are a lot of things to do with a scanner. More to the point: There are a lot of ways of keeping Bob alive. I miss Bob. I need to bring Bob down here as soon as possible. At the moment he's safe and sound at the South Side house, under the careful watch of Helen, the old lady across the street, who stops over to pet him and remind him how special he is. Helen is so great that way. As soon as I get this place organized, as soon as I actually move in here, I'll bring Bob. I should bring Helen down, too. It will be a shame to move away from Helen.

Anyway, electronics. I was talking about electronics. The electronics are a comfort. And out here on this farm, I think they'll be a whole new kind of comfort. The idea of living in the country and having the environmentally friendly use of electronics bringing the world closer, but not really closer, is about the most perfect relationship to solitude I can imagine. I feel lucky to be making this move just as the Internet is coming into its own. It's weird to think that I can be out here in the land of Joe Crowleys, and I can still have instant access to my editors in New York, the babes in Pittsburgh, my family in Philly, and all the libraries of the world.

In fact, as soon as Alex gets these phone lines hooked up, the libraries of the world will be closer than my own mailbox. Well, our mailbox. Our mailbox is a half-hour walk away, all the way at the end of Wilson.

I love the sound of that. "Our mailbox." I've never had an "our mailbox" before. So many of life's adventures are in the words.

"I'm going to take Betty on a walk to *our* mailbox," I say, grabbing her leash.

"You and Betty have your own mailbox?" he says.

"No, *ours*," I say. "Yours and mine."

"Oh. Well, I love the sound of that," he says.

"Me, too!" I say. "I was just thinking that."

"No, I was."

"No, I *was*!" I say. "I thought it first."

"Well, I thought it *yesterday*."

"Well, I thought it *five years ago*."

"You did?"

"Actually," I say, "actually, yes."

He smiles. He smiles a fifty-acre smile. "But what about Marley?" he says.

"Huh?"

"The mailbox," he says.

"You want a mailbox for Marley?"

"No. The *walk*. Aren't you going to take Marley?"

"Oh, they'll just get tangled up in the leashes," I say. "I hate that."

"You think you really need leashes out here?" he asks.

"I don't want the dogs to run off."

"All right," he says. "Leave Marley here to help me with the phones."

"Come on, girly girl," I say to Betty, clicking on her red leash with the reflector stripe. She looks at me. She looks at me like "You're kidding, right?" She looks at me the same way I scowled at my mother when I was forced to wear one of those huge puffy orange life preservers before even getting in the *car* to go to the lake.

"Betty, heel!" I say, as we head up the hill. Oh, this is fun. Are we going to yank our whole way to the mailbox? I should get a longer leash. I should get her a fifty-acre leash.

BOOM!

Okay, this is getting old.

Betty ducks, makes herself short, and runs between my legs.

"It's all right, girl." Poor Betty. She is not cut out for the fire-arm life.

That gunfire sounds a lot closer than surely it must be. Surely there are laws keeping hunters a safe distance from people's homes.

Betty and I make it to the top of the hill. The booms have encouraged her to stop pulling on the leash. Funny how the sound of battle makes the troops huddle together. We pass through the upper gate. We take the left onto the dirt road, which is now more mud than dirt, more mush than dust, and soon the woods opens up like a picture window to the Scenery Hill scene. All brown now, it looks like a bowl filled with butterscotch squares and brownies. The cloud cover has flattened the light so this really does seem more 2-D than 3-D. It reminds me of something. It reminds me of being in my parents' living room as a little girl. I am on the floor, lying on the scratchy rug. There is a flimsy movie screen towering over us. My parents are showing a slide show of their recent trip to England. We kids are trying to appreciate these sights, really trying. We must have been so very trying. We are sticking our hands up into the light, making hand puppets on the screen.

Standing here with Betty, I do it. I put my hand up in the sky, waiting for the shadow to appear.

But no shadow appears.

"This is real, all right," I say to Betty. "Can you believe this? Can you believe this is now the background of our lives?" But she seems a lot more interested in the foreground. She is sniffing uncontrollably, as if vacuuming the road.

"Betty, look at this *view*!"

Roo roo roo roo! she shouts. She senses something up ahead. Smells something? A rabbit? A groundhog?

"Betty, *heel*!"

Just then, from around the bend, comes the none-too-subtle object of Betty's barks: two guys in orange. Orange hats, orange suspenders, orange overalls, orange everything. And guns. Guns strapped all the hell over them.

Well, wow. Why do I suddenly feel like I'm a tourist in Bosnia having made a very wrong turn? Why do I feel like Gilligan stumbling into some scary native village where everybody has painted faces? ("We come in peace!")

The men approach.

"Hey," one says. "Where is your orange hat?"

"Hey," I say. It seems to be the way people greet one another around here.

Roo roo roo roo, Betty is saying. She is embarrassing me. This is horrible. She is not showing off her princess-self.

"Quiet, girl. Quiet!"

"What are you doing out here without orange?" the one man says.

"Um."

"You want to get shot?"

No, I don't. And I'm trying not to stare at the big knife attached to his belt, either.

"You can't walk around here without orange."

But this is my road. My property is on either side of this road. Does he mean to say I can't walk around my home without worrying about getting shot? Wasn't that supposed to be an inner-city kind of worry?

Betty has quieted. But she is sniffing the men. They are trying to figure out what to do about her.

"Her name is Betty," I say. "She won't bite."

"Is she sick?" one says.

"Huh?"

"Why does she need to be on a leash?" he says.

"Well, um." And I can feel Betty looking at me. I can feel her saying *See?*

"Pretty eyes," the one hunter says, bending over to pet her.

"Oh, she's a movie star," I say. "Can't you tell?"

He smiles.

"Ma'am," the first one says, "you really should wear orange if you're going to walk around like this." He extends his hand. "My name's Joe," he says. He is a tall, grandfatherly man with beautiful chiseled cheekbones and a wide brow. He has the markings of the Eastern European men I know so well and trust. Lithuanian, I think. "And this is my son, Joe," he says.

More Joes? Just how the hell many Joes live in this place? (Am I on *Candid Camera* or something?)

"Are you the new people?" Joe, the son, asks. He doesn't look like his father. He has jet black hair and a jet black beard neatly trimmed to give his features an English tidiness.

I nod and point toward the farm, even though apparently he and everybody else around here already knows where I live.

"You picked a beautiful spot," he says. "We've walked about every inch of your land."

They have? What for?

Betty is sniffing again. Joe gets on one knee and strokes her ears. "A movie star, eh, girl?" he says.

"Did you ever watch *Gilligan's Island*?" I ask.

"Huh? Well, um. Sure."

"Well, doesn't she remind you of Ginger?"

"Um," he says. He smiles. "Sure she does."

It's beautiful, I think. It's just plain beautiful how 1960s TV can form a bond between even the most diverse cultures.

"The people who used to live here," the father says, finally, "they never minded if we hunted."

He looks at me. He seems to know this is a sensitive subject. He says, "So, um, you mind if we hunt on your property?"

Our property? But . . . we *live* on our property. Or we're going to. Our property is for people. Surely there must be laws about not hunting where people live. Where, exactly, does hunting occur? Isn't it something that goes on somewhere else? Plus, I mean, dead animals? *Doesn't he know who I am?* Or who I used to be? I mean, there is no way. There is no way I am going to let anybody stalk

God's innocent little creatures on my property. Mine is to be a safe haven, a sanctuary, a place of love and happiness for all living things. I mean, *hunting*? On my property. On *our* property? I'll have him know that I am, or I was, a crusader for the eternal life of all animals. I blessed myself, in the name of the Father and of the Son and of the Holy Spirit, every time I saw a dead animal on the side of the road.

I'm not sure how to explain all of this.

So I say, *"My property?"* It comes out like a chirp.

He says it's one of the best spots around. "Do you know how many deer we pulled out of there over the years?"

No, I don't. I ask him how come there are so many deer there.

"Because of the multiflora, probably," he says.

"The what?"

"The multiflora rose bushes," he says. "You got the most around."

We do?

Multiflora rose, he explains, is a prolific thicket of flowers and thorns. A menace to farmers that also happens to provide a lush habitat for deer, birds, rabbits, and many other of God's innocent little creatures. Apparently, our farm is covered with it. I had sort of noticed it before. I mean, it's part of the green. Part of the postcard. Maybe a little darker shade of green when you look from far away. I just figured it was something you mowed in the spring.

He laughs. "You can't mow that stuff," he says, pointing to a bush, which is about ten feet tall, on the side of the road. He notes the thorns, the angriest thorns, half an inch long spread an inch apart on a long, slender branch that looks like a whip. He notes the tears all over his hunting jacket from these thorns.

"So how do you get rid of it?" I ask. (I have dancing visions of all-new tractor attachments in my head.)

"Multiflora?" He shakes his head, looks down. "Heh heh."

His son says, "Heh heh."

I tell him, well, my plan is to put sheep on the fields. Perhaps the sheep will eat it.

He says, "Where *are* you from, ma'am?"

I point north. Way, way north. "The city," I say.

"Ah," he says. "That explains a lot."

And so I listen for a long time while he offers multiflora advice. He tells me about poisons. He strongly suggests I seek professional help. He is a very nice man. We talk about tractor parts. We talk about sheep. He offers a dead deer in exchange for the privilege of hunting on my property.

"Ah," I say. Now, there's something I hadn't figured on. I wonder if any of the babes have ever been offered a dead anything in exchange for anything.

A dead deer. Hunters on my property. It occurs to me that I am really not prepared for this discussion. Up until a day ago, I'd never even known anyone who hunted. Up until a day ago, I'd never even considered the possibility of meeting a hunter.

I stand here thinking I should speak my mind. Because there is no way. There is no way I'm going to allow hunting anywhere near me. And I am a woman of the 1990s, active and independent-minded, fully in charge of my life. It is so important to me that I stand behind my beliefs and be heard, be known. This is a golden opportunity for me to spread my magnificent wings and soar.

I say: "I'll have to ask my husband. . . ." It comes out like a series of chirps, dying bird chirps.

"Well, heck, we'll just stop on by and meet your husband sometime," Joe says.

"That will be . . . nice," I say. And soon we say our good-byes and I head home, opting not to bother with the mailbox. Because now I'm worried about getting shot. Now I'm worried about stumbling on a dead deer. Now I'm worried about turning into a wussy woman who hides behind a husband she doesn't even have. "Betty, come!" I am saying. Now it's me yanking her along. "We have to *hurry,* girl." I need to get out of here.

By the time I get back to the house, I'm itching like crazy. Alex is in the driveway talking to two men. "This is Joe Crowley," Alex says to me. "He's come to look at the driveway."

"Hey," he says.

I look at the other man.

"And this is his assistant, Joe Crowley," Alex says.

"Oh," I say. "Um. Wow." Joe brought his dad? What is going on?

"We're no relation," the first Joe Crowley says. "He just works for me sometimes."

I stand there doing Joe Crowley arithmetic in my head.

"Joe is the son of Joe the mechanic," Alex says, pointing to the second Joe Crowley. "The one with the divorce papers?"

"Oh," I say. Alex is looking awfully at ease with this Joe Crowley proliferation.

"I have a friend," the first one says. "I'm going to bring him over."

"A friend?"

"He sells limestone, too," he says.

"Another Joe Crowley?" I ask.

"What?" he says.

"Oh, I wasn't sure what we were talking about."

"My friend has been hauling a lot longer," he says. "I'm just getting started, and I'm not sure how much to bring. This is a big job."

"Oh," I say.

"Well, then," Alex says.

And so Joe and Joe hop in Joe's white truck, which has a red hood apparently transplanted from another truck, and they roll down the driveway, toward the hills, back into the mystery that they emerged from.

"Don't you think the first Joe Crowley would have told us he also had a son Joe Crowley?" Alex asks.

"He does?"

"Yes. That short one was Joe's son."

"He was?"

"Yes! Aren't you following?"

"Not even a little bit. But speaking of Joes . . ." I tell him about Joe and Joe the hunters. I tell him that if any hunters stop by, he should pretend he's my husband.

"Huh?" he says.

"Just cover for me, okay?" And then I tell him about the multiflora, which is an even more complicated story. I tell him the take-home message of this day, thus far: "We are stupid."

"Oh," he says.

"Really stupid." And this multiflora is a symbol of our stupidity. We bought fifty acres of thorns. Thorns we can't get rid of. Thorny weeds that attract both wild animals and bloodthirsty hunters.

"Oh, come on," Alex says. "I'm sure we can get rid of it. How hard can it be?"

He heads into the barn. He gets out a rake. A *rake*? "I want to see something," he says. He goes over to a bush, a great towering thicket of thorns nearly twice his height. He pushes back the branches with the rake and looks at the base of the plant. It's thick. It's, like, a foot thick.

"See that?" he says, like he's got it all figured out. "Wait here."

And in a few moments he is back with the chain saw. *The chain saw?* He's gonna cut these things down one by one? There is an entire forest of these things.

"Okay, now you hold the branches back with the rake, and I'll crawl under there and cut it down," he says.

"Right-o."

I hold the rake while he tries to get the chain saw started. I've never actually been this close to a chain saw. There is an actual chain on that saw. Fancy that. Who in the world would ever have thought that a chain would be a good cutting mechanism? I have no urge to try the chain saw, or even figure out how the chain saw works. I am quite surprised at how little interest I have in all this mechanical gear. This is not like me. I must really be overwhelmed.

Zzzzzzt. Zzzzzzt. Alex gets that monster running. He grits his teeth holding this chain saw. This chain saw seems to awaken a whole new manliness in him. Maybe this is what chain saws are for.

Zzzzzzt. Zzzzzzt.

Nothing. I'm here holding this bush back with this rake, and he's lying down there on his belly with this monster machine with spinning teeth and—nothing. The chain saw does not seem able to cut through the multiflora trunk.

"Must be something wrong with the chain saw," Alex says, crawling out.

I drop the rake.

We stand there scratching our heads. Alex gets back on the ground, and we try the chain saw again.

Zzzzzt. Zzzzzt. You'd have to see how fruitless this is—the mighty teeth of the chain saw will not cut through that trunk—to understand why it seems so logical to proceed to the next idea.

"A forest fire," I say.

"Good idea," he says.

Alex gets kerosene, rags, and matches, and he begins making a torch. I go get a hose. I hook the hose to the basement spigot and run it the fifty-some yards to our intended forest fire area. "Better safe than sorry," I say.

We have no idea what we are doing. We are kids out for mischief with no parents in sight.

We sprinkle kerosene and gasoline all over the bush. We light the torch. I step back, way back, preparing for the conflagration.

"Betty, Marley—get back!" I shout.

I pick up the hose and prepare, should my firefighting skills, of which I have none, be needed.

Alex tips the torch on the branch. I have my eyes shut, waiting for the FWOOOM! that will accompany the explosion.

No FWOOOM happens. Alex moves closer with the torch. The gas burns. The rag burns. We watch with hope, but the flames . . . die.

Multiflora, it seems, cannot do a sustained burn.

I stand there holding the hose, looking at our failed experiment. Alex scratches his chin. He looks around. He looks around at all the acres and acres and acres of this stuff. It is like kudzu of the North, an angry red plague stretching up every surrounding hillside.

This is the first time that the scale of the farm really hits us. We surrender. To the multiflora and to something else, I think. We are smart, we are strong, we are brave.

And we are puny.

In the middle of this vast thorny nothingness, we need each other more than we ever could have imagined.

Under the thick sky, I breathe the air that feels like it could fill outer space, but also now stinks of burning gas. I feel the leafless trees holding me in their sway. I hear the booms in the distance, and I hear something else, I think. I hear the exhale in the hills.

ALL RIGHT, BOB. HERE YOU GO. THIS IS A CAT BED. *This is a bed designed specifically for your cat comfort. Do you like it? Here, come on, lie down in it, here, curl up in it. Bob, curl up! This is your retirement bed, Bob. No, here Bob. See how soft it is? Oh, all right. Whatever. You'll do what you'll do. . . .*

Bob, it turns out, prefers sleeping on my scanner, my HP Scan-Jet 4p. Something about the rounded top he likes. The scanner is right next to me, here in my new office, and Bob likes to stretch all the way out on it, rest his head on his upper leg, and alternate between snoozing and staring at me. If it were any other cat besides Bob staring at me like that, I think I might find it extremely creepy. But we are a unit, me and Bob.

He's losing weight, I think. But other than that, he doesn't seem sick at all.

My bringing Bob down to the farm signals a further commitment to this place. It's mid-December, only a few weeks since I moved my office down here, and already Bob has joined me. So have my bed, a bureau, and a refrigerator. Apparently I'm more ready to call this place home than I thought I was. I'm not itching as much; fear has given way to plain old confusion, as fear often does.

Bob, why don't you go off and explore this house? Why don't you go upstairs and see if there are some mice crawling around or something? Or, hey Bob! There are spiderwebs upstairs! Big spiderwebs to snoop around in. Remember how much you used to love those webs in the South Side basement and you'd come upstairs with your whiskers all tangled up in them? Oh, c'mon, Bob. . . .

Bob has shown almost no interest in his new surroundings. He's content to sit here and adore me. Maybe it's his nerves. I don't know. I'll give him time.

Betty, on the other hand, has decided that her real calling in life is to be a watchdog. She positions herself at the kitchen door in the morning, the door leading out of my office in the afternoon, and a hallway door at night. I do not think she is getting much sleep. She sees things outside. I don't know what she sees. But she barks, *Roo roo roo roo,* until I calm her down.

I can't blame her, though. I spend a lot of time distracted by the scenery outside, too. As a matter of fact, I am not getting a tremendous amount of writing done; I'm too busy looking out the windows. There is a semicircular window, high above the doors leading out to the yard. And this window is like a frame, a TV featuring the sky. A sky with folds of every shade of gray and blue and white, spiraling into each other, out of each other, all of it headed left. Don't look now, but the sky is moving. I've never had such a view of the sky. I've never known how busy the sky is all day.

And I never knew I could type without looking at my fingers, without looking at the screen. But I can. In fact, I can't not. I look to my right, and as far as my eye can see there are fields, then woods. And in the field across the road, I'll see a deer bounding now and again, and huge birds, the hugest birds, what are they, hawks? Turkeys? And outside to my left the solitary birch tree stands, as if impervious to the wind, and suddenly a yellow bird will be there, then a blue one, then a black-and-white-striped one wearing a red vest, all of these birds stopping by that tree looking for food. What do they eat? Are there frozen bugs in there? Seeds?

I have to get a bird book.

I have to get a bug book.

I have to get a seed book.

I have to get a tree book.

I have so much to learn.

I have learned some things about multiflora rose. I've learned that the plant was brought in from Asia in the early 1950s when the U.S. government came up with the brainstorm that this thorny stuff could work beautifully as a "living fence" during the postwar metal shortage. Farmers could throw some seeds down, and bingo— Mother Nature's barbed wire. What nobody figured on was that birds might eat the seeds and disperse them hither and yon. In no time, farms along the East Coast were covered with a good idea gone crazy.

By now, I have gotten good at identifying multiflora rose. I'll drive around and take in the scenery and note how we sure do seem to have more of it than most farms around. I have to wonder, but only sometimes, only at night when I can't sleep, if this awful menace is my penance, or if my penance is something much more obvious. Penance? Why do I feel I have to suffer something? As if happiness were some kind of sin.

I have a friend, Mark, who believes, really believes, that everybody has a balance between good and bad in life. That if you have a lot of good stuff happen, that just means you are due a lot of bad stuff, and vice versa. I used to argue this point with Mark. Because I thought it was a childish view. I thought there's no way God would design the universe using such an unsophisticated template.

Then I learned that Mark's father jumped off a bridge when Mark was fifteen, and that ever since Mark has been waiting, really waiting, for the badness to stop. He keeps thinking the next stage of his life will bring happiness, has to bring happiness, because there is no way a person can be expected to live his whole life in misery.

Sometimes nowadays when I'm looking out these windows, at the birds and the trees and the awesome sky, I'll feel as if I'm looking at the future. And the future is so pretty. Then I'll look at the multiflora rose and feel sad, but not really sad, because to tell you the truth there is plenty of beauty, plenty of might in that weed. I've been told that it smells beautiful in the spring. This property is going to be a perfume factory in a few months.

Then I'll look at Bob, and of course my heart will sink. I'll think Mark was right. I'll taste the danger. I'll conclude that you can't have happily-ever-after without first losing a piece of your heart.

Don't look now, but the sky is moving. Not falling, just moving.

The phone rings. It's Beth, one of the babes. She wants to know how I like it at the farm. Beth has a way of always getting to the point. I am trying to tell her about how beautiful it is here. I tell her about the sky and the fields and the turkey/hawks and the birch tree.

"It's like falling in love, isn't it?" she says. "I remember that from when I bought my house. Enjoy it now, because it won't last."

Yes it will! Of course it will. Now why did she bring this up?

"But you still love your house, don't you?" I ask her.

She doesn't answer.

"You do, don't you?"

She doesn't answer. Have I hit a raw nerve here? Jeez, I had no idea.

When she doesn't answer for the third time, I start saying, "Hello? Hello?" Then I realize we've been cut off. I click the receiver. Nothing. I try Line Two. I try Lines Three and Four.

This is weird. These phones have been working perfectly since Alex installed the lines.

I go out to the car and get my cell phone. (I guess that would be Line Five. Is this getting extreme?) I dial the phone company.

"Hello?"

"Is this the phone company?"

"Speaking."

"Well, my phone went dead."

"Hang on, I gotta get a pen. . . ."

The Marianna/Scenery Hill Telephone Company is not, mind you, one of your telecommunications giants.

"Okay," the woman says. "When Tom comes in, I'll let him know."

Tom? Who is Tom, and when does he plan on coming in?

"He's up on the pole," she says. "So I don't know."

Okay, a little technological snag. I can deal with this. It's one P.M., on Friday. Time to get the mail anyway. I wonder if Alex wants to come with me. He's off today, down in the barn trying to figure out how to stop it from collapsing. All the locals who drive up here say the same thing: "Hey, your barn is about to collapse."

At first I didn't really register the implications of this. Because all I could hear was "your barn." I loved the sound of that. Just like I love saying "I have to go down to the barn." Or "Alex is down at the barn." I love having a barn because I love the sound of it. I feel like the luckiest person alive, having a barn. Never mind that it may not be a *standing* barn much longer.

I head down to the barn, thinking: I am heading down to the barn! Alex is in there, scratching his chin again.

"I think I've got it figured out," he says. "I'm going to brace this whole section here with those old oak beams we found."

"Great," I say. "The phones are dead."

"Oh, jeez," he says.

"The phone company is checking into it. As soon as Tom gets down off the pole."

"Who?"

"I'm pretty sure he works for the phone company," I say. "Do you want to go with me to the mailbox?"

"Well, okay, sure," he says.

"Let's take the dogs," I say. "No leashes."

"A big day for the dogs," he says.

"A small day for the leashes," I say.

"Hey, our hats!" I say. Alex's kids sent us two orange hats they got at a Hoss's Family Restaurant. It was kind of a joke present, but not really a joke present. I run in to get the hats—because while buck season has ended, doe season has started. The hats are big, thunderous polyester numbers with "Hoss's" printed over a deer head. We put them on. We look at each other. And the strangest thing is, we do not look bad.

Actually, that is not the strangest thing. . . .

We head to the mailbox, and as we approach the corner of Wilson and Spring Valley, Marley veers off into the yard of our nearest neighbor. He starts staring up at a tree. He seems transfixed. What is so fascinating to him? He starts barking. *Woof, woof, woof.* I can see a tank of some sort in the yard, and a wheelbarrow turned upside down nearby. Why is he so upset? We get closer. I can see something hanging from a tree. Something red. It's about five feet long, and it's tied to a branch. It is something about the size, say, of a deer. . . .

Oh, dear.

An entirely skinned deer is dangling from the tree, twisting ever so slowly in the wind.

Oh, dear.

"Marley, get away from there!" Alex yells.

"Marley!" I shout.

Oh, great. So now Betty has been alerted. *Roo roo roo roo!* she shouts, for every one of Marley's *woofs*.

We stand there with our two dogs hysterical over a dead deer hanging from a tree, wondering what to do.

The neighbor comes out. Oh, great. She is carrying a big knife. Oh, great. Really great.

"Um, hello," I say.

"Marley!" Alex shouts. "Betty, come here!"

"Sorry about the dogs," I shout over the dogs. "They won't—"

"Oh, don't worry about the dogs," she says. "They can't reach. We love dogs. What kind of dog is that?"

"A poodle," I say.

"A poodle?" she says. "I thought—"

"A *standard* poodle," Alex says. "Not one of those little yappy things."

(Just how many times am I going to be involved in this conversation?)

She introduces herself. Sarah. She doesn't say why she is carrying the knife. She doesn't say anything about the deer, how it got there, or how long she plans to have it hanging there. I am trying not to notice the deer. I am trying not to notice that the deer's tongue is dangling out one side of its mouth, either. She welcomes us to the area. Then she says, "George doesn't love dogs."

"Who?"

"George over there," she says, pointing with the knife. "The guy with the sheep?"

"Oh." The farm now known as George's is the farm abutting our property along the ridge. It's George's sheep that are sprinkled on our postcard view. George's hills are the ones we fell in love with. It's George's land that won our hearts.

"George shoots dogs," she says. "Watch out for George."

Oh.

"Why on earth does George shoot dogs?" Alex asks.

"It's a sheep thing," she says.

A sheep thing?

She explains the dog/sheep dichotomy in these parts. Dogs chase sheep. A dog is capable of chasing a sheep to its death. Farmers have to protect their herds. If a farmer sees a dog chasing a sheep, the farmer will shoot it.

"Well, couldn't he *call* first?" I ask.

"He's shot plenty of dogs," she says. "Keep your dogs away from George."

"Okay."

I look at Betty. A sitting duck. A sitting dog. Does she have sheep-chasing bred into her? She has become bored with the dead deer she can't reach, so she is chewing on a stick. Well, I hope that's a stick. That better not be a dead deer bone. Marley is sitting staring at the dead deer, as if perhaps he is waiting for it to fall. Marley is developing a tendency to stare like this. Something about country life leaves him transfixed, at times for hours. He'll stand in front of a tree and stare at it. Maybe it's part of his sentry aptitude, I don't know. But when Marley is doing this, I think he's the one getting good at solitude, not me.

"Betty, Marley, come on!" Alex says.

We tell Sarah we have to be moseying along. I really don't want to stick around because I really don't want to find out what she's going to do with that knife.

On the way back from the mailbox, we say it's amazing how much you can learn just walking to your own mailbox around here. I think about how much of my day I spend in my office, at my computer, searching the Internet, singing the praise of the Information Superhighway. I think how much more exciting it is out here on the Information Dirt Road.

The walk home requires passing the entire length of one of George's fields—where there are no sheep today. Thank God. Do they make electric collars that keep dogs away from sheep?

When I get back, the phone is ringing. It's Ellen, one of the babes.

"Who's Tom?" she asks.

"Who?" I say.

"Someone named Tom just answered your phone."

"Oh," I say. "He's up on the pole."

"Where?" she asks.

My life is getting harder and harder to explain.

And so we mark the approach of the winter solstice by the size of the neighbor's dead deer. It keeps getting smaller. One day we walk by, and a shank is missing. Then a shoulder. After a while, it is just a head and a neck hanging there. This is right about the time the booms stop. Hunting season is over, and we are still alive.

We've had a lot of our new neighbors stop by. Apparently, this is what people do around here; they "stop by." At first you wonder what they want, but then you realize they don't want anything, except maybe a little human contact. Joe and Joe the hunters stopped by one day to meet my "husband," and they gave us two more orange hats as presents. We ended up giving them permission to *walk* on our land with their guns, just not to shoot anything on it. This actually was a compromise that pleased them since George, the sheep farmer, permits hunting on his property, and our place provides easy access to George's.

A lot of other people have stopped by. A baker who works up at the Century Inn stopped by with an apple pie, saying did we know that once upon a time a baker for the Century Inn lived in our house? No, we didn't. And what a delicious pie! Bob, the neighbor with the cow farm, which is next to George's, stopped by to commiserate about the price of beef falling to under fifty cents a pound. Alex was sympathetic but didn't really help when he compared the price of beef to the price per pound of a poodle. He did the math in his head. "Yes," he said. "These dogs go for about fifteen dollars a pound." Bob looked at him. Oh, Bob and I both looked at him. For a second there, I thought Bob might actually start talking to *me*. Which would really have been quite something. Because I am just "the wife." That's what Bob called me. Women around here aren't expected to talk much, to *understand* much. It's like the old days. Well, not the Madonna of the Trail old days, I don't think. Somehow I don't think the Madonna of the Trail would have tolerated that attitude at all.

I often think about that statue, about that stone lady holding that baby, never shivering in the cold and never sweating in the heat. Season after season, standing there. I think about her when I read about all the ways in which the middle of nowhere has been the center of everywhere.

I read about Marianna, a village less than three miles south of our farm, a town sharing our same telephone exchange. It was settled at the turn of the century. It used to be a famous coal-mining town, named after Mary Ann Feehan Jones, secretary and treasurer of the Pittsburgh–Buffalo Company. The company built the entire village in a matter of months, contracting the construction of 282 houses of matching yellow brick and a boardinghouse on the hillside behind three mine shafts: number one, "Rachel," number two, "Agnes," and number three, "Blanche."

Bricks, sewer pipes, everything arrived by rail. Advertisements for mine workers appeared in newspapers around the world. Prospective workers were assured living quarters, six dollars a month for a six-room house with a bathroom and a hot water tank. One tree was planted on each lawn. Each year the company would award prizes for the best-looking yard.

Marianna attracted Russians and Italians in great numbers, as well as Scottish, English, and Slavs. They were not disappointed. It was a most inviting town. And to make it more wonderful, the company built the Arcade, a massive, stately structure that contained a drugstore, an ice cream parlor, bowling alleys, pool and billiard tables, a dance floor, a skating rink, a movie theater, a gymnasium, and a reading and lecture room. It opened with great fanfare on July 4, 1910.

When President Theodore Roosevelt invited the big mucketymuck mining experts of Europe to inspect the coal industry of the United States, he culminated that tour with a visit to Marianna. Everybody applauded. The Marianna mines became known as the world's largest and most complete commercial coal plant, and Marianna was hailed as a model mining town.

I loved reading that. It made me feel like cheering. It filled me with pride about this area, *my area.* I loved hearing how these hills have drawn pioneers over and over again, that the middle of nowhere is no stranger to strangers. It made me feel at home.

Then I read that, four months after the Arcade opened, it burned to the ground. I hated reading that. I hated that so much. It made me think of my friend Mark. It made me think of Bob.

For a time, the wind was knocked out of Marianna. But the mines and the town of some two thousand people continued to prosper throughout the century, until Rachel, Agnes, and Blanche stopped producing as they once did, and a century of coal mining in America didn't matter anymore.

Fewer than six hundred people now live in Marianna. There isn't much there. A post office, a bank, a few churches, and a hardware store that is about to close.

· · ·

ONE CHILLY MORNING, THERE IS A KNOCK AT THE door. Someone else stopping by. Alex gets it. "Hey, Joe," I hear him saying. It's one of the Joe Crowleys. I go out to see that it's the Joe Crowley with the limestone who doesn't really know how much limestone we need but says his friend does.

He has brought the friend. Mercifully, the man's name is not Joe.

"Billy," he says, extending his hand. He has on dark glasses, so it's hard to trust him immediately. He's beanpole thin, except for his belly, a grand belly, a hard belly sticking out over his silver rodeo belt buckle. His left cheek also bulges forth, packed with some kind of impressive tobacco chaw.

"I got sixty ton of number two limestone out here for you," the man named Billy announces, his speech a bit slurred by the bulge, or the . . . He walks to the edge of the porch and spits a stream of brown juice into the boxwoods.

"*Sixty tons?*" Alex says. He is still grappling with the scale of this farm. He is starting to get a lot of headaches.

Billy takes Alex over to inspect the stone.

"That's great," Alex says. "Yep." You can tell Alex doesn't know how to inspect sixty tons of number two limestone, but he is doing his best. He is trying to fit in. I can only hope he doesn't ask for a pinch of tobacco.

We all stand out here shivering, talking limestone. Talking red dog. Talking about how cold it is. Soon, and inevitably, we get into a conversation about the multiflora. Because this is what all the locals talk about when they stop by. Because this is the most obvious thing to talk about. Well, this and the fact that our barn is collapsing.

"You gotta doze it," Billy says, and then he spits again.

"Doze it?"

"The multiflora," he says. "You gotta go at it with the bull-dozer. It's your only hope." He says he's cleaned up a lot of farms with his John Deere 350. Multiflora doesn't root very deeply, so you can scrape it off the face of the earth, leaving most of the topsoil intact. It would be something like giving the farm a shave, although he calls it "pushin' briars."

He spits.

He says, "Tom?"

Tom, his teenage son, hops out of the truck. He's a short, compact kid in a black cowboy hat, a ski jacket, and tight jeans. He spits, too. I've really never been around spitting, except for seeing baseball players do it on TV, so this is taking some getting used to.

"Tom, get the hats," Billy says. Tom goes back to the truck, leans in, and emerges with two hats.

"Here," he says to me. "Here," he says to Alex. The hats are, yes, orange, and they feature the phone number of Nichols and Sons Excavation Company. "You give me a call if you want us to push any briars," Billy says.

"Thank you," I say. "These are very nice hats." I put mine on. I'm acquiring quite a nice orange hat collection.

"You want this limestone?" he asks.

"Sure," we say.

"Well, move these cars outa here, and we'll get it down."

I go in for the keys. I put on another coat, the only coat I can find, Alex's wretched old parka with grease all over it that he calls his "barn coat." Phew. It stinks. It stinks of diesel fuel. But, oh good, there are gloves inside. Well, sort of gloves. They're . . . rags. Doesn't Alex ever throw anything out? I go into the basement and find some galoshes, then head out. We juggle the cars, and I end up in the pickup, halfway up Wilson Road. I think: Well, as long as I'm out here, why don't I go get us all some lunch? I hop out of the truck, yell out, yell over the pond, over the barnyard, to Alex. "I'm going to go get some food!"

"What!?"

"Food!"

"What?"

Whatever. We need to get walkie-talkies or something. It's hard to communicate over fifty acres.

I head up to Tradesmen's, the same place Alex and I went on

moving day. I've grown to like the place, the homemade chili, the fresh-baked bread.

I pull into the parking lot. I'm glad I'm in the pickup, now that I think about it, because now I fit in with all these other pickups. My pickup is empty just like all the other ones. I wonder if people drive pickups just because other people drive pickups.

A woman pulls in behind me. She is in a sedan. A Subaru. She looks completely out of place. She looks like she should be at a Taco Bell. It's weird the way I've so quickly become part of the pickup team, not that I am really part of the pickup team.

The woman in the Subaru steps out of her Subaru. She has on a skirt, heels, and pantyhose. She looks like I used to look, only months ago, back when I was thirty-seven years old and lived in the city and worked in the Benedum Trees Building. Back when I was a normal person. I am still that person, even though I now look like, well, this person. She looks at me, looks at me up and down, as I climb out of my Elly May Clampett truck with the bullet holes in it.

I peer ever so quickly up toward the sky to confirm that, yes, I am wearing an orange hat featuring the phone number of an excavation company. I am wearing a wretched old coat that smells of diesel fuel. My gloves are rags, and I have on a disgusting pair of galoshes.

The woman stretches her lips back with a fake smile, like you do with people you would prefer to avoid.

Okay, I need to talk to her.

I really need to talk to her.

I need to say, "Wait a second here. You don't understand. *This is not who I am!* No, no, no, you've got it all wrong. *This is not who I am.*"

I am still me. Aren't I still me? Yes, I need to tell this stranger who looks like the old me that I am still me.

Instead, and because I really have no choice, I hold the door for her and step inside.

EIGHT

THERE IS A LADYBUG IN THE KITCHEN SINK, THE tiniest creature. It's an odd thing to see in February, the dead of winter. But in the months since I've been at the farm, amidst all the craziness and confusion, there has always been this bug.

"Well, hello there," I say, as I do each morning when I'm putting the coffee on. "Dude, why do you insist on hanging out by the drain?" Drains are dangerous places for bugs. I pick the ladybug up and put it on the windowsill, where Bob is sitting. Bob loves this windowsill. And Bob never bothers the bug. *Thank you, Bob.*

I have gotten good at picking the ladybug up, confident. At first I would put my finger out and wait for it to crawl. But now I grab it by the shell and gently squeeze. It never flails its legs or anything. I am even beginning to believe it likes the attention.

I have decided, rather arbitrarily, that this ladybug needs a spider plant to live in. Maybe then it will stay away from the drain. The next time I go to the store, I'm going to buy a spider plant so the ladybug will have some entertainment. Maybe I can even find one with aphids.

My mother said country living would be lonely. I have barely even begun to settle in here, and already she is right. Alex has moved himself down here, and by and large I have moved myself down here, and this is our home. Still, there are days that go by when Alex is in town working, and I'm here trying to work, and all I do is sit in my office and dial the phone, reaching out. But I have to believe, really believe, that the loneliness is just a stage. I believe loneliness is a door you have to go through—a passage leading you to solitude.

Solitude is what I'm after. The kind of tranquillity that allows you access to your own imagination. Or at least, this is what I'm telling myself. I wanted to get away from those investment brokerage people staring at me like I was a zoo animal. I wanted to get away from the crazy neighbor brat with the lunatic eyes. I wanted to go to a place where I could think, really sink into my own imagination, or ride it, drift along with it, as in a balloon. The kind of place probably all writers crave. The kind of place where the outside world is still and quiet and you get a chance to listen, to peer, to go inward via something as tiny and seemingly insignificant as a ladybug, and witness divine glory.

Divine glory. Really? That's kind of a tall order. Am I here on this farm searching for God? I don't think so. I really don't think so. *"Am I?"* I ask, looking up. He doesn't answer. He never answers. But okay, I've gotten used to that. And me and God, we're doing fine. I mean, basically. I mean, we have our ups and downs like anybody else. But I can't say this has been a particularly troublesome time in our relationship.

"Divine glory"? What's that? Why did I even think that? That's borrowed lingo. That's probably Thoreau lingo lingering in my head. It's so easy to throw out words without worrying about what they mean.

I miss solitude.

I miss the kid in the shed.

That's what I said. That's what I thought.

But what am I really reaching for? That's what I'm wondering now, standing here in the kitchen watching this ladybug. It's running the length of the windowsill, back and forth, as if unhappy about this sill. I think it wants the sink. All right. I put it back in the sink. It seems happier here, although I cannot verify that.

Mildly interested, Bob looks down at the bug, and then he shuts his eyes, as if meditating. *Bob, you are so good at solitude.*

I think about that shed I went to when I was a kid, surrounded by those animals on the farm behind our house. What did I find there? Or what did I leave there?

And why did I even feel the need to run there in the first place? Why did I reach for solitude when I was ten? I didn't have the kind of home a person would need to escape from. There was laughter in our house on Lorraine Drive. There was laughter and kindness and love. And an awful lot of agreement. Everybody agreed with everybody else. On matters of food, God, presidents, baseball.

Did I agree? It was hard to know. Hard to separate. Hard to become an individual when bouncing along inside the bubble of the family.

At the farm, with those animals, and in that shed, I think I figured things out. I formed opinions, or at least the urge for some I could call my own. How can you know who you are, what you believe, where you are in relation to anything else in the world, when you are all knotted up with everybody else?

I think the call of the inward life starts here. Solitude helps you differentiate, define the borders of the self. Solitude helps you figure out where everybody else stops and you begin.

People figure this out in all different ways, of course. My friend Marie figured it out in her own way. She was my best friend all through college, one of the ones that got the Subaru and now has the minivan. Actually, she's moved on to a Ford Expedition and a vacation home at the seashore. She hated being alone. We were opposites that way. I would quote Thoreau: "I never found the companion that was so companionable as solitude." She would twist her lip and tell me I was nuts. She was an only child of older parents and couldn't seem to get enough noise in her life. She needed the energy of peers to make her whole. I'd get tangled up in the peers, caught up in the culture, lost.

Defining the edges of the self isn't something that happens once in your life, of course. It's not like you figure it out and then get on with things. It's a process. For me it's inward, outward, inward, outward. The turtle act. The turtle who needs to pull her head in when the light gets too bright.

But the problem with solitude, I am finding, is that it's really not an easy place to get to. Solitude is quite different from being alone. Solitude is the state of being alone *without losing your mind*. There's a fine line there somewhere. Or maybe a thick line. Because the only way to get to solitude is to step through the door of loneliness.

This is what I'm having a hard time doing here at the farm. I am lonely. Alex is in town all day, day after day, and I am here alone, working, writing. It's where I said I wanted to be. But I am lonely.

Maybe I'm no good at solitude. I don't know. Maybe I'm too weak. Or too needy. Or too frightened. Or too something.

"I never said, 'I want to be alone,' " Greta Garbo once commented. "I only said, 'I want to be *left* alone.' There is all the difference."

I love that.

I should exit my Thoreau stage once and for all and enter my Greta Garbo stage.

I should start wearing dark eyeliner.

Like Greta Garbo.

And Betty.

I should say to hell with solitude and start having some fun like Betty.

Okay, when you are jealous of your dog's life, you know you have a problem.

But look at her out there in that yard. Rolling on a dead thing. Look at the joy in her beautiful eyes. Look at that black goo all over her neck. She seems so happy about it. She appears so completely uninterested in understanding the essence of her inner dog. She's just . . . dog. And now here comes Marley. Betty prances over to him, leans in to him as if wanting to show off her new perfume. Marley sniffs. Marley leaps. Marley looks like a mechanical dog the way he can spring from a standing position up into the air. Soon the two dogs are wrestling, doing dog somersaults in the leaves.

Fun. They are having so much fun.

I look at the ladybug. I am starting to *identify* with this ladybug. I am sympathetic with the urge to go down that drain. Because intuitively I know that going down the drain is a lot easier than sitting here in solitary confinement.

To hell with solitary confinement. This is not natural. Maybe I am at the farm to find solitude, but on some level I am also at the farm to embrace the natural world, and this is not natural. Humans are pack animals, we crave each other, we grow and mature and flourish because of each other. We learn to swim, to ride bikes, by watching each other. We learn our values, our principles, by debating each other. We discover who we want to be in the eyes of God by singing praise with each other.

We need each other. Just like this ladybug needs more ladybugs, or at least some aphids to keep life interesting. I will bring it the spider plant tomorrow. There is nothing that can be done about it today.

Or is there? I mean, I could run errands. Yes, I am sure I have some errands to run. I could run errands and pick up a spider plant along the way.

"Okay, ladybug," I say. "You talked me into it."

I give Bob a scratch behind the ears, then grab my coat and keys. I get in the car and head to the stores. One thing I love about Scenery Hill is that it's far from the stores, but close at the same time. Far, in that you go for ten minutes over the hills and through the farms, past the sheep and the beautiful barns that make up this valley, and suddenly when the hills relax and become flat, there is a highway. Ten minutes down the highway, you have exited the past and entered the present. And in the present, all the shopping centers are contained, in one intersection of two highways. The present doesn't spill out into the past, at least not yet. Past and present are separated by a perfect twenty minutes of driving, about enough time for you to become emotionally prepared for either.

Okay, there's the Wal-Mart. It's a huge, low, flat, boring building with a blue top. I've never been in a Wal-Mart before. I've been in a few Kmarts, though. I didn't feel like I belonged.

The sign says that Wal-Mart is open twenty-four hours a day. This comforts me. I love knowing that anytime, day or night, when I need to see people, Wal-Mart will be here.

In the store, a lady in a blue apron greets me. "Welcome to Wal-Mart!" she says, rolling a cart toward me. I love her instantly. I love her because she is here.

I wonder how many people in this Wal-Mart are here for the same reason I am here. I wonder if anybody is here to pick up a spider plant for a lonely ladybug.

I navigate the aisles with my shopping cart and note one heck of a deal on dog food. One heck of a deal on paper towels and Diet Pepsi. The aisles are wide. The place is so well lit. The shelves are so neat. I am feeling so good about Wal-Mart.

I find the plant section. I see some spider plants in hanging wicker baskets. I look through them, looking for one with aphids. No aphids. These are healthy plants, darn it. Whoever is in charge of Wal-Mart's plant department is doing a good job. I put one of the largest ones in my shopping cart.

I pull out my cell phone. I have to call Alex, I have to tell him that Wal-Mart is *so much nicer* than Kmart. There is no comparison.

I am having a spiritual experience, all right.

I am becoming a person who appreciates Wal-Mart.

My cell phone battery is dead. Again? Something is wrong with this stupid battery. Well, that's convenient. Because now I get to go shop in the cell phone section of the store. A nice young man who introduces himself as Cal offers to help me. No, he doesn't have my kind of battery. But let's see. And he gets out his battery book, looks mine up. He tells me no, I'm not likely to find my battery at

Wal-Mart. Then he tells me about a cell phone store nearby. Pretty soon he is drawing me a map to the cell phone store.

I want to say "I love you, Cal." I want to say "I love you, Wal-Mart." But instead I say thank you and make a dignified exit. I pay for the spider plant and put it in my car.

At the cell phone store, which is so much more than a cell phone store, I see something. I see one of those new satellite dishes, eighteen inches in diameter, capable of beaming something like five hundred million thousand TV stations straight from outer space into your living room.

Jim, the salesperson, sees me eyeing those babies. He says, "May I help you?"

"Just looking," I say.

"Well, how many stations do you get with your cable TV?" he asks.

"We don't get cable where I live," I say. "I live on a farm." (I love saying this. Almost as much as I love saying "Alex is down in the barn.") "I live on a farm."

"Then you are the perfect candidate for a satellite dish!"

Which is true. I mean, we only get two channels on the farm TV, and even those are very snowy.

"Are they expensive to install?" I ask.

He says I could install a dish like this myself, no problem. "I put my mom's up in, like, a half an hour." He shows me how to hook the dish to the dual receivers and how the remote works off a special UHF antenna so you can change channels without even being in the same room as the TV. He shows me the on-screen channel guide, and he demonstrates the superb picture quality, thanks to 120 watts of digitally compressed signal.

I nod, and nod some more, never mentioning the nagging voice in my head: *Six hundred bucks for the privilege of watching a whole lot of stupid television?* Is this really in line with my values? Do I really want to be a person who has access to five hundred million thousand TV channels?

Well, yes.

But it's not something I would brag about.

I think of the ladybug, the drain. That ladybug needs a spider plant. And I need a satellite dish.

I hand Jim my Visa, and soon it is a done deal. I become a person with a satellite dish.

I bring the satellite dish and the spider plant into the house. I hang the plant over the kitchen sink. The ladybug is down by the drain again. "All right, little guy," I say. "The fun *begins*." I pick it up and put it on a leaf. It crawls back and forth, and I can't really tell if it's happy or not.

I call Alex and tell him about the satellite dish. I can't really tell if he's happy or not about it. But then again, he is not much of a TV watcher. But then again, he is working in the city every day and he sees actual humans, so he places less value on virtual ones.

ON SATURDAY WE TACKLE THE SATELLITE DISH installation. To get the ladder up, we have to make our way through the briars that have grown up against the house. We climb onto the roof, one at a time, me with the installation kit, Alex with the instruction manual between his teeth, and a belt full of tools around his waist, and the satellite dish, a kind of giant gray dinner plate, under his arm.

"I wonder what our neighbors will think when they see we have a satellite dish!" I say, excited.

"Hee hon ha hay heehor," he says.

"Huh?"

He spits out the instruction manual.

"We don't have any neighbors."

Good point. And I so love the way we are talking "we." More and more we are talking "we." It's becoming positively normal to say "we." Because we are blending our lives together, ever so quietly. We are blending our futures together, ever so gently. Maybe we needed the crashingly loud reality of this farm to help us work out the rest of things, as if in the background of a picture. The fuzzy part. The part you see but don't really see.

There have been no statements, no big talks, no big get-on-your-knee-and-ask-me-to-marry-you moments. And anyway, you would have to torture me with big flaming knives to get me to admit that this is what I want, this is what I wish, this is the dream come true that happens to other people, not me. But Alex, he's already tried the M-thing. I know he has no interest in trying it again.

But, Alex. I have Alex. I have a we. We have this farm. We have Betty and Marley, and even Bob is still alive. I have no reason in this world to complain. I love this life. I feel like I am alive, really alive, for the first time since I was ten. I think about that shed. What I found there, what I left there. I think about solitude, what it's for. I think about finding a place in which you can sit and differentiate yourself from the rest of the world. And I think: Why? Why does it matter? Why do you need to know the edges of the self?

Standing here on this roof with Alex, I have a notion. I think you need to know the edges of the self before you can begin to know how to knit them together with someone else's edges. Before you can really know how to love.

How strange to think that solitude and love have coexisted all along, like a coin has to have both heads and tails.

"Okay, do you want me to do something?" I ask Alex.

"Just stand there and look pretty," he says.

"Oh, please."

"But you do look pretty today," he says.

"But you're starting to sound like the locals around here," I say.

"Yeah, what is up with that?" he says. "The womenfolk in these parts sort of drape themselves over the men and don't talk."

"Womenfolk?" I say. *"Womenfolk in these parts?"*

"I'm starting to talk weird, aren't I?"

"You are," I say.

"I think I'm discovering my inner hick," he says. "This could get ugly."

"Get?" I say.

He hoists the bracket up to the called-for seventy-five-degree angle, reaching toward the southwestern sky. He holds the dish up, trying to see how it will fit. I'm not sure I like the way it looks. I'm not sure a satellite dish really goes with our new country image. Fifty rolling acres, a bank barn built in 1887 by Amish dairy farmers, a lily pond with a visiting blue heron dining on a resident frog, a stream meandering beneath a towering chestnut grove—and a satellite dish?

Even Eva Gabor on *Green Acres* didn't sit around watching TV, at least not that I can remember. And I hate it when I'm driving through some rural area, drinking up the pastoral landscape, imagining all the country people in their houses churning butter or weaving rag rugs or canning peaches—and then there's a giant satellite dish in the yard. It's like a billboard announcing a homeowner's priorities: "Hello, I am a person who watches a hell of a lot of TV."

It's a good thing they make these things so small now. That's what I'm thinking. Eighteen inches around will not be so . . . obvious.

"It's taking us a lot longer to install this thing than it took Jim to install his mother's," I say to Alex, after we've been at this for several hours.

He looks at me.

"But it's taking us, like, four hours longer than it took Jim to install his mother's," I say.

"I don't care about Jim's damn mother," he snaps.

It occurs to me I better shut up.

"Okay, let's try again," he says. "Go on in, and tell me what it says."

Alex is on the roof aiming the dish at the southern sky, while I clamber off the roof and head inside for the fiftieth time to watch a little red bar go up and down on the TV screen, indicating signal strength.

"Hey, we got sixty percent!" I yell. "Whoa, now it's forty. . . . Oh God, you're losing it! YOU ARE LOSING IT!"

"WHAT?!"

"YOU HAD IT, BUT NOW YOU LOST IT! Hold on! Okay, you are at EIGHTY PERCENT! DON'T MOVE!"

I run outside, climb the ladder. "Don't move an inch!" We are finally aimed directly at the satellite, and now all we have to do is put in the final bolt, a specially designed cylinder that will hold the entire four-and-a-half-hour project together.

Alex is balanced on his left knee, reaching for the bolt, which I am about to hand him but then . . . I drop it. It goes *tinkle, tinkle, tinkle* rolling down the roof. We watch it bounce off the lowest row of shingles, vault like that skier on the old *Wide World of Sports* intro, sail through the air as though in slow motion, and land, *plop*, in a pile of rotting leaves.

"Sorry about that, chief," I say, feeling myself in a total Maxwell Smart moment.

It is dusk by the time we find the bolt and finish the job. The stars are coming out. The amazing stars. You don't see stars like this in the city. Every night a display like fireworks. And the satellite dish is pointed at them. And somehow one of those stars is sending me TV, glorious TV.

I've never really considered TV a cosmic experience before. I mean, what's cable? A wire hooked to another wire hooked to a cable company. There is no mystery in cable. But now a satellite. More than 22,300 miles up, moving at the exact same speed as the Earth moves. And I have a path to it, through the sky, piercing the atmosphere, invisible.

I have never, ever thought of the transcendent quality of television.

I am, I think, desperate.

Desperate for TV.

Desperate for some kind of transcendent experience.

I am beginning to believe transcendence can happen only when you're not looking for it. It was the ladybug that led me to the spider plant. It was the spider plant that led me to the stars.

"Okay, it's working," Alex says, while I grab a blanket and a bag of Doritos and prepare for some serious Saturday night viewing.

"But we can't watch TV," he says.

"What?"

"We have tickets to the ballet," he says.

"We do?"

"Yes," he says. "It's, well, a surprise. Happy Valentine's Day!"

"Oh," I say, delighted and disappointed at the same time. I think about those five hundred million thousand TV stations. And Valentine's Day isn't, technically, until tomorrow.

"Can you be ready in a half an hour?" he says. "The show starts at eight-thirty, so we really should hurry."

"Oh," I say.

"If you don't want to go," he says, his shoulders starting to slump. "I mean, it's, well, *Romeo and Juliet.*"

I snap out of it, snap out of it like when you're driving on the Turnpike and about to fall asleep. Suddenly it hits you, just hits you: It is not an option to sleep now.

"I'd love to go," I say. "What a wonderful surprise." Here, after all, is the man I love making a most loving gesture. I think of how many Valentine's Days I've spent home alone, with a bag of Doritos and a blanket and a TV.

So we get all dressed up. Alex puts on his new gray suit and his new tie with the tiny geometric petunias on it. I put on the slinky black number I wore when I was recently a judge at the Miss Delaware pageant. That's kind of a long story. I was there to write a magazine story about it. It was my first time judging a beauty pageant. And actually, I had something of an epiphany at that pageant. Many of the other judges were former Miss Delawares. On the elevator, headed to our first judges' meeting, one of them turned to me and said, "You look great! What year are you?"

"Huh?" I said.

"What year?"

Then the most fantastic truth hit me: *She thinks I am a former Miss Delaware.* It was beautiful. It was interplanetary. Because I never even knew I *wanted* to be a former Miss Delaware.

Later that evening, I told Alex, who had joined me on the assignment. I said, "Hey! One of the other judges thinks I am a former Miss Delaware!"

He looked at me. He said, *"You?"*

And right then the sky dropped on my head. He saw me go limp. He saw my spine go all wobbly. And he knew he was sunk. He knew it right then and there.

"It's just that, well, you hardly ever even *go* to Delaware," he said. It came out like a tweet.

Oh, please.

But well, whatever. I picked myself right the hell back up again. I ignored him. I sent him to the beach to think about his sin. And so then naturally, the whole rest of the weekend I hung around the lady who mistook me for a former Miss Delaware.

For the record, I wanted Miss Dover to win. Her platform, "Milk: From Moo to You," was quite informative. But she lost out to Miss Rehoboth with the flute act.

Anyway. The black dress. The ballet. The city. Alex and I head into town on this horribly cold February night. The city is so alive. How strange it all seems. All the lights. My God! Blinding lights! And all these people around doing all these . . . people things. Everybody going about their lives, hailing buses, sleeping on steam vents. I am reminded of Mark, the one who believes in the fifty-fifty split. A few years ago, Mark moved to Alaska. Just fled in a pickup truck, late one December night. It took him days to get there. He came back for a visit about a year later—via airplane—and kept complaining about how overwhelmed he was by Pittsburgh. The noise. The traffic. The tension. I thought: *Pittsburgh?* Sweet little Pittsburgh? I didn't actually believe him. I didn't think you could lose all those filters you created for city living so quickly.

But here in town, I believe him. I feel so unfiltered. We park in a big indoor lot. The elevator doesn't work. It makes me cranky. I'm cold. I go clicking in my fancy Miss Delaware heels down a stairway that reeks of urine.

In the concert hall, my mood is supposed to . . . shift. I mean, that's what you have to do in the city. You have to forget that you just walked down a stinky stairway and passed all those people on steam vents, and you have to immediately start feeling good. Okay. And sure, yes, it's beautiful in this concert hall. Opulent. Our seats are magnificent, ten rows back, center section. Perfumes swirl in the air. This is the first ballet I've been to in years. It feels wonderful to be here, next to Alex, holding his hand. The lights go out. The dancers emerge. And soon . . . Juliet.

A most delicate Juliet.

A butterfly.

There is desperation in the arch of her back, fire in her legs. The music lulls me. I feel desperation in the arch of my back. Fire in my legs. For a time, I become Juliet, a twirling Juliet. By the time she wakes up, sees Romeo dead beside her, I am in tears.

I've never cried at a ballet before. I never knew a ballet could capture me in this way. Maybe it's the filterless life.

Afterward we go for a late-night bite, and then Alex says let's go back to the farm. Even though it's an hour's drive, even though we could so easily stay in the South Side house, even though this is exactly the sort of occasion I kept the South Side house for.

"I need us to be at the farm," he says. The farm has come to represent something to Alex that it hasn't for me. For him, I think it really is an escape. A kind of church. He's so much calmer there, so much gentler in his view of himself. Sometimes when we're at the farm, I'll look at him and see an inner-city kid blossoming at camp.

It's midnight by the time we pull into the driveway. A moonless midnight, dark as ink. The clouds have moved in, moved in tight. It's cold. It's damp. We rush toward the door, and Alex grabs me.

"Let's take a walk," he says.

"*What?*" I say. "Honey. It's *February*."

"Right."

"And I'm in *heels*."

"Right. But I want to go to the top of the hill with you," he says.

"There is no way I'm walking up that hill in this cold," I say, sounding like my mother.

"All right," he says.

When we get inside, I move toward the TV. There are five hundred million thousand TV stations beckoning, and I have yet to try one.

"Don't," he says. "I have to ask you something."

"Well, what?"

"Well, wait here," he says.

I sit on the couch, fling my shoes off, look at the blank screen. That poor TV. That TV needs me. Bob jumps up, curls himself next to me. Bob wants to watch TV, too.

Alex comes back into the room with flowers. Wow! A dozen pink roses. "Wow!" I say. He's really doing this Valentine's Day up. What did we do last year? Did we do anything? A fancy dinner maybe? Nothing like this.

"Thank you!" I say, standing up to hug him tight. "They're gorgeous."

"Oh, God. Look at this floor," he says. "I should vacuum."

Huh? Is he okay? Alex cleans when he's nervous, sort of like I itch when I'm scared. He gets out the vacuum, pulls the cord, turns it on. Bob scrams. The dogs leap. The dogs are wearing my same expression: *What the hell?*

He vacuums the whole house, does a really good job, as I doze in and out of vacuum noise. He says we really should buy a Shop-Vac so we can vacuum the basement.

"Uh-huh," I say, half-expecting him to suggest that we now go to the twenty-four-hour Wal-Mart to look at Shop-Vacs.

"Are you okay?" I ask.

It's now two A.M. And he's standing here staring at me.

"Maybe we should turn in for the night?" I suggest.

"Wait here," he says.

And he darts away again.

I lean my head back on the couch, close my eyes.

"Ahem." I open my eyes. He's back. He's standing there holding a tiny black box.

Oh.

He hands it to me, gets on one knee.

Oh.

"Okay," he says. "So. Um. Will you marry me?"

Oh!

Much to my delight, I do not go into full cardiac arrest.

Will I marry him? But . . . he's already tried the M-thing. He doesn't want to do it again. I've been walking around assuming he'd never do it again. But he knows I want to. And he staged this whole event.

Soon I am in tears, holding him, clinging to him. I cry the same tears I cried when I was Juliet, only not those tears at all.

NINE

THE RING IS PLATINUM, A CHANNEL SETTING WITH seven small diamonds. It's too big, which is perfect. Because *engaged*? This is big. Really big. This is so not me. Isn't it? Hell, I hardly ever even had boyfriends.

I call Nancy, one of the babes, to tell her about the ring because I know that of all the babes, she loves this sort of thing. It's good to have a girly girlfriend. It gives you permission.

"Weeee! Woooo!" Nancy squeals on the phone. She wants details. She wants to know how he did it, what he said, where we were sitting. I tell her about the ballet and the roses, which she loves. I tell her about the vacuuming and the satellite dish, which makes her laugh. She thinks Alex is perfect for me.

"So when is it happening?" she asks.

"What?"

"The date?" she says.

"For what?"

"The wedding!" she says.

Oh. A wedding? Well, now. Isn't it enough that Alex and I have gotten the courage to use the E-word? And even the M-word? Now she's talking the *W-word*?

"Where will you have it?" she says. "Do you think you'll wear a gown? I'm definitely wearing a gown. I don't care if it doesn't happen to me until I'm sixty, I'm wearing a gown."

Nancy and I are around the same age, but we are in somewhat different stages. Nancy has a long history of unsatisfying relationships, a series of men she longed for and with whom she rarely made it past the bait-and-switch trick. She thought there was something wrong with her. It never occurred to her it was the men. She went for dangerous men, only the dangerous ones. Over and over again.

About a year and a half ago, Nancy's mother got sick. Really sick. "Bone cancer," the doctors finally said. Then within a few months, her father got sick. Really sick. "Bone marrow cancer," they said. It was the most hideous coincidence imaginable. Both of her parents, one in one bed, one in the other, dying. Nancy would trade off which bed she would curl up in. Nancy's friend Jack started hanging around. He'd lost his parents already, so he had an inkling of what Nancy was going through. He stayed with her. He walked the parental death march with her. Jack was a friend. Not Nancy's type, in that there was nothing particularly dangerous about him, but none of that mattered. He wanted to help her. She needed help. Nancy's father died on a Monday. Her mother died Tuesday of the next week.

And Nancy and Jack fell in love.

It seemed so unfair and yet so oddly and cruelly fair. It seemed like Nancy had to suffer the ultimate sacrifice—losing her parents—before she could find love.

It made me think my friend Mark was right.

Nancy and Jack have been a couple for about a year now. We all know he's going to pop the question any second; it's obvious. I suspect that Alex's little surprise might be just the spark Jack needs.

And we're all going to be so happy for Nancy. We are going to squeal like baby pigs and eat bonbons and make a fuss. Because this is what you do for Nancy; this is what Nancy loves.

"So what are you two going to do today to celebrate?" she asks.

Um. Celebrate? I hadn't actually thought of that. And anyway, wasn't it kind of dangerous to call the attention of the universe to my happiness? I mean, if we go with the Mark theory. Perhaps I should keep a low profile with my joy so as not to call in the agony patrol to even things out.

I tell Nancy that, rather than celebrate, we're thinking of calling Billy today.

"Billy?"

"The guy with the bulldozer."

"Bulldozer," she says.

"The best time to push briars is winter," I say. "And it's already the middle of February."

"Uh-huh."

But I can tell I've lost her. She starts talking about ice-skating. She's lost me.

Maybe the idea Alex and I have of attacking the multiflora now is bigger than February. Maybe it's a way for Alex and me to prepare the farm for our future together, a way of cleansing our hearts of the thickets of the past.

Or maybe it's one big itchy vacuuming project needed to calm our nerves.

Before I call Billy, I call my mother to tell her the E-news. I just blurt it out. I am not good at talking to my mother about such things. My mother is sort of the anti-Nancy. No squealing. None of that girly crap. My mother wanted to be a Chaucer scholar before she met my father. My mother had no intention of ever marrying, especially if it took her away from Chaucer. My parents have been married for fifty-two years, and it is the happiest marriage I have ever seen.

My mom and dad are thrilled with the news that Alex and I are getting married. The phone starts ringing off the hook. My sisters, my brother. Everybody is thrilled. First of all, because they all love Alex. They know he's good for me. But I also think they're relieved. I think they're sick of the way I've always been so mysterious, so private, about matters of romance. I rarely brought guys home— except the ones from foreign countries whom no one could actually converse with.

I don't know why I held the truth of my love life so close to my heart. My sisters did not do this. The whole family lived through Claire's divorce. And Kristin had a new boyfriend around every few months. But I was embarrassed by love. I was embarrassed to admit I wanted it or needed it. I'd get prickly if anyone asked.

Perhaps this was the unintended fallout of some of my mother's guidance. She seemed to harp on me, more than she did on the others, about being independent. Learning to live your own life, that was the most important thing. Not a life in the shadow of some man. My mother would never actually call herself a feminist. But that's what she is. She's a feminist in the same way a nun is a feminist: someone who hears the call to do something, become something, and who does it without worrying about what anybody has to say about it. For my mother, the call was to be a wife and mother. It was something she never expected, never wanted. It was completely out of whack with her plan. But that's what it was, so that's what she became.

She didn't let us play with Barbie dolls. That was no role model for a little girl. She didn't let us watch the Miss America pageant. (And yes, I told her about the Miss Delaware comment. She said, *"You?"* Now perhaps you can see why she and Alex get along so well.)

Beauty queens, Barbie dolls, these were no role models for women. "Don't depend on your looks because your looks won't last," she would say. She was not big on makeup or jewelry. I waited months and months for her to help me bridge the gap between childhood and adolescence by telling me when to start shaving my legs. She never did tell me, so I just started doing it. The same way with dating. I figured she would say something. Something like,

"Okay, it's time to start." But she never did. So I went ahead and did it. But somewhere along the line, I got the idea that it was wrong. Like shaving my legs was wrong. Because she never actually gave me permission for any of this.

And she talked over and over again to me about independence, about being independent. Why did she pick me to give these lectures to? Because I was the youngest? The last one? The public school experiment? Because she saw something of herself in me? I have no idea. But it stuck. I would not allow myself to get too attached to men, because attachment itself was a threat.

So maybe this is why I rarely brought boyfriends home. I don't know. I am only figuring this out now, when it doesn't matter. But it does matter, because this is who I am, or this is who I was. How much of who you were do you have to take into who you will be?

I finish the call with my mother. Alex calls his kids. First Amy, then Peter. They both say the same thing everybody else has said so far: "Hooray!" and then, "When is the wedding?"

I wish everybody would just stop at the hooray part.

Eventually, I call Billy. It feels good to talk about something else. Who knew bulldozer talk could be a breath of fresh air?

Billy says, "You got coffee on?"

"I'll put it on," I say.

"Me and Tom will be right over," he says.

And all I can think is: They're going to come inside? But where will they spit? I wonder if I'm supposed to have some kind of spitting thing here in my house for these people.

THE THERMOMETER HAS NOT HIT FIFTEEN DEGREES today. When Billy and Tom come over, they take off layers and layers of clothing, draping them by the fireplace. There is no spitting at all. We have a good time. They tell me stories of Billy's life. Some great moments in bulldozing, including the many times Billy nearly died.

"He's got scars on his legs that are tire tracks," Tom says. There is a softness to Tom, a padding on his face that lends him innocence. His eyes don't line up right. Or no, there's something about the two sides of his face that don't quite match. There is an awkwardness to Tom.

"I've been shot at," Billy says. An ex-con came after him with a .22. The bullet hit a can of Skoal in Billy's breast pocket, diverted, then skimmed across his chest before lodging in. It lodges there still.

"So now we only chew Skoal," Tom says.

Everything is beginning to make an uncomfortable amount of sense.

We talk about snow. We've been so lucky this year with snow.

"I can remember Fran, the lady who used to live here, getting snowed in for a week once," Billy says. He says he used to plow the driveway for her. "Because that tractor you got, you can't really drive that on this property."

We can't? But I love that tractor, that giant skinny rooster standing in the barn.

"You'll kill yourself on these hills," he says. "It's a good tractor, but it's for if you got smooth land, like in Ohio. With your property, you need four-wheel drive, and you need a roll bar. And a seat belt. You'll kill yourself without four-wheel drive and a roll bar."

I look at Alex.

"Oh," he says.

"You sell that tractor," he says, "and I'll find you a new one."

But exactly how does one go about selling a tractor?

"You want me to, I'll sell it for you," he says. "I'll find you a new one." It is, he says, the neighborly thing to do. "Meantime, you get snow here, you call me. I'll plow it. Don't you do it on that tractor. I'd hate to see new neighbors ending up dead."

One thing you have to say about country life versus city life is, there are a lot more things that can kill you in the country.

We work out a deal with Billy. He says if he can keep his bulldozer parked here for the rest of the winter, and if he can work on our briars when the weather is okay and when he's got a free day, then he'll reduce his sixty-five-dollars-per-hour rate to fifty dollars.

"Sounds good," Alex says, having no real basis for comparison.

Billy and Tom start putting all their clothes back on so they can go outside and get started. Betty and Marley come over to sniff them and their clothes.

"What kind of dog is that?" Billy says, looking at Marley.

"That there's a poodle," Alex says.

That there?

"A poodle?" Billy says. "I never seen one like that."

"A standard poodle," Alex says. "Not one of those yappy things."

"You don't see a lot of poodles around here," Tom points out.

"He's a great dog," I say. "Really, um, smart. Poodles were used as sentry dogs in Vietnam, you know."

"I flew a helicopter upside down in Vietnam," Billy says.

"Upside down," Tom says.

They head out into the bitter air. Soon they are heave-hoing with a lot of heavy chains, moving the bulldozer off the trailer. Then they drive away in their big red truck, leaving the bulldozer an ominous presence in our yard.

They start the next morning at dawn. I know this because the low rumble of the machine wakes me up. I climb out of bed, following the sound to my office window, the one with the birch tree outside it and the scanner underneath it, which is still Bob's bed. Alex follows, and so do the dogs.

Through the dim morning light, I can see Billy driving the mighty yellow machine. It is spewing black smoke. Tom walks ahead of it, breathing white clouds, and he makes a lot of hand motions, like a coach in a baseball game. The roar of the bulldozer rattles the windows. Bob has been interrupted from his slumber and is sitting on the windowsill, watching. I am watching. Betty is here, watching, and Marley and Alex, too. All of us, a unit.

The blade of the bulldozer comes down, and Tom motions for it to come forward. As it does, the huge thicket starts moving, too. First a little jostle, and then, with virtually no oomph on the part of the bulldozer, the giant evil bush is on its side like some pathetic little tumbleweed. Billy keeps driving forward, pushing the bush into a ravine.

Behind him, nothing. Just space, glorious space. A blank canvas for nature to fill.

That's what I see. I don't know what Bob or Betty or Marley or Alex sees. We all stand here a long time watching. There's something soothing about watching the brambles get scraped off the surface of your life. It's like going to confession, getting all those black spots wiped off your soul. It's like starting a new life, one free and clear of all the thick nonsense that used to strangle you. All the things you used to believe about yourself that weren't true, not really, they were just good ideas gone crazy.

I find myself transfixed, but not by the machine. Not by the briars in motion. I find myself transfixed by . . . nothing. After the briars are gone—once cover to deer, rabbits, and other timid creatures—nothing. Nothing never looked so beautiful. Nothing is something. Nothing is a patch of rich, beautiful topsoil. What's going to happen when the sun reaches this unclaimed place? What's going to happen now that the prickly cover has been stripped away?

SHEEP ARE STUPID

TEN

SHEEP, I AM TOLD, ARE STUPID. I'M NOT SURE WHY this matters. But every time we tell someone around here that we're thinking of putting sheep on these fields, we get the same response: Sheep are stupid.

Sheep are so stupid, one neighbor told me, that if they get scared, they'll keep running and running and running, headlong into a fence, and die of strangulation.

I don't know why he didn't blame the fence instead of the sheep, but that is neither here nor there. The main thing is, we're soon going to have about fifteen acres of multiflora-free land, and we need to decide what to do with it—before Mother Nature does.

It's April, and Billy has been out there pushing briars for two months. The sound of the bulldozer has been good company. The roar of the diesel reminds me I'm not alone here. Sometimes when it's close, it even makes the kitchen sink vibrate. When I worked in the city, I remember, there were guys renovating a parking lot outside my office window. How I cursed those workers and their jackhammers. How strange to find myself embracing bulldozer noise.

Every afternoon at about four, Billy knocks on my door. He'll say, "Well, come on out and see what we did." And so we'll wander together over the mounds and mounds of clumpy earth and broken trees. Betty and Marley race ahead, sniffing several generations of recently unearthed sniffs. Billy likes to tell me which areas were the toughest to negotiate and where the surprises were. He's buried a lot of the uprooted briars in ravines, while the rest have been pushed into enormous piles that are set on fire with a combination of diesel, gasoline, and old tires. The tires, apparently, are the key to making briars burn. Some of these piles have been smoldering for weeks now. It's quite stunning to see how many new views we have now that a lot of the briars are gone. We can even see the pond now from the top of the hill. "It's gorgeous!" I'll say to Billy, when we're out there looking around.

"Thank you," he'll say. "I'm glad you like it."

It's something we have in common, seeing the beauty in the briar-free hills. It's something I have come to value. Because I have invited several of the babes down to see how the land looks now that the briars are gone. "Isn't it *gorgeous*?" I'll say, as we hike over the mud, and they hold on to branches to keep their balance on the slippery surface. "Um, gorgeous," the babes say, unconvincingly. The babes curl their lips. The babes tend to focus on the thirty-foot-high piles everywhere with stinky smoke coming out. "This is sort of how I imagine Germany just after the war," one said.

Billy's son, Tom, comes to work with his dad most days. He's a senior in high school—which doesn't get in the way of his work schedule too badly. Schools around here still let kids out to help with family farms and family businesses. Schools around here consider it a service to the community, which is still reeling from the loss of coal mines; to the family, which has more work to do than anyone can do alone; and to the kid, who is learning a trade. Tom never drives the bulldozer, though. He stays on the ground and directs traffic. When Tom is not needed in this way, he often sits in the mud and pets Marley. Tom has taken to Marley; in a way, I think he feels sorry for him. Like Marley is the village idiot or something. A lot of workers who stop by to help Billy, they'll make poodle jokes.

Dumb jokes, like Marley would get eaten by a sheep if we got sheep, or Marley better watch out lest a giant groundhog fetch him. Well, I didn't say they were funny jokes or even clever jokes, just Marley-is-a-wuss-dog jokes. But Tom always defends Marley. He'll say, "Stop picking on him. He's a good dog."

Tim, our FedEx guy, is another person who has taken to Marley. In the city, you never know what FedEx man or woman will show up, but here it's always Tim. What a sight it is to see him come moseying up Wilson Road in his rectangular white truck. It's like civilization coming. It makes my heart leap, sort of like I imagine it would be for a person lost at sea finally seeing land. Marley and Betty bark like crazy at the arrival of that truck. Well, Tim brings dog treats. He usually lingers with us for a while. Mostly he talks about cars. What car he wants to buy, what car he used to have, his favorite cars. And as he talks about cars, he sits on the back bumper of his truck, stroking Marley. "This is the first poodle I've ever known," he'll say, smiling curiously at Marley.

It's a good thing Betty is not the jealous type, because Marley sure gets all the attention around here.

These small events leave me feeling happy. I seem to have acquired a whole new talent for feeling happy, or maybe I've rediscovered an old one. The tiniest things delight me. Like this ladybug. Can you believe this ladybug is still here? You have to admit this is a long time to have a bug in your life. It moves between the sink and the spider plant and a porcelain frog next to the sink that I have for putting sponges in.

In my new bug book, I found out that this ladybug is a Multicolored Asian Ladybird Beetle, *Harmonia axyridis,* and that it can live up to three years. It's supposed to hibernate in the winter, though. So I don't know why this one is so peppy. In the cool weather, it's supposed to find a dark crevice to sleep in and then emit an "aggregating pheromone," a chemical attracting other ladybugs. This is another thing my ladybug apparently hasn't done, since it is still very much alone.

Sometimes I think about emitting an aggregating pheromone.

Sometimes I think about what it would be like if I could turn this farm into a neighborhood—I'll bet all of South Side could fit in these fifty acres—with friends close by and neighbors making neighbor noise, reminding you that you are part of a larger whole. But mostly I project these longings onto the ladybug, which seems, at least for now, to be living out my loneliness for me.

The other bug I really like reading about in my bug book is the seventeen-year cicada, *Magicicada septendecim,* which has the longest life span of any bug. Now there's a bug. It lives underground, sucking on tree roots—for seventeen years. Then, as if magically, it somehow knows that its seventeen years are up. It crawls out of the ground, anchors on a tree, molts, flies around in a swarm of its pals, makes the most awful racket, finds a mate, mates, dies. According to my book, I'll be forty years old when the *Magicicada septendecim* appears here the next time. I can't help but wonder what it's doing now, underground. I can't help but wonder who or what tells it that it has reached its seventeenth birthday and that it's time to go, time to flee, time to start an entirely new adventure.

These are the kinds of things I wonder in the daytime, as I sit here reading bug books, working on my stories, petting Bob on that spot on his spine he likes, and plunging ever so timidly into solitude.

My evenings are with Alex. He'll come home, and we'll eat dinner and talk about our days. Here at "home." Is that really what this place has become? Yes, I believe it has. It's hard to pinpoint the exact moment at which I began to think of it as such. Home doesn't happen that way. Home, I think, is a yanking you feel, a push and pull away from your previous home, a gradual drift. I don't know that you ever necessarily completely leave your old home, or if you even can. You bring a piece of it with you, if only in your heart, your dreams, or some other combination that makes up memory. I am always surprised to note that every time I have a dream set in a place that is supposed to be "home," it actually takes place at 810 Lorraine Drive, the suburban house that I grew up in. In the dream I may be thirty-eight years old, but I am in that house.

I wonder if the South Side house will ever replace Lorraine Drive in my dreams. I sort of doubt it. But South Side will always be a part of me, so much so that I still cannot even imagine selling that house; I am finding all kinds of ways to rationalize keeping it. Lately, Alex and I have been talking about his moving his office there. That little red brick house would make a great place for people to come and dump their misery. That house would understand. That house would never judge, laugh, or betray secrets. I think of that house as a cradle that kept me safe for a decade, and now I don't mind lending it out.

Alex and I have been so busy planning. Planning, planning, planning. No, not wedding planning. We'll get to that. I don't actually know quite what to do about that W-thing, and I do sort of wish the babes would stop nagging me about it. "I am not the bride type!" I remind them. I didn't grow up with dreams of marching down an aisle in a big flowing gown and a droopy veil; as far as I know, I have no inner princess that I long to get in touch with. Or if I do, it is stupid.

But Alex and I are planning. We talk sheep versus goats versus cows. We talk about the pond. It could be a much bigger pond, a five-acre pond instead of a one-acre pond, if we had Billy come in here with even more of his excavation equipment and build the dam up. We talk about building a greenhouse. We talk about how we're going to renovate the house. We talk about getting a horse. Alex says he wants a mule. A mule? Why does he want a mule? He has no idea. Maybe he just likes the sound of the word *mule*. We are like two excited travelers landing in some foreign place, planning our itinerary, overdoing it.

And if there is a nagging in me at all—a vague, almost superstitious sense that this dream is way too good to be true—I am blaming it on spring. Where in the hell is spring? Shouldn't it be here by now? I don't know; maybe I'm used to the mall. At the mall, April is ushered in with colorful new displays in pink and purple and lime green. Out here in the country, the colors seem to wait a lot longer.

We are enveloped in brown. A brown foreground and a slightly lighter tan background and a deep chocolate horizon. Brown. One thing I've discovered about the brown is that, close up, the brown is . . . mud. I've never known such mud. Mud that will suck your boot right off. I understand shoelaces in a whole new way. I even have a much more sympathetic view of concrete. When I go to the city, every other week or so to visit the babes, I like to slap my feet on it. "What a great invention!" I'll say. "Look at that. You can put your foot down and pick it up again, and you still have your shoe on!"

Bleeep, bleeep. Okay, there's the phone. Line One all the way back in the big room. I go charging, and so do Marley and Betty. We have a conditioned response to Line One, my office line. *Bleeep, bleeep.*

"Hello?"

It's Alex. "So what's for dinner tonight, honey?" he says, with only a hint of irony. Suddenly we've been behaving like Samantha and Darren on *Bewitched,* only without the twitching nose part. A smiling husband going to work, coming home to a smiling wife and a pot roast.

I'm on dinner duty. Of course I'm on dinner duty; I'm home all day. Well, I'm working the same hours he's working, but I'm home doing it. And I am soon to be "the wife." I don't mind the idea of "wife." Something about having a full-time man in my life has opened up a domestic side of me I have never before met. I've never been one to make a meal, unless it was a very special occasion in which I had to actually open a jar of spaghetti sauce and actually dump some pasta in a pot of boiling water.

When you are a single person living in the city, you are a restaurant person. You meet your friends for a drink after work and order the low-fat nachos. Or you get take-out Chinese.

And now look at me. Now I'm thinking pork chops. And homemade applesauce. And sauerkraut. That's what we're having tonight. I find that I like cooking. The country makes me appreciate the kitchen. Because the country, or at least this farm, is a place of such vast chaos, and the kitchen is a place I can comprehend.

I tell Alex about the pork chops and the applesauce and the sauerkraut.

"That sounds good," he says. "Listen, can you come into town next Friday with me?"

"What for?"

"My doctor wants me to get a test," he says. "And she says I won't be able to drive."

"What?"

"Well, you know I went in to her today," he says.

"I thought it was just a checkup."

"Well, it was," he says. "But she found something."

"What!"

"I'm sure it's nothing," he says.

"But you just said it was *something*," I say. "What is it? Where is it?"

"Please don't panic," he says. "Really. She said it's probably nothing."

He tells me it's some bleeding, something in his intestine.

"What?"

"I'm sure it's nothing," he says. "She just wants to rule everything out. I swear to you she said it's probably nothing."

"All right," I say. "If you say so. But I don't like the sound—"

"Next Friday," he says. "We have to be there at, like, seven A.M. or something."

"Well, it's a date," I say.

He says he's got to go. He's busy. Another client is about to pop through his door with another hour's worth of misery.

I go back to the kitchen and finish the dishes. Bob is here, rubbing against my legs, weaving himself in and out and between.

Nothing, Bob. He said it was nothing. So then why does he need me to go with him if it's nothing? I'm not liking the sound of that. "Nothing." But okay. I'm not going to stand here and get worked up over nothing. Bob seems to agree. Well, he is not challenging me on the notion. He is purring so loud, I can feel it in my ankles.

I look at the ladybug. The French call ladybugs *"les bêtes du bon Dieu,"* creatures of the good God. In Italy they're called *"vacchette della Madonna,"* cows of the Virgin. In most every culture where ladybugs are found, people regard them as symbols of good luck.

La bête du bon Dieu. A good God. A God who has placed me gently in this place. Well, maybe not gently, but affirmatively. I look beyond the ladybug, out the window. Beyond the window, I see Billy and Tom and the bulldozer. Beyond them, woods and sky and the vast brown unknown. And beyond that: spring. That's one thing you can count on. You can never know what's next in your life, but you can know that spring comes after winter. You can trust, even though it looks impossible right now, that the green and the pink and the purple will come. You can trust the rhythm of the seasons.

Are there other seasons, other rhythms? Colors and sounds we can't see or hear? There must be. There must be hundreds of them going on all at once. I think of the mysterious seventeen-year seasons of the cicadas. I think of drought and flood, of fire and wind, of tornadoes and meteor showers, all kinds of rhythms playing some syncopated beat we can't hear, much less understand. A rhythm heard only by angels, perhaps, only by seventeen-year cicadas, only by souls over centuries, for all we know.

I think how you can feel cozy and snug and in love and like the happiest person alive, with your very own good luck ladybug to seal the deal, but you can never know what's next.

Now Billy and Tom are running down the hill. Well, that's weird. It's not even two o'clock yet; are they finished for the day? Why are they running? Why are they running so funny? It's an awkward jog. Tom is holding his father's arm, holding it with the kind of urgency you hold injuries. Oh, God. Has something happened? They see me looking out the window, and Tom motions for me to come outside, to hurry.

I grab the cordless phone, Line Three, because I think: Oh God, I better dial 911. Does 911 even work out here? I think, by the strange way they are running and holding Billy's arm, that perhaps Billy's arm has been amputated. Or half-amputated. I can't see it from the elbow down. I don't know what else to think.

Betty and Marley run outside with me. *Roo roo roo roo! Woof, woof, woof.*

"Here!" Tom is yelling. "Here!"

I am sprinting toward them as fast as I can in this mud. I am out here with my slippers on, as you do in times of emergency. As Billy and Tom come into closer range, I can see that Tom is not holding Billy's amputated arm at all. He is holding . . . an animal.

"A possum!" Tom says, as they come closer.

Oh.

"Tom caught it by the tail," Billy says, smiling. "We thought you might want to see it."

Oh.

Billy is holding the animal by the back of the head, and he is squeezing around its jaws tight, to prevent it from biting. The animal is licking its tongue back and forth, for lack of any other flailing possibilities. Tom has the animal by the hips. It's not a very attractive animal. It has a very thick, scaly tail.

Roo roo roo roo! Woof, woof, woof.

"Betty, get down!" I shout. "Marley, sit!"

"You want to touch it?" Tom asks. He's got his blue coveralls zipped down to his belt, and an undershirt showing.

"Um," I say. "Actually, no."

"The fur is really soft," Billy says.

"And she's pregnant!" Tom says. "Did you know her babies will fit into a teaspoon, that's how small they are?"

"Is that right?" I say, standing here in the mud, in my slippers, holding a phone, wondering why we're doing this.

"Possums have a pouch, like kangaroos," Billy says.

"Is that right?"

Billy and Tom spend a good long while giving me possum facts. This seems to be some sort of educational bonus, an extra service thrown in with their bulldozing work. They tell me about some of the other animals they've seen while scraping the multiflora. They tell me about a tiny doe and its mother. They tell me about countless pheasants and turkeys and a beaver. They tell me about "millions and millions" of groundhogs.

"Is that right?" I say.

No, the irony is not lost on me. In fact, I've kind of been

avoiding this issue. I've been sitting here all these weeks watching this multiflora get scraped away, cheering the vast nothingness left behind—and I have done nothing about the fact that I am responsible for the destruction of perhaps hundreds of little birdie homes and rabbit warrens and Bambi bungalows and, now I see, possum maternity wards. In the hierarchy of ecological awareness, Little Miss No Hunting is no higher than the hunters. They kill a deer or two. I order the displacement of entire villages.

"We should get the possum away from the dogs," I say, feeling pity for the rodent. Or the marsupial. Or whatever. Betty and Marley are enthralled by the sight—or smell—of this thing, sitting here at Tom's feet, as if waiting for him to release dinner.

"Yeah, this thing would kill a dog if the dog didn't know what it was doing," Tom says. "See those teeth?" The possum is now drooling.

"Well, I don't think Betty or Marley would know how to battle a possum, so—"

"All right, Tom, go put her in the briars down there," Billy says.

Billy hands the jaw to Tom to hold, which he does with one strong hand, with the other balancing the animal's rump. He waddles over to a ravine and bends down, releasing the animal gently, respectfully.

"What time is it?" he says, returning.

"About two," I say.

"I gotta go," he says to his dad. "I'm going to be late. I have to go home and get cleaned up first."

"Then you go on," Billy says.

Today is the day for Tom to go to the army recruiting station. Both his father and grandfather have done their duty to their country, and Tom hopes to follow in the tradition.

"Well, good luck," I say to him. He smiles and gives a salute.

"You want to put some boots on?" Billy says to me, looking down at my fluffy yellow slippers, now covered with mud. "And I'll show you what we did."

"Sure," I say, and head back to the house to get outfitted for an-other mud-walk.

When I return, Billy is leaning on the fence, pinching some to-bacco out of a little round container. He tucks it in his lip, then puts the container in his back pocket.

"You warm enough in that?" he says, looking at me.

"Yeah," I say, opting not to explain that this jacket is made of a special insulating fabric that the Lands' End company has promised will keep me warm in subzero temperatures.

"Well, we're almost done for this year," Billy says to me as we walk. Now that mud season is here, he says, he's going to have to quit pushing briars because that bulldozer could slide sideways down that hill and kill him. So he'll give it another week or two, but that's it until next year.

I hate hearing this.

I want to believe he feels disappointed, too.

I mean, I know it's stupid. Clinging to a bulldozer driver for company. But I've come to think of Billy and Tom as part of this place I now so casually call home.

Billy and I continue walking, kicking mud balls as we go. The sky is a shock of blue, and there are no clouds. I take a deep breath, as if hoping to catch a whiff of spring. Well, that's stupid, because I get a noseful of burning rubber and diesel smoke. I choke, cough, collect myself, waving my hand in front of my face as if to get air.

"You okay there?" Billy says.

"I'm fine," I say. "I'm tough."

"Yeah."

We walk in silence.

"Well, I hope Alex don't mind," Billy says.

Mind?

"You being his woman and all," he says. "I hope he don't mind the way we're alone like this every day. If you'd like, I could explain to him."

We are alone?

Well, yes, we are alone, just me and Billy and God knows

how many pregnant possums out here. But I never thought of it that way.

"I don't think Alex will mind," I say to Billy.

"I just thought I should say something," he says. "You being his woman and all."

There is nothing flirtatious in his manner. The look in his eye is more of genuine concern. It's the same look he has when any of the guys who come by say curse words in front of me. He'll correct them, he'll say there is a lady present, and then he'll look at me and say, "I am very sorry you had to hear that."

Sometimes I worry about Billy meeting the babes; some of them have mouths on them far fouler than the mouths of those workers. I don't want Billy to know this. I don't want to disillusion him. Sometimes I look at Billy and see him as a mighty bull with the thickest hide that protects him from the briars of the country but, were he to wander into the city, would only look foolish.

A lot of times, as we walk through the mud, Billy and I talk about life. He tells me more about his life than I tell him about mine. Some friendships are like this. Billy is forty-nine. He grew up in the mountains of West Virginia in a home without running water or electricity. He has lived a lot of lives since becoming the owner of an excavation company. He was a helicopter pilot in Vietnam, got gunned down twice. The second time he was the lone survivor. He was hurt. He was hurt bad. He crawled past seven of his buddies, all dead. He crawled under a stump in the bank of a stream. "Crawled under there to die," he told me. He could see the Vietcong as they searched for survivors of the wreckage, he could see their feet in the water. He had a .45 and he had a .357 Magnum and he had a grenade under this arm. He pulled the pin on the grenade, positioned it just so. "So that when they pulled me out, I'd take half of them with me." But they didn't see him and walked on by. He was rescued days later by some Australian soldiers.

When he got home from the war, Billy worked a few years on the river as a crane operator for a barge company, then got sick of having a boss and set out on his own. He bought a two-seater airplane and got a contract to fly dead people back home from the scenes of distant auto accidents. "Well, how else would they get home?" he explained to me. His airplane could accommodate only him and the dead person, who would be strapped in, seated next to him, just like any other passenger, except it would be dead. Once he had to take home a very beautiful dead woman who kept flopping over onto him. It was a long flight. He felt bad for her. "I felt so bad for her, I had to quit that line of work," he told me.

As we walk up toward the apple trees, all leafless and gnarly, Billy tells me he's been tractor shopping. "I found a tractor for you," he announces. "To replace that death trap you got. You want to go look at it with me next week?"

Something in his tone. He's nervous.

I look at him.

"I know it's unconventional," he says.

Unconventional?

"But I asked Patty already, and she said it's all right if I take you to the tractor store," he says.

Patty is Billy's "woman." I haven't met her, but he's referred to her before. Tom's mother left Billy when Tom was just a toddler. Patty has been in his life for a few years now.

"Well, where is the tractor?" I ask him, completely circumventing the subject of him being a man and me being a woman and us being alone and him inviting me on a tractor-store date.

"Up there in Dry Tavern," he says.

"You think it's a good tractor?" I say.

"I do. Four-wheel drive. A roll bar. And it has a front loader."

"Well, what color is it?" I ask.

"Um. I think it was blue," he says.

"Did they have any red ones?"

"Um. I think they did."

"Let's go see them," I say. "What day do you want to go?"

"I can't go till the end of the week. Thursday?"

"I think that's good for me."

"You'll have to ask Alex if he minds," he says.

"I really don't think he'll mind," I say.

"But you'll ask him?"

"All right."

We walk over to the new area that Billy and Tom got cleared today. It's not a very large area, maybe the size of a football field. "We had trouble here," Billy says. "You see them logs? They used to be over there. We had to pull them out with chains, and the one chain snapped, and Tom, I thought he would cry."

"Cry?"

"He's not as tough as my other boy, you know. But he's a good boy."

Billy's other son, his oldest, is also named Billy. He just got out of the Marines. Now he is a professional bull rider in North Carolina.

As we head back down the hill, I ask Billy about how Patty came into his life.

"Oh, a couple of years ago I got cancer," he says matter-of-factly. "I got cancer in my prostate."

"Oh," I say. "I'm sorry."

"It's life, you know," he says. "You can't really do nothing about it. But I'm okay now. And I have Patty to thank." He tells me about being sick, the operations, the chemo and radiation treatments. He got sicker. He couldn't work for months, couldn't leave the house. Patty, who works at a nursing home, nursed Billy. She was a friend, nothing more. But it got so Billy needed more nursing, and more. And maybe Patty needed some nursing, too.

"She got beat up pretty bad where she was living at," he says.

"Beat up?"

"Like a man will do," he says. "A bad man."

Billy rescued Patty, right there from his sickbed, although he doesn't quite make it clear how he did this.

"Put it this way," he says. "I got over 190 guns in my house. I got an *elephant gun*."

"Oh," I say, trying to conjure an image of a Dumbo-sized weapon.

Billy rescued Patty and Patty rescued Billy. And pretty soon Patty was at Billy's house all the time. "So I told her," he says. "I told her, I said, 'You're here all the time. Why don't you just stay?' " So that's what she did.

"That's a nice love story," I say.

"She's a good woman," Billy says. "I would never hurt her. I would never let anybody hurt her."

"Sounds like she got herself a good man," I say.

Just then Betty comes charging up. She has a skull in her mouth. Some dried-up thing. Apparently, she and Marley went after the pregnant possum, but all they got were some body parts. Maybe an old possum, maybe an old raccoon, maybe an old muskrat; I really don't know my skulls. Billy tries to get the skull out of Betty's mouth so he can identify it, but there is no way Betty is giving up that thing.

I think how I used to pay a dollar twenty-nine at the pet store for one dried pig ear. I think how there used to be baskets of pig hooves and cow bones to choose from by the cash register. I think how disgusting I used to think that was.

The dried-up jaw still has its teeth. That much I can see.

I think how gentle we want to believe the natural world is, but how unapologetically savage it is.

Then there's Marley. He shows no interest whatsoever in the skull. Instead, he is sitting by the edge of the woods, staring. Doing his transfixed act. Motionless, frozen. Just sitting and staring.

"Marley, come!" I shout. He doesn't even flinch. "Marley, you are starting to scare me."

ALEX GETS HOME A LITTLE AFTER SEVEN. HE ALWAYS looks so rushed when he comes in the door, as if his drive here were some desperate escape.

"Ugh," he says. "I have a horrible headache."

I give him a hug. "Okay, you're supposed to say, 'Hi honey, I'm home,' and then I'm supposed to hand you a martini," I say.

"I'll have to work on that," he says. "So what happened today around here?"

I tell him about the day's briar-pushing show, and about the possum education.

"Uck," he says.

"But it was very informative," I say.

"I guess the dogs liked it," he says. "Did they have possum for lunch?"

"Actually, a possum could kill a dog," I say, as I chop carrots at the sink.

"Are we having possum for dinner?" he asks.

"No, still pork chops," I say.

He opens the cabinet and takes out plates, begins setting the table. "But maybe you're just *telling* me it's pork," he says, elbowing me as he passes. "But you're trying to slip me possum."

"Maybe!" I say, delighted that he's come up with a new game. A disgusting varmint food game. Tomorrow night I'll make stew and hint around about a muskrat that I saw.

I love being a farm wife. Or an almost-farm almost-wife. It feels like the most wonderful game. It feels as silly and nonsensical as when Claire and I used to play "church" in the basement. We made Communion hosts in the Easy Bake Oven, a flour and salt and water concoction we invented, and Claire pretended to be the priest. "Body of Christmas!" she would say, and I would kneel and stick out my tongue. We didn't think it was right to say "Christ." We thought that might be pushing it.

Alex and I sit down to our pork chops and sauerkraut and homemade applesauce. Betty curls up under the table, in a tight little circle. Marley is stretched out flat as a rug over by the door, and Bob is snoozing on the windowsill. How wonderful. How complete it all feels. Here is my family, everyone safe and sound, snug in our farmhouse.

"So," I say to Alex, "Billy says he's going to have to stop pushing briars soon because of the mud."

"Did you ask him what we're supposed to do with fifteen acres of mud?" he asks.

"Actually, I did. He said we should go up to Scenery Hill Hardware and buy, um, he said three hundred pounds of grass seed and a broadcast spreader. He says we have to get the seed on before the warm weather comes."

"Three hundred pounds?" Alex says.

"That's what he said."

"And what's a broadcast spreader?" Alex says.

"I have no idea."

"Oh, and Billy wants to know if you mind if I go tractor shopping with him next Thursday," I say.

"Do I mind?"

"That's what he said."

"I don't get it," he says.

"Well, I barely do," I say. "And have you noticed all I talk about anymore is Billy?"

"Maybe you're not watching enough TV," he says.

"Good point."

"What kind of tractor?" he asks.

"There's a blue one there Billy likes," I say. "But he says there's some red ones there, too."

"You think we should pick a tractor based on color?"

"I'll just let Billy pick it," I say.

"Yeah."

"Did you know Billy had cancer?" I say.

"He did?"

"Prostate," I say. "I think it was a few years ago."

"So he survived it," he says.

"Yep."

"Are you going to be able to come to town with me next Friday?" he asks.

"Of course."

"I'm sure it's nothing," he says.

"I know."

ELEVEN

NOW, COWS, I AM TOLD, ARE DISGUSTING. BUT THAT isn't the way anybody puts it. Instead, whenever I mention to anyone around here that we are thinking of putting cows on our fields, they start telling me cow facts, eventually landing on something truly awful.

"I saved two cows last week," a neighbor said. He was explaining how cows have a problem when they eat too much. "They blow up and fill with gas and can explode," he said.

"Yikes," I said.

"So I do what my daddy did," he said. "You get your knife and you count the ribs, you count down to the seventh and eighth. And right between the seventh and eighth rib, you put your knife in. Poof! It's like popping a balloon. It beats paying a vet's bill, that's for sure."

No matter what else happens in our lives, Alex and I agree we will never be able to pop cows.

On Thursday, tractor-shopping day, Billy pulls up at precisely eight-thirty A.M. in his Ford LTD, an unmarked police cruiser. I've never seen him drive this vehicle. Usually he's in his bright red pickup. The cruiser even has one of those police lights on the dashboard. There are a few guns in the front seat that Billy has to move so I can sit down.

"I am the constable of Deemston Borough," Billy announces. I was not aware of that. He tells me that Patty is the assistant constable. "I used to be the *police chief* of Deemston Borough," he says, "but I got tired of it. So now they have no police department, because they never really did, except me. So now I'm the constable, but I'm still sort of the police."

"I see."

I get in the car, and Billy says he talked to Bob, the tractor store man, who has put the blue tractor on hold for us.

"Great!" I say. "So let's go give 'er a look!" I like this adventure already. I think of what I used to be doing at this hour, back in my old life. I'd be walking down Eleventh Street, hailing a bus to my office downtown. There was a time when I loved that bus. What an adventure that bus ride felt like! I'd never taken public transportation before. I don't even think we had public buses in the suburbs where I grew up. I thought that bus was amazing. Someone would pick you up a few blocks from your house and, for a dollar and twenty-five cents, drop you a few blocks from your office. What a concept! I loved that bus.

But then one day a lady in the back threw up. Everybody rooted in their pockets and purses for tissues. But it was no use. Another time two teenagers got into a fistfight. Thank God no one had a weapon. And often that bus was so crowded, you had no space you could think of as personal. Often I'd have to stand in the aisle, crammed there with all those other riders, sniffing someone else's smells. One time I let go of the little handle thingy so I could scratch my nose, and just then the bus came to a screeching halt, and me and about twelve others went tumbling like bowling pins.

I took to wearing sunglasses on the bus—my first attempt to shield everybody out. Then I started making sure I had my Walkman in my ears playing Bob Marley or something else reggae, a beat that would calm me down. And I remember standing on the bus one day, behind those sunglasses, listening to that music, and thinking how far, far away the bus world had become. I remember noticing that I was no longer living *in* the world but outside it. In the city I was doing everything and anything I needed to do to keep that world from touching me. I thought: That's not right. That can't be right.

Billy drives the back roads toward the tractor store, heading past Marianna on windy lanes I've not yet traveled. We go under low, abandoned train trestles, left over from the glory days of mining. Soon we are in the deepest woods. "It's like a national park back here!" I say to Billy.

"It's the *country,*" he says. And then he picks up an emptied glass bottle of Lipton's iced tea, which he spits into.

"I don't know how I'll ever learn these roads," I say. "All I know so far is Route 40."

"The *highway*?" he says. "Oh, we never take the highway. Too crowded. We use the hard roads, or the tar and chip roads, or the red dog roads." A lot of people around here refer to roads by their surfaces. *Red dog* is the name they use for dirt roads, since the dirt used for dirt roads is a reddish-brown byproduct of coal mining. A highway is any road that has a yellow line on it, even Route 40, which really is just a two-lane skinny thing meandering through farms and villages.

"A *highway*?" I say. "Crowded? I don't suppose you've ever done rush hour through the Squirrel Hill tunnels in Pittsburgh."

"Pittsburgh?" he says. "Why would I go to Pittsburgh?"

Billy drives me by ponds he has dug, fields he has cleared, barns he has rebuilt, red dog he has hauled and spread. He seems to know every farm, who's who, and what's what. He shows me coal mines that have closed, and he tells me what it was like when they were open. He shows me thousand-gallon septic tanks he's buried, which you can't actually see. But I trust Billy.

"You want to see my house?" he asks. And so we stop at a small green house with cross-hatched windows and a porch decorated with plastic butterflies. The yard is covered on one side with many pieces of enormous excavation equipment and on the other with neat piles of stone, mulch, sand, and other things people might need.

"Okay, President Lincoln drank out of this well," he announces, as we get out of the car by a rickety old pump. He draws some water and fills a Dannon yogurt cup with it. "You want to taste?" I sip the water and think I'm supposed to feel connected to President Lincoln, but I'm not sure so I don't say anything.

"Okay, this is a log house," Billy says as we approach the door. "Come on, I'll show you. Because this was built long before you and me was born. I put siding over it to modernize and whatnot." There's a garage attached, which Billy has made into an office. Well, at least one corner of it. The rest of the office space is taken up with a giant hot tub sitting there gurgling. There are pictures of Billy stationed in Vietnam. There are pictures of Billy's son Billy in his Marine Corps uniform, and other pictures of him as a bull rider. There is a stunningly handsome picture of Tom, all done up in a suit, which seems to shout: "You know what? I am not like the rest of them." More and more I am beginning to understand Tom's attachment to Marley.

Billy shows me a vine that Patty has trained to go all along the kitchen window, and he shows me some of his guns he is proud of, most of all the elephant gun, a black-and-silver hunk of machinery that looks too heavy to carry. "It's nice just to say you have it," he says.

I tell him that, with the exception of a few hunters I have met since moving here, he is the only person I have ever met who even has one gun.

He looks at me, shakes his head back and forth. "Shooooey!" he says, unable to comprehend what planet I've come from. "When I was a kid, everybody took a gun to school," he says. "Not with the intention of shooting anybody. But just to kill supper on the way home. What else was there to do with your spare time?"

"Um, well, we watched TV," I say meekly. "Did you ever see *Green Acres*?"

He smiles. "I'm a little older than you," he says. "But I've seen reruns."

I feel instantly happy, instantly bonded, instantly in touch with the human condition.

We get back in the car, and on the way to the tractor store, Billy tells me about some of the people he has shot, most of them when he was a young man. There was, for instance, those boys who beat up his kid brother. That got Billy mad. "I knew where they was going," he says. "They was going to a house of ill repute. And that's where I found them. I said, 'Hi, boys.' And I shot each one of them. None of them died. I didn't intend for none of them to die. I just intended to bruise them up real proper for a long time."

"Of course," I say.

"They healed up," he says, sensing my concern.

I wonder what Billy thinks when he watches *Green Acres*.

When we get to the tractor store, Billy walks right up to the blue one, which I think is particularly ugly. There is not even a hint of charm to it, especially compared to our red 1958 Farmall. This one is sort of square and functional and a garish blue. I am told that it is a 1986 Ford 1710, diesel, with a roll bar, huge "Ag" tires, four-wheel-drive transmission, power steering, nine million pedals to figure out, and one amazing hydraulic front loader. You can make the bucket go way over your head with the tug of a lever, then make it tilt down and dump stuff with another tug.

"It's a bargain," Billy says. The guy wants $13,000. Buying a tractor is like buying a car. At least on this level. The farmer down the road from us has a $75,000 tractor with an air-conditioned cab.

Billy says I should try to drive the Ford 1710.

"No thanks," I say.

"Get on there," he says. "You gotta try it."

So, well, okay. I hop on. It's a lot shorter than our red tractor. I don't feel so high up. And the seat is, well, wow. The seat is quite luxurious compared with the bony seat on the red one. There's a thin layer of grease on the steering wheel, human grease, I think, the grease of the farmer who once plowed his fields with this machine. Billy pushes some buttons, and the thing fires up like a dream. He shows me how to put it in reverse, how to back it up to a shiny yellow brush hog put there for demonstration purposes. I find this to be an amazingly complicated procedure, what with all the pedals I am told to push in an exact sequence. He teaches me about hydraulics. I find myself not caring. This is disappointing. I thought I was going to take to farm machinery. I really thought I was going to discover some great release of my inner tomboy.

Instead, I think of Alex on this tractor. I think of how much he would love all these levers and pedals. I am so glad he likes tractor things so I don't have to. Maybe I've been clinging a little too tightly to this idea of an inner tomboy. Who knows. Maybe I actually do have an inner princess that would like some attention. (As if.)

Billy has a hard time believing that I can make a tractor-buying decision without first showing the tractor to Alex, but this is what I do. I write a check from a line of credit we got from Farm Credit, a bank serving local farmers. Alex and I have found that it's awfully easy to get money if you are a city person trying to become a farmer. Bankers around here seem dazzled by the idea of customers who make a living outside of farm income alone. It doesn't seem to matter that we have, well, no farm income.

But we are thinking: sheep. We are thinking: cows. We are thinking of these animals as cheap labor, free grass mowers. But someone told us about the tax implications—for example, every farm thing you do is deductible—if you make even a tiny farm income, and so we have been thinking about livestock in a whole new way.

As Billy drives me home, I thank him for all he has taught me.

"It's been my pleasure," he says. "And when the tractor comes, you tell Alex I'll come over and teach him how to run it."

I wonder if Billy is this generous to everyone, or if he's taken us on because he truly worries about our ignorance.

When we pull up to my driveway, we can see that Tim, the FedEx guy, is here. Hmm. I'm not expecting anything. I wonder what he's brought.

"Hey, that truck is sliding," Billy says.

"What?"

"The truck!"

I look and see that, in fact, Tim's truck is sliding backward down a slope.

"Oh God, he's told me about those bald tires!"

As we approach, Betty is out there barking like mad. *Roo roo roo roo!* Even Marley is pitching a fit. *Woof, woof, woof!* It's "The truck is sliding!" in dog language. Tim is gunning the engine. The tires are spinning. The truck is on a slope that has turned into some sort of mudslide. Tim must have backed up too far over the edge of the driveway, where the stones stop, where the mud starts, where the hill starts. If it goes much more backward, it's going to go kaput into the pond. This is obvious to me and Billy and Betty and Marley and, I hope, Tim.

Billy leaps from his police cruiser. "This way! This way!" he shouts, indicating to Tim to turn his wheel sharply to the left, which Tim does. The truck stops sliding.

It lands, *thunk,* in a ditch. A really big ditch.

Tim hops out of the truck in his little FedEx outfit, climbs up out of the ditch. He is blond and trim and clean. He is not the ditch type. "A ditch," Tim says, looking at the ditch, Billy, the ditch.

"A ditch is better than the pond," Billy says.

Tim looks at me.

"It is," I say. "Think of your packages."

Tim stands there scratching his brow, wondering now what.

Without so much as a word, Billy heads over to the bulldozer and fires it up. He comes rumbling over.

I grab the dogs and put them in the basement. I grab my car keys and move my car out of the way, making a clear path.

Billy charges into the woods with the bulldozer, swings around, and threads that giant machine into a spot just behind the FedEx truck. He puts the bucket down, then inches toward the FedEx truck.

I'm sitting in my car, watching this. My car phone rings.

"Hello?"

It's Beth, one of the babes.

"Hi!" she says. "Where are you?"

"Actually, I'm sitting in my driveway," I say.

"Why are you in the driveway?"

"I'm watching the FedEx truck," I say.

"Watching it?"

"Oh, Billy is such a nice guy," I tell her. "I mean, this is *amazing.*"

Huh?

"The bulldozer guy," I say.

"Uh-huh."

"The bulldozer is lifting the FedEx truck," I tell her. "Clear off the ground!"

"Uh-huh."

The babes are learning not to ask for explanations.

I tell Beth I have to call her back.

Billy succeeds. He lays the FedEx truck ever so gently back down on the driveway.

"Thank you!" Tim is saying. "Thank you!"

They're shaking hands, as I approach. I tell Tim I'm really sorry about the ditch.

"Aw, it's okay," he says. "I got the baldest tires. And you know, I was only here to drop off supplies. I got some mailers with your name on them. I put them on the porch."

"But everything is back to normal?" I ask.

"Thanks to Billy," he says.

"It was nothing," Billy says.

And we say our good-byes. They head out, one by one, their tires going *crunch, crunch, crunch* over the stone driveway. I am starting to hate that sound, the sound of people leaving.

I call Beth back.

"Is everything okay?" she says.

"Oh, everything is back to normal," I say.

"Babe, normal in your life is getting really abnormal," she says.

"Do you think so?"

"We still love you," she says. "When are you coming to town next? Do you want to get together for lunch or something?"

"Actually, I'm coming in tonight," I say. "I'm staying overnight in South Side."

"Great! So are you free for lunch?"

"I sort of doubt it," I say. "I have to be at Shadyside Hospital at seven, and then I'll probably head back here."

"The hospital?" she says.

"Alex has to get some test," I say. "They said it's nothing. I don't know, some intestinal problem. They said it's nothing."

"Oh. Well, all right. Call if you want to have lunch."

"Okay."

"And have fun with the FedEx truck or the bulldozer or whatever."

"Oh, that's over—but, well, okay."

I click the little off button on the cell phone and head up to the house. I take a quick look around as if to check, as if I've missed something, as if there must be one bud on a tree, or a crocus sticking up, or the faintest haze of green on the forest's tip. But there isn't. This must be the slowest spring on record. I'm glad I'm going into town. I'll see stores with displays of pink and green and purple. I'll get in the spring mood. Maybe I'll buy a bonnet. I would love to wear a bonnet. I wish people still wore bonnets.

TWELVE

THE WAITING ROOM OF THE GI LAB AT SHADYSIDE Hospital is packed with strangers at seven in the morning. These strangers calm my nerves, help me realize this is no big deal. This is a routine test that a lot of people get. This is just Colonoscopy Day.

Alex and I take the two remaining seats in the waiting room. The TV is on, blaring a morning show.

"Are you nervous?" I say to him quietly.

"I can't say I'm looking forward to it," he says. "You want to go home and have waffles afterward? They said I'm going to be pretty much out of it for the rest of the day."

"Sure," I say. "I'll whip you up some waffles with, um, melted muskrat fat. It tastes like butter!"

"Sounds good!"

He refuses to get grossed out by my varmint food talk. I should have known.

"Waffles with melted muskrat fat and seventeen-year cicada sprinkles," I say. "Very crunchy."

"Mmm," he says. "And how about some raccoon gut syrup?"

Okay, I never should have started this. I should have known. I wonder if anybody in this waiting room can actually hear this conversation.

A nurse pops her head through a window and calls some names. One by one people get up. When they call Alex's name, he stands and walks toward the door to the lab, and just before he enters, he turns and looks back at me, flashing me the funniest face, a clown face, a clown hollering for help before he does some silly stunt into a ring of fire.

I smile, blow him a kiss, and then settle into my chair, get comfortable. They said it would be at least an hour before he's out of there. I've brought a book. I've brought magazines. I've brought a paper. There is plenty to do. I look at the TV. A commercial about fake eggs. I look around the waiting room. There are a lot of posters about colorectal cancer on the walls. There are also several huge underwater photographs of fish. The photographs were taken by one of the hospital's favorite colorectal surgeons. It says so right underneath. I think that's an interesting hobby for a colorectal surgeon, exploring a world where few people go and looking for exotic life forms.

It is getting boring, waiting here. I really wish one of us in this room was brave enough to stand up and turn off the TV. The morning show is over, and now it's *Jenny Jones*.

Oh, here's the doctor. Oh, good. Here's news. He calls Mrs. So and So. She stands up and heads over to him. But before she is even out of our earshot, the doctor says, "Everything is fine!" And Mrs. So and So is led back to the recovery room.

I think they should have these little meetings in private, I really do.

The doctor calls another Mrs. So and So. "Everything's fine!" And then a Mr. So and So. Everything is fine in his life, too. That's three down.

"Today, folks," Jenny Jones is saying, "today I want to introduce you to some teenage girls who want to be supermodels but their mothers think they're too fat. Come on out here, Miracle!"

"Miracle?" an old man next to me says. "Her name is Miracle?"

"Aw, she's not fat," says another.

"But she has to work on her walk," says the first.

Suddenly the doctor is here again with news. He calls Mr. So and So. "Everything is fine!" He calls Mrs. So and So. "Everything is fine!" One by one these people are led back to the recovery room. I wonder why he's not calling me. I look around at all the empty seats, feeling like a kid playing musical chairs, but in reverse.

He calls the next person. And the next. Everything is fine. Everything is fine.

Soon I am alone in this room.

"I did not say she was fat!" says Miracle's mother on national TV. "My boyfriend is the one who said she is fat. And he used to be a model!"

I turn the TV off.

I look at the fish pictures.

I look at the platinum ring on my finger. I twirl the ring around. I love this ring. I love Alex. I want to get married. We should make wedding plans. We should just go ahead and do it. A wedding. I could do it. Even though I am not the inner princess type. Now that I think about it, that lady mistook me for a former Miss Delaware, and it sure didn't take me long to get in touch with my inner former Miss Delaware.

The doctor calls my name. I stand up. "Are you Alex's wife?" he asks.

"Fiancée," I say. It's the first time I've ever actually used that word in public.

I look at him. He's not saying anything. He's not saying "Everything's fine," as he did with everybody else. The silence lasts four years, maybe five.

"Tumor," he says, finally. "We found a tumor."

It hits me like a punch.

"Oh," I say. "A big tumor?" It is the only tumor question I can think of.

"Yes," he says. "Quite big."

"Oh," I say.

He takes me back to Alex. A long shiny hallway that smells of glue. The doctor pushes back a striped curtain, as if presenting the results of his magic act. I half-expect him to say, "Voilà!" Alex is behind the curtain, asleep. He has tubes up his nose and a hospital gown on. Jeezus. He looks like an eighty-year-old man. It's as if aliens have captured him, have captured us, have in the blink of an eye swooped in and taken us away from the life we thought we were creating. I take his hand. His same soft, strong hand. But not the same at all. Jeezus. This is not the same man. This is not the same man who was just talking about raccoon gut syrup. Or beaver butter. Or muskrat waffles, or whatever the hell. . . .

He opens his eyes.

"Hi, baby," he says to me. "They found a tumor."

"I heard," I say.

"Well, what do you think it is?" I ask the doctor, careful not to even bring up the C-word.

"I don't know," he says. "I did a biopsy. We'll know more by Tuesday." Then he goes on and on about how large the tumor is, maybe the size of a golf ball, about how, no, this is not a polyp but a full-grown tumor, a large tumor, and when polyps become tumors, they, yes, typically they become cancerous, and it appears this one has been growing for quite some time. . . .

"Well, this isn't good news at all," Alex says.

"That's what I'm trying to tell you, sir," the doctor says. And then he reaches out and grabs hold of Alex's other hand.

W E DRIVE BACK TO THE FARM IN SILENCE.
"It could be nothing," I say, finally.

"It could be."

We are staring straight ahead.

"I'm sorry," he says.

"Sorry?" I say.

"I'm so sorry."

I don't think he has to apologize for having a tumor. There is little other tumor conversation between us.

When we get home, I make an omelet. I skip the whole waffle plan. It feels like everything we ever said to each other before he walked into that GI lab is now stupid. Uninteresting.

I make a huge omelet with big wads of ham in it. A hearty farm omelet. Alex had to fast for twenty-four hours before that test, so he's got an appetite. I have none. I stir my food. We sit in silence. All you can hear is silverware clanking. Bob is on the windowsill, sound asleep.

"I'm so sleepy," Alex says, halfway through his meal. "I'm still hungry, but I think I'm going to fall asleep on my plate."

"You should lie down," I say. "You're drugged."

"You're right, dear," he says. He looks at me, waiting for my smile. "I said, '*You're right, dear.*'"

I smile, but it takes effort.

He leaves the table and lies down on the living-room floor. I don't know why he picked that place. It seems as though any horizontal surface would suffice. Within seconds he is sound asleep. Marley sees him, goes over, and lies down next to his shoulder. Then Betty comes over, claiming his other shoulder. I clean up the dishes, and the next time I look over, I see Bob curled up at Alex's ankles.

All of them there, snoozing together. A unit. My family.

I don't quite know what to do with myself. I'm not going to call anybody and tell them. Because it could be nothing. It still could be nothing. We won't know until Tuesday if it's something. So still, technically, it is nothing. Why get all worked up over nothing? And anyway, this isn't how I do fear. I don't blab it all over the place. I get quiet. I get shy. I shut down. I go blank. I go inward.

Where's Billy, anyway? Aren't those guys supposed to be out there? Oh, no. Friday. I think he had to dig a sewer line or something up at the high school.

I look out at the hill. The hill of mud. I try to imagine it green. I try to imagine spring. Where in God's name is spring? I should put the grass seed on. Maybe that would give spring a boost. I decide to leave everybody here snoozing and go up to Scenery Hill Hardware and get a broadcast spreader and three hundred pounds of grass seed. That's something I can do. I need to do something.

A broadcast spreader, it turns out, is a cloth pack you wear over your shoulders, with a crank at the bottom. It holds about twenty pounds of seed, and you turn the crank, and it sends the seed flying.

"Well, I'll take two," I say to Jim, our hardware guy. He's a handsome young man, maybe thirty. He has curly hair and a relaxed physique. He's someone you automatically feel comfortable around. His German shepherd, Inga, comes to work with him.

"Nothing like His and Hers broadcast spreaders!" I say to him.

He smiles. "Actually, me and my wife both have broadcast spreaders," he says.

"There you go," I say.

"And actually," he says, "we're not using them. Why don't you just borrow ours?"

"But—"

"I got them right here in the back because last week George was using them at his place."

"But, Jim, I am going to *buy some* from you," I say. "How are you going to stay in business if you're always lending stuff out?" He's already lent us a snow shovel, a diesel fuel can, a hacksaw, and a set of wire cutters.

"Why would I sell you something that I have right here I'm not using?" he says. "It just seems dumb." He heads into the back room and emerges with the broadcast spreaders.

"All right," I say. "I think I'm going to take four hundred pounds of seed instead of three hundred." I don't know if we need four hundred, but I want the guy to make some money. Generosity begets generosity. That's one thing I've learned in Scenery Hill, PA.

"Well, pull your truck up," Jim says, "and I'll load up."

I thank Jim for his generosity, give Inga a pat, and head out.

Back at the house, I startle all the snoozers with my arrival.

"Hi, baby," Alex says, opening his eyes. "What time is it?"

"A little after three."

"My God," he says. "I slept that long?"

"You were drugged," I say.

"Whew. My head. What did they give me?"

"I got you a present!" I say. I show him the broadcast spreaders.

"Oh," he says, unsure what he is looking at.

"Broadcast spreaders!" I say. "His and Hers broadcast spreaders!"

"Wow," he says, through several yawns. "Why are they so dirty?"

"I borrowed them from Jim, up at the hardware store."

"He wouldn't sell you any?"

"I tried," I say.

"How is that guy ever going to stay in business?"

"That's what I said. Anyway, I bought four hundred pounds of seed."

"*Four* hundred?" he says.

"We'll need it eventually. We'll leave the extra hundred in the barn."

He yawns. "So should we try these babies out?" he asks, spinning the crank on the spreader.

"I don't think you're quite up to it," I say.

"I'm fine. The air would do me good."

"Well, okay then."

We change into jeans, J. Crew flannel shirts, Eddie Bauer hiking boots, and head outside. We try on our broadcast spreaders. We look at each other.

"We look like twins," I say.

"This is getting embarrassing," he says.

"It is," I say, laughing. It feels like a great release, this little laugh. It feels like my head is a pressure cooker and somebody finally opened the lid.

There is no tumor talk between us at all, and I am glad.

We drive the pickup loaded with grass seed to the top of the hill. We strap on our broadcast spreaders. And we start spreading the seed on the western face of the hill, the part Billy has finished smoothing. We climb up and down that giant hill like goats, spinning our respective cranks, watching the seed fly. I notice that I am spreading the seed about a hundred times thicker than Alex is. His is sparse, little flecks here and there. He seems to trust the seed. He seems to believe in the seed.

I am plopping mine in clumps.

There is a pessimism in me. A thud of hopelessness.

Soon it is dark, and we are still out here trying to get the seed down. It takes a long time to spread three hundred pounds of seed, even longer than we thought.

"You know, it's really light out here for being dark," Alex points out.

"It is."

We look up at the moon, the brightest moon. You don't get moons like this in the city. The light is strange, flat, blue, almost fluorescent. It's a glowing light, and it leaves a halo on everything it touches. I've never really done anything under the moonlight before, least of all planted grass seed.

Alex points to the western sky. "Hale-Bopp," he says. "The comet. Isn't that the comet?"

I suppose it is! That's the comet everybody has been talking about on the news. A glowing white cloud in the night sky—with a tail. It hasn't been visible for 4,200 years. It won't be visible again for 2,380 years.

We stand here a long time with our heads tilted back, looking at the comet. I can't help but wonder what kind of rhythm it represents. There must be so many rhythms. There must be hundreds of them going on all at once. I think of drought and flood, of fire and wind, of tornadoes and meteor showers. And now Hale-Bopp. A rhythm spanning millennia. Who would ever be able to hear the beat of that gigantic song?

THIRTEEN

IT'S TUESDAY. THE DAY WE'RE SUPPOSED TO HEAR.
Alex is in town, at work. I'm here in the big room with Bob, staring
at Bob, watching Bob swat a paper clip with one paw, then swat it
back with the other, as if trying to make that paper clip come alive.
The clip makes an unexpected flip, and Bob goes in for the kill,
rolling on it until he's all confused in a surprise somersault.

Bleeep. Bleeep. There's the phone. Line One.

Hello?

It's Dawn, a woman I've hired to come clean the house. She's
supposed to start today. She tells me she's sorry, but she's going to
have to cancel and start next week instead.

"A sheep emergency," she says.

"Oh?"

"Three of my ladies just went into labor," she says. "They
need me."

"Oh," I say. I tell her we're thinking of getting sheep.

"Sheep are stupid," she says.

"Yeah, well." (Do people think I expect intellectual stimulation from my livestock?)

"You know, sheep are so stupid that if they're facing uphill, they get stuck," she says.

"Stuck?"

"They think they're laying down because their eyes are closer to the ground. And they can't get up because they're already up."

"Stuck," I say.

Dawn says she is getting sick of always having to go up and turn her sheep around.

It is getting harder and harder to defend sheep.

It is getting harder and harder to plan anything.

Bleeep. Bleeep. Line One again. Why doesn't anybody ever use Line Two?

"Hello?"

It's Alex. There is news.

"Well?" I say.

"Inconclusive," he says.

"Huh?"

"The doctor said the test was inconclusive."

"Oh, God. Well—did he have a *guess*?"

"He said, 'Inconclusive.' "

"Did you tell him he's torturing us?"

"I don't think I had to. He seemed concerned. I mean, for a doctor."

"Oh."

"He said I shouldn't wait for another biopsy. He said I should call a surgeon right away and get it out."

"He thinks we have to move this fast?"

"It was like he was trying to convince me it was . . . bad."

"Oh."

"Do you want me to call the surgeon?"

"I just did. They were waiting for my call. The doctor had already sent over the chart. They gave me an appointment for tomorrow."

"Wow."

"Everybody seems really on top of this," he says.

"That's good," I say.

"Can you come with me?" he asks. There is fear in his voice. For the first time, fear.

"Of course!" I say. "They're going to take it out tomorrow?"

"No, no, no. They're going to do some tests, and schedule the surgery. I mean, I think it's complicated. Oh, I don't know what they have to do."

"It doesn't matter," I say. "I'll be there. Just hold on, baby. I'll be there. I'll pack you some clothes. I'll pack me some clothes. I'll meet you at the South Side house, and we'll have a nice quiet dinner together."

"All right," he says.

"Just hang on, baby."

"I'm hanging," he says. "Bye-bye."

I look at Bob. He's scratching his ear, *thump, thump, thump.* He is starting to look more healthy, not less. But that could be because I have another patient to worry about. "You hang on, too, Bob," I say as I push back my desk chair.

I look at the birch tree outside. A cardinal on a branch, a pretty flash of red, is pecking feverishly. Everybody seems so busy. Time seems to have stopped for me, but not for anyone else. Not even Bob.

I head back to the bedroom to get my suitcase out. All I can think, through my fear, are the stupidest thoughts. Stupider than sheep thoughts. I think maybe I should run out and get Alex another poodle. I think I should have bought him a set of dishes with poodles on them. I think of decorating the entire farmhouse in poodle art. I think of a poodle weathervane on the barn.

Bob wanders back into the bedroom to watch me pack. After all these years, Bob knows.

Yes, Bob. I am packing again. What are you looking at? It's no big deal, Bob. Just one night. I'm going to town for one night. You'll be okay here. I'm going to leave you a big bowl of dry, and I have another can of Fancy Feast I'll put out. That's a treat, isn't it? I got you the kind with liver. . . .

Bob jumps up on the bed, sits. Soon he is washing his feet. He's going nibble, nibble, nibble on his paw. Thank God Bob is still here. That's all I can say.

That is all I can say, Bob. Thank God I still have you, Bob. And I mean thank God. Thank God you are not dying. That's all I can say.

If he were a dying cat, he would be dead by now. I mean, obviously that vet got it wrong. That vet didn't know what he was talking about. It's been, what, nearly a year since the vet said, "Bob is dying." When you say someone or something is "dying," what does that mean? How much time do you get? Because, I mean, obviously, Bob is not dying.

Dying is just a word, Bob. A word. You are not dying, Bob. Thank God we finally got that straight. Because if you were "dying" a year ago, then technically you would already have died. Right? And you haven't. So there's no reason to keep using the D-word.

I feel better about Bob. I feel so much better. I can hear Betty scratching at the back door.

"All right, girly girl," I shout, and go to let her in. "Come on," I say to her. "But only for a few minutes. Because I have to leave again. You and Marley are going to sleep outside tonight. Just for one night." If it were more than one night, I'd bring the dogs. But these long car rides are really tough on Marley, so it's best to leave him home. "Aw, I know, Betty. But Marley needs you here. You two did okay last time, didn't you? Of course you did. It was like camping. Wasn't it? Did you roast marshmallows? Or did you and Marley sneak in that liquor cabinet? Not that we have a liquor cabinet. Not that you know this. . . ."

I am babbling. Betty is looking at me, trying to comprehend. She has her ears perked up. She is the most alert dog. When you talk to her, she looks as if she's trying, really trying to understand. I half-expect that one day she is going to open her mouth and "Mama" is going to come out in a tiny little voice.

Now Marley is at the door. He has something in his mouth.

Something green. I open the door. "Marley, drop it!" I say. He is, if nothing else, obedient.

He drops the green thing. It's long and skinny. It's . . . a piece of asparagus. A piece of asparagus with dog teeth marks in it.

"Marley, where in the hell did you get this?"

He looks at me. There is nothing whatsoever alert about his eyes.

In the morning, Alex and I arrive at the surgeon's office. We're holding hands. We're not looking at each other. We're not talking to each other. We're holding hands. They take him away from me. They take him back to the examination room. My hand feels empty. Cold.

Another waiting room. But no fish pictures. I sit here feeling sick, feeling as if I have no right to feel sick, since Alex is the one who is sick. Or supposedly sick. Or sick even though he doesn't feel sick. Or not sick at all. It could be nothing.

The surgeon comes out.

"You're his fiancée?" he says.

I nod. It is the first time anyone has ever used that word to describe me in public. I am starting to fear that word in a whole new way.

"Why don't you come back here and we'll . . . talk."

Great. Super. I'd love to.

He takes me into the examination room where Alex is sitting, looking down. Alex can't even seem to make eye contact with me.

"Okay, this tumor," the surgeon says to me, picking up a piece of paper. He has drawn a picture of the tumor for Alex to see, a picture Alex is apparently now processing in his head. "This tumor is not on a stalk as we suspected," the surgeon says. We had been told by the first doctor that it was on a stalk. We were told the stalk kind was the good kind, the kind least likely to be malignant. I had been clinging to that stalk information as my ray of hope.

The surgeon says no, this tumor is embedded flat as a pancake in the walls of Alex's intestine. And yes, it is huge. Larger than a golf ball. He says from the size and the shape and the way it's embedded, he says yes, it is most probably cancerous.

"But it could be early," he says. "We won't know anything for sure until we get it out of there and do the biopsy." He starts drawing pictures of intestines, showing where he'll cut, what he'll do, what he hopes for, what he fears.

Great. Super. Fine. Uh-huh.

He says our best hope is that it is "early." He says colorectal cancer, if caught early, is curable. Especially if there is no family history of it.

Alex is still not looking at me. Alex is looking down at the floor. Alex's father died of colorectal cancer, and so did several cousins.

There is talk of lymph nodes and liver involvement, of blood levels and CT scans, of chemo and radiation.

Finally, Alex looks up, peers at me with glazed eyes. "I think I should call the kids," he says. "I have to tell Amy and Peter."

WE DRIVE BACK TO THE FARM IN SILENCE AGAIN. The deadest silence. We make no mention of the rolling vermilion hills coming toward us, the hills you expect to see depicted on canvases in museums. We make no mention of the amusement ride, the great adventure in sight-seeing. We make no mention of the most adorably stupid-looking donkey standing on an overturned wheelbarrow, as if posing for a surrealist painting. We make no mention of the desolation in our hearts that seems to color everything.

"I'm sorry," Alex says, finally.

It's as if his only worry is me. But really, there is nothing to worry about. The sadness that is filling me will surely find its way out. How much can one person contain?

I think of those cows and what a relief it must have been to get popped.

FOURTEEN

THE LADYBUG IS GONE. I CAN'T BELIEVE THIS. I can't find it anywhere. It's not in the sink, and it's not in the spider plant, and it's not in the ceramic frog sponge holder either.

It's mid-April, and the surgery is scheduled for next Thursday at Shadyside Hospital, a stone's throw away from Alex's old house. We have a whole week to wait. They said Alex will then be spending at least a week in the hospital recovering. Amy and Peter are coming to town. We called Riva, Alex's cousin, who lives in Is-rael, and we asked her to pray. Alex has no other family. His sister, Marina, who was a sickly person most of her life, died five years ago. We called my family. We called the babes and other friends. We've asked everybody to pray, even if they don't believe in prayer.

And now the ladybug is gone.

The good luck ladybug. The ladybug that held my loneliness for me. The ladybug that was supposed to carry me toward or through or beyond or swirling in and around some joyful solitude ride.

Yeah, well.

Solitude schmolitude.

That's what I'm thinking. Solitude is a luxury for the lucky. For people who don't have sick cats and lost ladybugs and very possibly dying loved ones to worry about. For people who don't have to worry about getting their hands dirty with the everyday goo of ordinary suffering.

I couldn't care less about achieving whatever it was that solitude was supposed to help me achieve. It all seems like a juvenile indulgence now.

I am home alone, sitting at my desk, trying to work, trying to pretend nothing has happened. Because it still could be nothing. But now all I seem able to do is Internet searches for colorectal cancer. Wow. You can learn too much. You can read too much. You can read only so many times how quickly that cancer can spread if it's caught too late. You can read only so many times that polyp leads to tumor leads to bigger tumor leads to cancer leads to death if it's caught too late, especially if there's a family history of the disease. You can read only so many times that the man you are in love with has every bad indicator possible.

Yesterday I got some Joe Crowley news that, at a minimum, took my mind off my news.

What happened was, Joe Crowley—the first Joe Crowley, the mechanic Joe Crowley—one day he collapsed. It turns out he needs quadruple bypass surgery, or, as he calls it, "a real serious valve job." But, like so many other people around here, Joe doesn't have health insurance. So he has to get in line. He has to wait for a bed to become available at the VA hospital. They said the wait might be six weeks or more and Joe's doctor, well, he's not at all convinced that Joe's clogged heart can keep pumping that long.

You never know what's going to happen next. I mean, Joe? He seemed the picture of health, back when he was smacking his lips from those pineapple pancakes that the wife made. And if he's only charging people $16 for a state inspection, how in the world is he supposed to afford health insurance? Now I wish he charged us a lot more.

I feel bad for Joe. Which actually is good. Because sometimes, when things are going wrong in your life, it can feel good to hear that things are going wrong in someone else's life, too. But this doesn't feel that way. And that's good. I feel good that I feel bad for Joe. But I feel bad that I feel good for feeling bad about Joe.

I could be stuck in this loop all day. I need to get out more. Solitude is making my brain loopy.

Betty is outside barking. *Roo roo roo roo.* Maybe someone is here? Tim? Someone to distract me?

I look out the window, and it's . . . Joe Crowley. No, not that Joe Crowley. One of the other Joe Crowleys. The one with the limestone who didn't really have the limestone. He's done some work over here in the past months, some plumbing and wiring.

I head outside.

"Hey," he says. "Did I leave my socket wrenches here?"

"Not that I know of," I say. "But look around if you want."

There are two other guys in Joe's truck. I recognize one of them, the skinny one with the crooked bangs. I don't like that one. He gives me the creeps.

"How ya doing?" I say to him.

He doesn't answer.

Joe ducks into the basement to look for his socket wrenches, while I wait here with his friends.

"Check this out," the skinny one says to the other one, a short one, one I've never seen before. "A *poodle.*"

Oh, please. Not more poodle jokes. They really picked the wrong day.

The two guys hop out of the truck and commence teasing Marley.

"You can put leaves on him and they stick," the skinny punk says, demonstrating with some dried maple leaves.

"Hey," I say. "You know, he doesn't actually like it when you do that." I am beginning to understand the urge to own a rifle. A quick *pow!* right at his feet, just to bruise him up real proper for a long time.

Poor Marley, sitting there with dried maple leaves on his head.

They find some other leaves, toss them at Marley, seeing if the sticking works from a pitching distance. I don't know what to do. What to say. I wonder if they know this taunting is about to put me over the edge.

It works, throwing leaves at Marley. They stick fine. Poor Marley. But the weird thing is, Marley doesn't seem to mind. Which only makes the guys laugh harder. Because Marley is in one of his trances. He is sitting there motionless, frozen, staring off into the brush, oblivious to his crown of debris.

"What is he doing, communicating with the mother ship?" one says.

"He's daydreaming about becoming a German shepherd," the other says.

Oh, they are having a great time.

Poor Marley. I'm going to cry. I feel like I did when I was in grade school, trying so hard not to cry. The harder you try, the more your head takes on the size and pressure of a giant Hawaiian volcano.

Joe comes out of the basement and gives a shrug. No socket wrenches. He joins his friends. "Aw, Poodle Dude," he says. "What's up, Poodle Dude?" He leans on the pickup. He's a nice guy; he's been nice to Marley up until now. I hope his rotten friends haven't contaminated him.

"He's communicating with the mother ship!" the one says to Joe.

"No, he's dreaming about becoming a German shepherd!"

What, these guys can't come up with new material?

They're laughing their guts out. They love their own humor. It occurs to me that they might be drunk.

Just then, Marley leaps like a windup toy to his feet. Whoa. And what? He takes off—*fwooom!*—like a bullet. He is a black blotch streaking through the sky. Now we're the ones transfixed. Soon he is taking one giant leap into the brush, and before any of us know what is happening, he is swinging back around, like a gymnast that can both lunge and spin at the same time. As he swings around, we see it: a live groundhog in his mouth. Not any old groundhog. A groundhog a good six times bigger than Marley's big head. We stand there motionless, all of us, even Betty, watching this poodle wrestle this mother of all groundhogs to the cold earth; he seems to know right where to go, just how to snap its neck, because within the next blink of an eye, the groundhog is on the ground, dead. Marley stands over it, huffing and puffing.

Huffing and puffing.

"Cripes!" says one of the guys, who looks at me. "Does he always do this?"

"Actually, no," I say, my eyes bugged out.

"Hey, that ain't no wuss dog," Joe Crowley says.

"Shoot," says the skinny guy. "And I could use me a huntin' dog."

When the guys finally drive away, I think: This is it. This is the day Marley wins respectability. The world has sacrificed one groundhog so Marley can show what he is made of, that he may be a poodle, but he ain't no wuss dog. I feel, um, really proud of Marley. But I do sort of hope he'll go back to the way he was before.

Marley sits by the groundhog all day. He spends the next day sitting next to it, too. Like it is a favorite stuffed toy. A most cherished prize. A toy he *picked out on his own* and got to bring home. I really can't say why he needs to be near it. I wonder if he has to keep reminding himself it is true, or if he wants to make sure it doesn't leave.

On the third day, I am sorry to report, Marley eats the groundhog.

"Okay, that's gross," I say to myself. I am sitting here watching this, wondering what I should do.

The phone rings. Line One. It's Nancy.

I decide instantly not to tell her about Marley's feast.

Not that I get a chance to.

She is crying. For a moment, I can't tell if this is happy or sad tears, but soon it is obvious. She says Jack did it. He proposed! She is squealing. The diamond is an emerald cut. The wedding will be next October. She asks me to be her maid of honor.

Whoa. A wedding. With bridesmaids and everything? Just like

that? It's like bowling balls falling on me. I wonder if this is some great cosmic rearrangement, all the happiness over there, and all the sadness over here. I wonder if Hale-Bopp could possibly have had anything to do with this. Or some murmuring below by the seventeen-year cicadas. Or Mark.

I'm happy for Nancy. Of course I am. But it's weird to hear her do all this wedding talk when I was supposed to be the bride. *Bride?* I am not the bride type. Nancy is the bride type. Nancy has been the bride type ever since the day she was born, and it's about time she got to be one. It's only right. It's only fitting. Yes, this is good news indeed.

"Congratulations!" I say, and invite Nancy down to the farm to help her make wedding plans.

"And we can plan your wedding, too!" she says. "Have you and Alex set the date yet?"

"All of that stuff is sort of on hold," I tell her.

"I think you should plan a wedding," she says. She pauses. You can hear a breath of seriousness overtake her. "I think you should stand up in the face of this thing," she says. "I think you're giving this whole tumor thing way too much power."

Maybe. I remember telling her a similar thing when her mother was diagnosed. And then when her father was diagnosed. And then I didn't know what to say. There comes a point when there is nothing you can say. I am already planning for that stage. I am going to do all of my friends a big favor and leap right to that stage so they don't have to stand around feeling awkward.

"So, what have you guys been doing down there all weekend?" Nancy asks.

"Waiting," I say.

"Oh, God," she says. "You guys have to get out."

"Alex is out driving the tractor," I say. "It's his new addiction." That tractor. Thank God I bought that thing. Because Alex loves that tractor. Yesterday, and again today, he got up early, went out there, and fueled up. He got out the chain saw, all kinds of tools, put them in the bucket. He strapped the weed whacker to the roll bar, and then he rode off, like a kid running away from home with all his prized possessions.

"Where does he go?" Nancy asks. "I mean, what is he doing out there?"

"He's working on an apple tree," I say.

"A tree?"

"That's what he said."

"What's he doing with the tree?"

"I don't actually know."

When we hang up, I decide to go find out. I put on my hiking boots and head outside. The air feels good; Nancy was right. I look around for green. Or how about one stinkin' stalk of forsythia ready to pop? Nothing. Just brown, brown, brown. I'm about out of patience with this spring.

I follow the roar of the diesel engine. I hike to the top of the hill, and I can see the black smoke from the tractor. I can see a rustling of the brush. I make my way through and spot him there, with his tree. We have, perhaps, fifty apple trees on this property, and there is nothing special about this one. Like many of them, it is smothered in briars. Well, less so now. Alex has been freeing the tree. I stand and watch him back in with the mower and chop up some of the briars. I watch him hop off the tractor, pull the string on the chain saw with all his might, prune some of the tree's branches. I watch him get back on the tractor, sweep away the mess with the loader. I watch him stop, look at the tree, as if planning his next attack.

It feels good watching him go to war with nature like this. I'm sure the tree appreciates it, too.

What kind of apples will we get? What will we do with them? Will we make applesauce and pie? And what about our peach trees? What will we possibly do with all those peaches? We had hoped to be talking about these things at this point in the season, about what kinds of lettuce to plant and how many onions and where the broccoli should go. And what about the pond project? What about building a greenhouse? What about our sheep? And our goats? And I want a horse, and he wants a mule, and what about all our plans?

We have made mention of none of these things. In fact, as a topic of discussion, we are finding the future to be highly overrated.

THE NEXT DAY, A SUNNY APRIL SUNDAY, NANCY comes down to the farm, her arms loaded with bride magazines. She got her hair streaked and a manicure and a pedicure to celebrate her engagement. She looks terrific. She's a pretty woman, blond with deep, green eyes, and a cheerleader's body and manner. It's fun to watch her flip through the pages and make judgments about silk versus tulle and Chantilly lace versus Venise. Nancy has one heck of an inner princess. And she doesn't seem embarrassed by it at all.

She takes over the whole family room with her magazines and her joy. I love that she feels at home here, like a sister. Like a roommate.

She wants me to join in with the wedding planning, but I tell her I really am too busy. I have to go outside and sit on a bench and wait for spring. This is getting serious. I have been spending a lot of time on this bench. I've waited for daffodils that never show. I got teased by a magnolia ready to bloom, until frost wiped out that plan. It seems Mother Nature has gone on vacation, and the person she left in charge is stupider than sheep. Sorry, sheep. I am having trouble eating and sleeping and concentrating—even on my prayers.

I sit on this bench, this rickety old thing sure to give me splinters. I sit here and think: Our Father who art in heaven, *I should have bought him those poodle dishes.* Thy kingdom come, thy will be done, *I should have told him the truth six years ago, or four years ago, or whenever I knew.* Give us this day, our daily bread, *We would have had more time. We would have had a wedding. I could have gotten him a mule.* Forgive us our trespasses, as we forgive those who trespass against us. *It's all my fault. It's all my stupid fault for waiting. Never wait. Never wait just because you're scared, you idiot, you wuss.* But deliver us from evil. Amen.

Nancy sleeps over in the guest room. In the morning, she and Alex and I have bagels, and Nancy gets his opinion on wedding gowns. I'm surprised to see he *has* opinions on wedding gowns. But he does. He tells her he likes the basque waist the best.

When they both pack up and leave to go to work, I listen to the *crackle crackle crackle* of the cars over the driveway. I am alone again. I feel it like a thud. I look for the ladybug again. No ladybug. I sit on the couch with Bob on my stomach and watch stupid TV, which technically I need to watch, because I'm working on an essay about 1960s sitcoms and need to brush up on my sitcom lingo, so at least I have a good excuse.

Roo roo roo roo! That's Betty the doorbell. "Excuse me, Bob," I say, standing up. I look out and see Billy's truck. Oh, good. I haven't seen him in weeks. I hope he wants coffee.

"Hey there," he says when he reaches the door. He doesn't look good. He's lost weight. He's pale.

He looks at me. "Have you been sick?" he says. "You've lost weight." We stand there sizing each other up. I'm not sure why he's here. He's not even in his work clothes. He's gussied up the way guys around here gussy up: tight Wranglers, plaid shirt, shiny, pointy boots, and white cowboy hat.

"My brother died last week," he announces. He says it was leukemia that was diagnosed too late. "And my mother is dying," he says. He asks why is it that everything comes at once.

I look at him. I want to tell him about Alex, but I don't seem able to.

"You want some coffee?" I say.

"If you got it made," he says.

I pour him half a cup and then fill the rest with hot water, remembering that Billy finds my coffee unbearably strong.

We sit in the kitchen and talk about everything under the sun, except for his brother and his mother and Alex. We talk about sheep. Billy says there's a reason they're stupid. Because the farmers shoot the smart ones. Because the smart ones will figure out how to get through the fence, and then all the dumb ones follow. If you get rid of the smart ones, you don't have to worry about losing your sheep.

"So it's really not the sheep's fault that they're stupid," I say.

"The smartness is bred out," Billy says.

Poor sheep.

We talk about pigs. "Don't bother with pigs," he says. "Pork prices are down. Nobody around here is doing pigs."

We talk about his dad, who passed away years ago. He drove a school bus. He met Billy's mom on that bus. She was a student, a little kid. He loved her instantly and without reservation. He waited until she got to be sixteen, and then he married her.

We talk about Billy's Uncle Ophie, who lives in the mountains of West Virginia, near where Billy grew up. "Only he lives the old way," Billy says. "I mean the *old,* old way."

"How's that?" I ask, settling in for what I have come to know will be another good Billy story. Sometimes I wonder if any of these stories are true. Sometimes I think they should hire Billy to write a remake of *Green Acres*.

"That barn you got out there?" he says. "That would be a palace compared to Ophie's house. He lives in a shack, and the snow blows in." Billy says Ophie is an old man, perhaps ninety. His hair and beard haven't been cut in many decades, according to legend. He bathes twice a year, at which time he gets sewn back into his red long johns, which he wears until his next bath. He's married to Corey, an American Indian, whom he met when she was a little girl, an orphan. Ophie raised her, then married her.

"That seems to be a trend in your family," I say.

He smiles. "Ophie and Corey live together in that shack, at the end of a creek road," he goes on. "You can't drive to Ophie's. Because the road is a creek. Ophie's got the bank of that creek rigged up with cans and wires so if anybody comes by, he'll hear. He'll shout, 'Who's down there!' And if you don't answer, he'll start shooting. He's killed a few men. That's why I always make sure to answer."

Billy visits Ophie several times a year, just as he did when he was a boy. "I remember when I was little being so cold in the winters in that shack. I'd wake Ophie up and I'd say, 'Ophie, I'm cold!' And Ophie would say, 'Well, pull up another dog, boy.'"

Billy says he visited Ophie last week, when he was home for his brother's funeral. "And Corey, she had a big pot going over the fireplace," he says. "She poured me some. I said, 'Corey,' I said, 'Corey, now what is in this stew?' She said, 'Muskrat, groundhog, and a pork chop.'"

I slap my hand on the table and laugh. Laugh so hard, I think I'm going to pop. Wait till I tell Alex this one. It seems we weren't so off base with our varmint recipes.

"Corey cooks whatever it is that runs by the house," Billy says. "Or *in* the house. She'll grab it and cook it. But you know, that stew really wasn't too bad."

That reminds me of my news.

"Marley killed a groundhog!" I say. I tell him the whole story. I ask him to please tell Tom, because I know Tom will be so pleased.

"Well, there you go," he says.

I think how far I've come in just six months, that I would be sitting here swapping dead groundhog stories with a man dressed like a cowboy.

"Hey, you know, you should think about horses instead of sheep or pigs or cows," Billy says. Billy would himself love to have a horse farm. He tells me about a man in North Carolina who he knows who is a good source of saddles. "He has one arm," he says. "And he's always wanted to make saddles, so this is what he does. It's what he always wanted to do. I wish I could do that. Instead I gotta be in the mud.

"But you should think about horses," he goes on. "You could fit, what, ten horses in that barn?"

"No," I say. "Remember? The barn is collapsing, so at the moment we can't fit any." There is no headroom in the bottom floor, which is the place you would stall a horse. The foundation is crumbling, and so the barn floor is sagging nearly to the ground.

"We could shore it up," he says. "I seen worse." We talk about the size of the stalls, and we get out a piece of paper and a pencil and try to calculate how much money I could bring in by boarding horses for city people who are always looking in the area for stables.

It's the best idea yet, and I feel excited. I've always wanted a horse. And Alex wants a mule. I imagine having nine beautiful horses to look at every day, and one mule. I imagine a briarless farm, rolling green fields, and beautiful geldings bounding—only the truth is, I don't know a gelding from a filly from a colt. But I can learn. It feels great to get my mind in the future, and I wonder if Billy has any idea what his visit has brought.

Afterward, I walk him out. He looks at his boots, tips his hat, and says he's going to go see his mom. He thanks me for being home.

Marley comes sauntering up. He has a groundhog in his mouth, he has it by the neck; it's floppy and soggy and one leg is missing. It's not as big as the first one. But it is every bit as dead.

"Looks like the poodle got himself a new hobby," Billy says.

FIFTEEN

O N THE DAY OF THE OPERATION, IT RAINS. I AM here, but I am not really here at all. I feel as though my head is in an upside-down fishbowl, like a cat in a cartoon. I have no idea what is going on.

I sit in the waiting room with Nancy, who is with me because she knows how this feels. I think of how many times she waited for her mother, then her father to come out of surgery. I wonder how in the name of God she survived all that. Seeing Nancy now, alive and happy and flipping through bride magazines, gives me hope.

I hate hospitals. I come from a medical family, and I hate hospitals. My father, brother, and sister Claire are all physicians. My mother, sister Kristin, and I come from a different gene pool. My mother is a painter, Kristin is a television producer, and I'm a writer. I like our gene pool better. I get sick around sick people; I start imagining how it would feel to be them, and soon I want to curl up, or throw up.

When I was little, Claire fell off her bike while zooming full speed down the big hill in front of our house. She broke her arm and went to the hospital and came home with a million bandages everywhere.

I refused to go into her room. I refused to breathe her same air. I was convinced she was contagious.

Then she got toys. She got stuffed animals. She got Mouse Trap, the game I wanted my whole entire life. She got Baby First Step, a doll that actually walked. I started sleeping in Claire's room, hoping she was contagious.

It is three hours before the surgeon comes out. He doesn't look happy, but I can't say he looks sad, either. He's in blue scrubs, and he has that face mask thing hanging around his neck. "He's doing fine," he says to me, and then he holds up a photograph. An actual picture of the actual tumor that was once in Alex. What is with these colorectal surgeons and photography?

"Okay, as you can see, this tumor is quite large," he says. "This tumor is even larger than we expected. Let's say, the size of a tangerine?"

Uh-huh. I see. Why doesn't he tell me the tumor is as big as the United States of America? As big as Hale-Bopp? I am getting sick of hearing about the size of this tumor.

He says they've sent it to the lab. He says we'll know in a week. He says the surgery went well, and Alex is strong and healthy, so he expects no complications. He feels confident about having removed the entire "mass."

"Well, good," I say.

"Hang in there," he says, placing his hand on my shoulder. It's reassuring, a small touch like this. They should teach all doctors to touch like this.

Shortly after Alex is wheeled up to Room 402, Amy and Peter arrive. Amy appears ready to burst into tears. She rushes over to her father, looks at him, looks at me. She has her father's chin. Her father's back. Her father's hands. She is a fair-haired version of her dad, with clear blue eyes.

"He's sleeping," I say. "Everything went okay."

Peter gives me a hug. Skinny Peter. They say he's built with piano wire, he's so strong and so skinny at the same time.

"Are you okay?" he says to me.

"Oh, I'm fine," I say. "New glasses, huh? Very cool."

"Thanks," he says. The glasses are tiny, barely as big as his eyeballs.

Alex is waking. Peter goes over to him, takes hold of his hand. Amy has his other hand.

"Hey, sugar," Alex says to Amy, then turns to Peter. "Hi, sweet pea."

Amy and Peter stand over him. I stay back, watch them stare at him.

Alex motions with his head for them to come closer, to lean in. So this is what they do. I step closer, too.

Alex takes a breath. Then he speaks, in the tiniest, post-op voice: "Did I ever tell you," he says. Then he swallows, takes another breath. We lean in closer. "Did I ever tell you about the time," he says. "About the time I walked into the men's store and saw a sign that said 'All men's pants half off'?"

"Daaaaad!" Amy shouts, a shout that rings throughout the fourth floor of Shadyside Hospital. Peter folds over, laughing. And so do I. We crack up for a century.

"Ouch . . . ," Alex is saying. "Don't make me . . . laugh. . . ."

"Don't make *you* laugh!" Amy shouts. "We'll make you laugh, Daddy. Oh, now we've got you!"

Alex looks at me, as if for help.

"Don't look at me," I say. "I'm on their team."

Eventually, we make ourselves comfortable, settle in to Room 402. Amy and Peter and I stake out the hospital and find the cafeteria and the quickest routes to it. When he is awake, Alex spends his energy telling Amy and Peter that this is no big deal, that he doesn't believe he has cancer, that it's probably nothing. At one point, I think he even has them convinced of it.

IT'S RAINING AGAIN. WE'VE BEEN HERE FOR THREE days, and it's still raining. The gutters above the window of Room 402 don't work right, so the water falls in heavy streams, like at Niagara Falls. Well, not really, but it might as well be. Even inside, everything is starting to feel soggy. We've spent our time watching old movie classics and marveling at all the tubes in Alex's arm. He says he feels fine. He wants to go home. The only reason they're keeping him is because he's not allowed to eat, not even a smidgen, giving the healing time to happen.

On the fourth day the rain stops, and I take a day off from sitting in the hospital and drive down to the farm to visit Bob, whom I've left alone to fend for himself for these days. Billy said he would stop in and check on him a few times, and I trust that he has. The dogs are staying with me at the South Side house; it's easier to leave cats alone than it is to leave dogs.

As soon as I turn onto Spring Valley Road, I notice that something has changed. Something huge.

Green!

When I pull up to the farm, I see buds on the locust trees and blooms on the apple trees. I see a gentle green hue surrounding the pond, where water lilies are sprouting. I see the thickest mass of bright yellow forsythia lining the woods. There is even a lime green haze on our hillside, our newly seeded hillside. "Our grass!" I shout, leaping out of the car. "Our grass!" I can't wait to tell Alex.

Spring!

It's as if Mother Nature has come home and the rest has done her good.

I throw my arms up in the air and twirl around, like Julie Andrews in *The Sound of Music*. I feel a sudden and intense urge to sing the theme song from *Petticoat Junction*. But as quickly as the urge comes, it goes away. It's no fun singing stupid songs without Alex here to beleaguer.

The rains have also encouraged the grass around the house to grow. And grow. And grow. It is up to my knees in places, making the farm look neglected and sad. I will have to do something about this. I will have to do something right away. I head into the garage. I look at the tractor, the Ford 1710, and wonder if I might be able to actually run this thing.

I stand in front of the tractor. A ton of steel, taller than me, and far wider. This tractor shouldn't be blue. This tractor, I think, should be yellow with black stripes. Because it looks like a lion, an angry lion. The front grille is its fangs. The loader hanging below is its mane. And the roll bar up top is its ears, all perked up. I am terrified of this tractor.

I look out at all the long, sloppy grass. I look at the tractor. Okay, it's stupid to be afraid of a tractor. I need to conquer the tractor. I need to cut the stupid grass. And really, if I were to ride this tractor, I wouldn't be battling a lion. No, no, no. I have the power to change that image. The imagination is far mightier than a lion, or even a Ford 1710. I close my eyes and change the image. Erase it. The tractor is not a lion.

When I open my eyes, the tractor is a bull. Still a huge, dangerous animal, but, well, not a carnivore. A grazing animal. This tractor is hungry. I am going to let it out of this garage and give it all this grass to eat. That's all I'm doing. This is no big deal at all. What a nice bull.

I climb onto the tractor. It takes me a long time to get it started because I can't remember how Billy did it at the tractor store. It seemed so simple then. Um. There. It goes. It runs. It snorts. Wow. It's loud in this garage. I need to get it out of this garage. I forget how Billy taught me how to do this. I should have paid better attention. Um. This pedal combined with this lever. *Fwoom!* Okay, not very graceful, but there we go. Whoa, boy. Slow down there, pal. I am going back and back and back. I jam on the brakes, take a deep breath, and bring the beast to a halt. Okay, good. Tractor out of garage. Very good. The tractor bellows, and the fumes hit me in the face. It occurs to me that I have no idea how to make this thing go forward.

I look around at all the hills. All this grass. I don't have the foggiest notion how to negotiate these hills. I'll kill myself on these hills. Hills that once delighted me and hills that need me and hills that now terrify me.

I need Alex.

I fold my arms on the steering wheel, hang my head. And sob.

Thick, heaving sobs. I sob the way I sobbed for Bob in my living room that day, wailing like an infant. Only not like that at all. When it comes to death, I am a baby. *I am not ready for this lesson. And, God, I know. Yes, I know, God, I know as well as anyone how you are getting a headache up there from all those prayers coming at you for people. People, people, people. But please, let me have this dream. And, let's see. If you want, I'll go back to my work with the roadkill, of course. Or maybe there's something else you'd like me to do? Whatever you want. Name it. All I ask is that you please waltz into that lab—or, I don't know how you do these things—but make those cells not be cancerous. I know, I'm not supposed to bargain with you, but . . .*

Oh God, I am babbling. Babbling at God. Babbling a child's babble. Does God prefer more intelligent prayer? Does He downgrade your request if you sound like an idiot?

And why am I thinking so much about me? I should be thinking about Alex. If I really loved him, I would be thinking about him, his terror, not mine. I guess I don't really know how to do love. I am a baby at love, too. Jeezus, why does fear make you hate yourself so much?

My legs are wet from all these tears. And diesel exhaust, I am discovering, is quite a terrible atmosphere for crying. I taste it. It tastes like burned chicken. How do you turn this tractor off? I don't know how the hell you turn it off. I push buttons, eventually choking the engine. I hate this tractor. I climb down off the tractor, leave it right the hell here. I'll call Billy and ask him to come over and get it back in the garage. He won't mind. He won't laugh. He'll understand. Some friendships are like this.

I head inside the house to visit Bob. This does not cheer me up. This does not cheer me up one bit.

Bob, please stop howling. I'm sorry, Bob. I am sorry to leave you alone here. I had to stay in town. You know I wouldn't have left you if I didn't have to. Okay, up here. Right here. God, you're so skinny, Bob. When did you get so skinny? Do you want some tuna? Would you eat tuna? Please? I really need you to eat, Bob. Please stop howling, Bob. I am here.

I go into the kitchen and open a can of tuna and drain it into the sink, which is stupid, because Bob would have liked the tuna juice. But I am not really thinking.

And, oh. Well, look. The ladybug. The ladybug is back. How about that! I wonder if I am supposed to jump for joy and feel a sudden surge of good luck, or if I am too old for that.

"Well, hello!" I say. "I am really glad to see you."

I think: *"Les bêtes du bon Dieu,"* or creatures of the good God. I think *"vacchette della Madonna,"* or cows of the Virgin. Cows? What in the world does that mean?

Then I notice something. There are two ladybugs. "Hey!" I say.

Wait a second, there are three ladybugs. Wow. All these ladybugs. I can't even tell which is mine. Or maybe none of them is mine. Maybe mine deposited its aggregating hormone and split, and these bugs moved in. How many ladybugs are here? Four ladybugs? Five, six ladybugs? Wow. Where are all these ladybugs coming from? Is this some sort of good luck infestation?

I consider taking one of the ladybugs, putting it in an envelope, and bringing it to the hospital. But then I think, no. They must have rules about bringing bugs in.

I put the tuna in a bowl for Bob and sit on the floor and serve it to him.

He turns away. He comes over to me and curls up in my lap.

"Bob!" I say. "It's *tuna!*"

He has no interest in food.

E XACTLY ONE WEEK AFTER THE SURGERY, THEY release Alex from the hospital. There is still no word on the biopsy. Amy and Peter head back to New York; we'll call them as soon as we hear. Alex and I drive together out of the hospital parking lot, stop at South Side to pick up Betty and Marley, and head back down to the farm.

"Wow!" Alex says as we drive up Wilson Road. "It's like magic! *Isn't it like magic?* I mean, when we left, it was brown. We come back, it's green! It's like a freak of nature or something!"

I consider pointing out that this, in fact, *is* nature, but decide not to interrupt his reverie. He is a city boy blossoming at camp again. I love it when he is a city boy blossoming at camp.

"Spring!" he says, trying to take it all in as we come up the driveway.

I open the car door, and the dogs leap out. It's their first whiff of spring at the farm, too. Marley throws up. Betty races toward the pond, *roo roo roo*ing at the blue heron nesting on the bank. The bird takes off, flaps the loudest flaps. That bird is twice the size of Betty.

"Spring!" Alex says, stepping out of the car, pointing at the rhododendrons and azaleas in bloom. "Spring!" he says, pointing to the amazing shock of color put out by the red maple down by the barn.

"Well, I told you!" I say.

"Well, you were right!" he says.

"What?"

"I said, 'You were right, dear.' "

"Thank you very much."

When we get inside, there are more ladybugs in the kitchen. There are ladybugs in the living room. There are ladybugs in the dining room.

"Oh, my God," Alex says. "What are we supposed to do about these bugs?"

"Ladybugs are good luck," I say.

"But—"

"We can't kill them," I say.

He gets out a broom and starts sweeping ladybugs into a dustpan.

"Be careful," I say.

"I'm giving them a better life," he says, stepping out onto the front porch and dumping the bugs in the zinnia bed, or the soon-to-be zinnia bed. I can't wait to plant zinnias.

I go at the kitchen ladybugs with another broom, another dustpan. My God. There must be ten thousand ladybugs here. Can you have so much good luck, it is downright disgusting?

"Okay, this is beyond gross," Alex says, after his third trip to the zinnia bed. He opens the pantry and reaches for the vacuum cleaner.

"You're not going to vacuum the ladybugs!" I say, imagining all my little friends getting sucked into a vat of common dirt, imagining all my good luck getting sucked out of the universe.

"What are we supposed to do?"

The phone rings. Line Four. Alex's line. It stops us in our tracks. We look at each other.

"It's probably Peter," he says.

"Or Amy," I say.

"Of course," he says, and answers.

"Hello?"

Not Peter. Not Amy. Too long a pause.

"Yes," he says. "That's correct. Uh-huh. Well, what is the . . . ? Uh-huh. I see. And they are sure? Is there any other way to . . . No. Okay. Well, then. I understand. I mean, of course. I'll call in the morning and schedule the appointment. Thank you, doctor. Thank you for . . . calling so quick."

He hangs up.

He looks at me. He doesn't say anything. It's as if he's in shock.

"Well?" I say.

"B-9," he says.

I jut my head forward, like, "Hello?"

"B-9," he says. "Like in Bingo."

"Benign?" I say.

"Benign," he says.

"But . . . what about the size, I mean a *tangerine*—"

"He said they sliced it every way they could. He said, 'You

don't have cancer.' He said he was happy. He said it doesn't usually turn out this way.'"

It takes an awfully long time for this news to sink in. You'd think we would spin around, jump up in the sky, shout hallelujah. You'd think I'd break into one heck of a medley of stupid songs.

But that is the music of joy. What is the music of humility and awe? Of praise and thanksgiving? Of promise and commitment?

I step toward Alex, wrap my arms around him. We hold each other so tight, our muscles quake. We stand under the wagon-wheel kitchen light, holding on. There are ladybugs crawling all the hell over the place. There are ladybugs crawling in the wagon-wheel kitchen light. Soon it is raining ladybugs.

"Uck," he says, letting go, looking up.

"There is no way you're vacuuming these things," I say.

"What if I used the little hand-held Dustbuster?" he says.

"Resist!" I say. "Resist the urge to vacuum!"

And so we spend many hours sweeping ladybugs, which may sound like an odd thing to do to celebrate a future that suddenly becomes intact. But to me it feels like harvesting luck, offering it back to a most holy wind.

Soon, a howling wind. Cool air moves in without so much as a warning. Rain comes down, water in sheets. I wonder what ladybugs do in the rain. I think about the drain. I hope Mother Nature has a better configuration out there than a kitchen sink drain. There is a flash of lightning, as the wind and the rain join together in a full-blown storm, a chorus. I stand at the kitchen sink, looking out, watching the trees on the ridge sway as if made of rubber.

The electricity goes out.

Roo roo roo roo! Woof woof woof. A symphony of barks, howls, and rolling thunder. Finally, a flash so bright and so close, it seems the lightning has certainly touched the earth, and later we learn that a tree has fallen and crushed a section of fence. In no time, our fields of delicious high grass are full of happy sheep.

The neighbor's flock has taken advantage of the chaos, and I think that's pretty smart.

CUE
THE MULE

SIXTEEN

Obviously, the thing to do now is to buy a mule. That's what I'm thinking, as I zoom like a maniac down Daniel's Run Road, one of the pretty tar and chip roads Billy showed me. I am getting good at back roads. I am loving back roads. Back roads make you feel like you belong.

A mule. I should get Alex a mule. Okay, but what exactly is a mule? I see cows and sheep and a few horses passing by my window, but no mules. At least none that I can identify. What exactly does a mule look like? And why did Alex say he wanted a mule? Did he even have a reason? Does he even know what a mule is? Well, I don't know. Details, details. I should get him a mule. The mule will be a surprise. A wedding present! The mule will come clippity-clopping up the driveway at precisely the right moment on September 13—exactly nine days before my thirty-ninth birthday. My wedding day.

It's June. So much has happened since the ladybug invasion, since spring arrived and the warm winds blew away bad news, blew it away as if it were nothing. Nothing! A nothing that opened our really has had everything to do with new life. I think back to that first day when we watched the bulldozer give this farm a shave. How I stood there transfixed. Not by the machine. Not by the briars in motion. But by nothing. A nothing that has made room for everything.

And a mule.

SEVENTEEN

I'M AT MY COMPUTER, DOING AN INTERNET SEARCH for *mule*. A mule, I read, is a cross between a horse and a donkey. Well, I knew that. I mean, I sort of knew that. A mule has the body of a horse and the extremities of a donkey. Long ears, short mane, long legs, short tail. Pound for pound, a mule is much stronger than a horse. Mules have tremendous stamina, can live on frugal rations, and are exceptionally surefooted. Mules, I read, are loyal, intelligent, affectionate, stubborn, obstinate, and/or aloof, depending on the author of the mule description. People seem to have strong opinions about mules. Horse people laugh at mules. Maybe because horse people tend to think in terms of bloodlines, in terms of "showing." Mules are sterile. There are no bloodlines. Mule people seem to think horse people are snobs. Mule people love the way each mule is unique. Mule people think mules are woefully misunderstood. Mules, it seems, are the underdogs of the equine world.

The more I read, the more I come to think Alex is definitely a mule person. I wonder if there are many mule people out there who are also poodle people.

Mules are available in small, medium, and large. You can pick one up for about a thousand dollars.

But where? And how quickly?

Billy will know. Billy knows how to get anything around here. Good idea. I'll go down to the barn and ask him. Billy and Tom and Butch, another helper, have been down there sawing and banging and heave-hoing for a few weeks now, shoring up the barn in what turns out to be a fairly complicated project. I like having the guys back. I like going down there and bringing everybody iced tea.

I head into the kitchen and fix a tray with three cups. Extra sugar. Spoons. Fresh lemon slices. I'm getting good at the work of womenfolk. I swing the kitchen screen door open with my hip and head down to the barn, careful not to spill the refreshments.

"You guys thirsty?" I say as I duck my head and enter.

"In a minute," Tom says, hoisting one end of a beam over his shoulder.

The guys are covered in sawdust that sticks to their sweaty T-shirts. Tom is by far the neatest of the three. He wears his shirt tucked into his Wranglers—which are ironed—and he's sporting a new, hip haircut, real short on the sides, longer on top. Tom seems to have aged years over these past few months. Aged in a good way. I'm surprised. Because he seemed so depressed when he got the news: He didn't get into the army. He couldn't pass the physical due to an eye condition. He's legally blind in one eye, and nearly so in the other. I thought he was going to collapse when he heard. Because he would say he *needed* to be in the army. Because this is what his father did and his grandfather. He needed to serve his country. But Tom didn't collapse, at least not for long. He decided to become an EMT and enrolled in night school. He brings his books to the barn and reads when he gets a moment or two. "I'm gonna *do* this," he said to me one day. "I'm gonna save lives."

"You guys like extra sugar in your tea?" I say, wishing someone would see what a nice little tea service I've made here. "Lemon?"

"In a minute," Billy says, hammering.

They're never too talkative when they're working. I rest the tray in the wheelbarrow, find a seat on a sack of cement, and wait for them to take a break.

Billy seems to have aged a lot in these past few months, too. But not in a good way. He's thin and frail, practically as thin and frail as Bob. And he hasn't told me one tall tale since he started this barn project. Not one. I suppose losing both his brother and his mother has taken its toll. He doesn't talk about it, though. Then a few days ago he stepped on a rusty nail that went right through his foot. I insisted he go get a tetanus shot. He fought me on that point. He said he would be fine. He said how about I go up to Kenny's Grocery and buy him a can of Skoal instead. Which I did. Because it made him feel better. But then I came back and nagged and nagged and nagged until he got in his truck and drove off to the clinic for the shot.

I notice that today, the old wood—the wood with the rusty nails sticking out—is stacked neatly outside the barn, stacked in a place where no one will step on it. I suspect Tom did this.

Sitting on this sack of cement, I look around and try to imagine where Alex and I might hang a sign that says "Sweetwater Farm," the name we have decided on. Farmers use "sweet water" to refer to the sap of maple trees, and we have more maple trees on this property than any other kind of tree. Sweetwater Farm. A good name. We should definitely get a sign.

"All right, Tom," Billy says, "leave it set right there." Billy wipes his forehead on his sleeve and says, "I'm thirsty," signaling a break.

I hand out cups. Nobody wants sugar. Nobody wants lemon. One, two, three, they down those drinks so fast, you can hear the clunking sound come out of their throats. I watch three Adam's apples bobbing in unison.

"So guess what," I say to them. "I'm thinking of getting Alex a mule."

Dead silence.

"A mule," Butch says finally. "But why?" He is a beefy young man, with several missing teeth and sandy blond hair. He is the kind of person you look at and get the urge to say "hown' dawg."

"Because he said he wanted one," I say. "Do you know where I can get a mule? I don't want to pay too much."

"Don't, don't, *don't* get a mule!" Tom says. "Mules are ignorant, and they bite." He says his grandfather had a mule that refused to be ridden unless it was primed with a quart of beer.

"Aw," I say. "That's kind of endearing."

"Don't get a mule!" Butch says. "Mules aren't like horses. You know, horses, they'll forget. A mule, he'll hold a grudge against you his whole life."

But I would be nice to the mule. He wouldn't have a reason to hold a grudge, I point out.

"You ever been around mules?" Butch says. "Mules will outsmart you time and time again until you can't help but yell."

Billy listens. He considers these comments. He pours himself more tea. He looks at the tea, as if finding an answer there. He says, "Alex wants a mule. Get him a mule."

I love Billy.

I ask him to please be on the lookout for a mule; I need one by September 13.

"Okay, I'll find you one," he says.

I know better than to ask him how, or where, or any such details. Billy is a man of action, a man of his word.

I see Alex heading down from the house, all done up in his cute overalls, his tractor-riding outfit. God, he looks so . . . clean compared to these guys.

"Sssshhhh," I say. "He's coming! Quick! Change the subject!"

"SO HOW ABOUT THIS BEAM?" Billy says, real loud.

"WHAT IS THAT? AN EIGHT-FOOTER?" Butch asks.

"YES, BUTCH. YES, IT IS."

Alex comes in.

"What's going on?" he says.

"Nothing," Tom says, real short, clipped. "We're not talking about anything."

"Nothing!" Butch says. "Why would somethin' be goin' on?"

Alex looks at the guys, me.

Okay, these guys are not good at this. Really not good. No more secret mule conversations.

"Well," Alex says to me, "we should leave here by four to pick Riva up at the airport."

"Okay," I say. "I'll be ready."

"And the sheep are back," he says.

"Oh?" I say.

"There must be fifty of them on the hill."

"Uh-oh," I say. "Let's get the dogs in." The sheep belong to George, the farmer next door, the one who allegedly shoots dogs. Those were his smart sheep that came exploding through the fence last spring after that storm and started chomping on our grass. They've been back several times since.

"Must be one heck of a hole in that fence," I say.

"Or else one very smart sheep leader," Alex says. "Where are the dogs?"

"Has anybody seen the dogs?" I say to the guys.

Nope.

"You sure they aren't chasing the sheep?" I say to Alex.

"We would have heard by now," he says.

"Then they must be over visiting the cows again," I say. They like hanging out at the neighbor's dairy farm. Jay, the farmer, doesn't mind. He doesn't shoot dogs. But then again, our dogs don't chase his cows. But then again, we've never seen our dogs chase a sheep.

"Well, let's get the sheep out of here before the dogs come back," Alex says.

"All right."

"You want us to help?" Tom asks.

"Nah," Alex says. "We're getting good at this."

We head up the hill. I wish I had better shoes on. I have my iced tea service shoes on, these little Keds. You should have thicker soles when you herd sheep. The sheep are all hunched over, bundles of curly wool. Beautiful animals, really. Peaceful and fluffy. I have had no desire whatsoever to shoot them, even though, technically, they are trespassers and apparently I am allowed to. I mean, if George is allowed to shoot my dogs.

It occurs to me that I am very angry at George, a person I've never even met. I start clapping my hands at his beautiful, innocent sheep.

"Come on, sheep!" I say.

Herding sheep is not a complicated procedure. You walk up to the sheep. One of them sees you and walks away from you. The others follow. The only real trick is steering. First, you have to know where you're steering them, and then you have to jog a ways to cut off the leader so she'll point in the right direction.

"Baa," I say to the sheep.

Baa, one says. Only it comes out more like *mehhh.* But people are conditioned to hear *baa.*

I love these sheep. I love the way they waddle. And when they walk, you can hear the grass go *swish swish swish.* Kind of like the sound of a satin ball gown, now that I think about it. But I am in my bride stage.

"Let's go, girls!" Alex says to the sheep. "Time to go home."

We wave our arms in the cool afternoon air, around and around, a rhythm like a windmill's. The sheep keep moving.

"I'm not sure where the hole in the fence is, though," I call to Alex, who is herding from the back, while I'm up here with the leading lady sheep.

"Just head up to the gazebo spot, and walk along the fence line," he calls.

The gazebo spot. Ah, yes. The invisible gazebo. The gazebo that has not yet materialized. That was supposed to be the first thing we did when we moved to the farm, put a gazebo on the hill. It was going to be so beautiful. So simple. Who knew we would get busy hiring a bulldozer driver, buying a tractor, buying tractor attachments, getting a satellite dish, getting engaged, discovering a tumor, taking out the tumor, getting a new dog, getting the barn renovated, planning a wedding, herding sheep—before we would ever again even think of the gazebo? The gazebo was part of the post-card, the 2-D version of the dream. One thing you can say about 3-D is, it is a lot more expensive.

Eventually, we get the sheep all together, a great curly mass of sheep, mashed up against the fence. I hear something. A motor-cycle? "Someone is coming," I say to Alex. I can't tell exactly where it's coming from, but it's getting closer. Suddenly, from over the rise, comes a man driving a four-wheeler.

"I think that's George," Alex says.

"Uh. Oh."

The man waves. He stops in front of us. The four-wheeler sputters and shuts off.

"Hi there," he says. "Sorry about the sheep." He's a stocky, rugged man in a white T-shirt and a torn fisherman's vest. He has a ring of tobacco juice around his lips. His belly is big, like there's a watermelon sitting in his shirt.

"Well, we got them all up here in one spot," Alex says.

"Thank you kindly," he says. "I'm George."

"Hello," Alex says, extending his hand. He introduces me. I don't extend my hand—I look around for the dogs. I look to see if George has a gun on that four-wheeler, if perhaps he is toting a dead dog. I don't see any gun. I don't see any dead dogs.

Soon Alex and George are deep into farmer talk, sheep talk, al-falfa talk, while I stand here and do the womenfolk thing: stare blankly, stupidly.

But George keeps looking at me as he talks, as if he's trying to actually include me in the conversation. As if he might actually be-lieve that I understand what's going on. Well, that's kind of re-freshing. One point for George.

Soon we are all talking together. Talking fence.

George tells us something we never knew. This fence isn't his. Or, not only his. This is "our" fence. In the tradition of these hills, neighbors split ownership and responsibility for fences. Fence lines, he says, are sacred matters, set by ancestors.

"Yeah, my grandpap put in these posts," George says, kicking one. He lifts a section of wire off the post, providing a passageway for the sheep. "Heee-yaaaa!" he calls at them. "Come on, heeee-yaaa!" The sheep scurry. I jog this way and that to keep the little ones in line. Soon all the sheep are home again.

"Yeah," George says. "My grandpap and old man Collins, the one who built your house, they put these posts in together." The two farmers divided the labor, shaking hands on an agreement that would last more than a half century. The part near the road was to be maintained by one family and the part near the forest by the other. They planted a tiny oak tree to mark the spot where one part became the other.

"And that's the tree," George says, pointing at a towering oak arching magnificently over both sides of the fence.

As it happens, the damaged portion of the fence is on our part, making it our responsibility to fix it. Hmm. I wonder if he's made this whole story up to try and get us to fix his damn fence. I start looking at him as a dog murderer again.

"But you know what," George says, rubbing his lips, as if he can feel that tobacco juice stuck on there. "I'll fix it. It's no big deal to me." He says he has the equipment. He knows we don't. Plus, he's used to it. "Two generations of the Collins family," he says. "We got along fine." He says the next owners of the place, the people who sold it to us, they wanted the fence agreement in writing. "They brought lawyers in here," he says. "They came over to my place with a contract, who would pay for what, and when, and how. Finally, I said forget it. I said I'll take care of it myself."

The question George is asking is more implied than explicit. And to me it feels like an invitation. Would we like to become part of the tradition of these hills? A tradition of oak trees and neighborliness, of expectation and commitment. A culture in which the nature of responsibility isn't some mental exercise for litigators but rather a matter of one very powerful handshake.

"Hey, why don't I help you patch the hole," Alex says, offering his own symbolic gesture of cooperation. "I mean, I'd like to learn how to put a fence up, because I think eventually we're going to get sheep at our place."

"Oh, I can show you," George says. "And I can sell you some sheep when you're ready. I can teach you a lot about sheep. I went to college for sheep, you know."

Sheep college?

"Penn State," he says. "Bachelor of science in agriculture."

A college-educated farmer. This is not even close to how I imagined the man who shoots dogs.

Roo roo roo roo!

Speaking of which, that's Betty's bark. My, her voice carries. She's off in the distance somewhere, her bark filling the valley with echoes.

I look out over our land and can see the FedEx truck rumbling up Wilson Road, and then comes the inevitable *Woof, woof, woof, woof* of Marley.

"Those are our dogs," I say to George. It feels like a big deal to use the actual word *dog* in front of him. "We have three dogs," I tell him. It feels like a confession. I describe Betty and Wilma and Marley to him. I give him very explicit dog detail. I wonder how I might pop the question.

"You know, your sheep have been in our field several times now, and our dogs have not so much as barked at them," I say. Which is true. "So I don't think our dogs will ever go after your sheep," I say.

He's looking at me. He's scratching his belly.

Alex isn't saying anything. I wish he would chime in here. I don't really know how to say this. I mean, how do you ask a person to please refrain from murdering your pets?

"So there's no reason to, you know, worry about our dogs," I say to George. "Heh heh."

"Naw," George says, straddling his four-wheeler, revving the engine. "Not if you keep 'em home."

He smiles, says stop on over any time for sheep lessons. He tells

Alex he'll be up here working on the fence tomorrow if he wants to help. He waves and sputters off.

"Well," I say to Alex.

"Nice guy," Alex says.

"I wish he didn't shoot dogs," I say.

"Let's head back. It's getting late."

I look at my watch. "Four o'clock!" I say. "Riva!"

"Oh, God!"

We were supposed to *leave* at four.

We jog through the gate, down Wilson Road, the quickest way home.

When we reach our driveway, we can see the FedEx truck is still here.

"Tim's still here?" I say. "Well, that's weird."

The truck is parked funny. Like it's not really parked at all. Just stopped.

"He's parked funny," I say.

"I doubt it's another mud slide," Alex says with a laugh.

"Which is a good thing, because it looks like Billy is gone for the day."

As we get closer, we can see Tim sitting on the ground by his truck. Well, that's weird. He's hunched over something. Something black. Something about the size of . . . Marley.

"Oh, my God!"

We run. We run as fast as we can, our feet kicking the rocks and dust into the air.

"I am sorry," Tim is saying. He has Marley in his arms. A flimsy Marley. A seemingly lifeless Marley. "I love this dog." His voice is tiny and squeaky, and his face is bright red, as if he's ready to burst into tears.

"Marley!" Alex cries. "No, please, not Marley!"

"He was going in circles," Tim is saying. "I thought he was on my right, I heard a thump, oh, I love this dog. You know I love this dog."

Marley's eyes are open. He appears to be breathing. But he is not moving.

"Oh, Marley!" Alex cries. "Okay, boy. I'm here. . . ."

"He was going in circles," Tim is saying. A shrunken Tim. A weakened Tim. "I thought he was on my right, I heard a thump. Oh, God, I'm so sorry."

Alex scoops Marley up and carries him like a baby up to the house, Betty trotting behind.

"Come inside," I say to Tim. "Come inside and calm down. It's not your fault. He's been crazy around that truck. Just crazy."

"He was going in circles," Tim says. "I thought he was on my right. I went left. I heard a thump—"

"Come inside," I say to him.

"I'm going to sit here," Tim says. "If you don't mind, I'll just sit here." Wilma is at his feet, her head tilted back, her tail thumping. Wilma doesn't seem to know whom to comfort, either.

I head inside. Alex already has the vet on the phone. He's placed Marley on the couch. There is no blood. His eyes are open, blinking. He seems alert. But he is not moving.

Bob comes out. Skinny, scrawny Bob, a flimsy string where once a mighty tail stood. He walks so carefully, so slowly, because he can hardly see.

I pick Bob up, hold him, cradle his bony body. I kiss him on the head. We go over and sit beside Marley. "It's okay, Marley boy," I say. "We're going to take you to the doctor, and everything will be okay." Marley is whimpering quietly.

Alex hangs up the phone. "They gave me an address." he says. "An emergency hospital."

He is holding the piece of paper, unable to figure out what to do with it. Well, I don't know what to do, either. We should go together, with Marley. Just like we went together that day Betty got stung by the bee, the day we realized we were in love. But we have to go to the airport and get Riva. Or he has to get Riva. Or I should get Riva. Um. Love is getting so complicated. And at the moment, I have to take charge.

"You go," I say. "I'll get Riva. Just go."

"What am I going to do if something happens to Marley?" he says.

I stand up, put Bob down, fold my arms around Alex. "Go, baby. Just get him to the doctor." I hold him tight, smell his farmer smell, diesel plus cut grass plus sheep. I see Marley on the couch, Bob on the floor.

I am starting to feel as though I need much, much longer arms.

GATE A-19, THE MONITOR SAYS. "ARRIVED," IT SAYS, blinking. I charge. Riva is there, leaning on a water fountain. She is a short woman, under five feet tall, with a body that advertises her passion for food, her joy for living. She wears her hair in a jet black page boy, and her eyebrows are carefully penciled in, giving her the look of an exotic silent-film star.

She looks saggy, sweaty, bedraggled, as a person should look after a fourteen-hour transatlantic flight. She sees me and lights up with a smile. She hugs me and kisses me and tells me several dozen times how very much she loves me. She looks around. "And . . . Alinka?" she says. "Where is my Alinka? Why is he not standing with us?"

"Oh, everything is fine," I say, downplaying the drama unfolding back home. "Alex had to take the dog to the vet. He'll meet us at the farm."

"*Oh, my Got,*" she says. "He is okay? Please, say me he is okay." Riva often confuses the words *say* and *tell*. She is fluent in eight languages; her accent is Lithuanian with a little Russian and a sprinkle of Hebrew. In the style of Eastern Europe, she has many pet names for people. Alex is Alinka or Alushinka or sometimes Alushka.

"Everything's okay," I say. "You've had a long trip. You look exhausted. Let's get you home." I keep her mind on matters of suitcases and carry-on bags, and on the ride home I elicit stories of Tel Aviv. If I breathe a word to her about Alex, about Marley, about the fact that for all I know Alex's beloved poodle is paralyzed, is dead, Riva will explode with panic. Riva is a worrier. Riva is a caretaker. Riva is the universe's grandmother, believing herself to be single-handedly in charge of the health and welfare of anything and anyone she loves. And she loves Alex more than anyone else in the world.

She comes to be with Alex several months every few years because she feels that it is, at a minimum, her duty. Her duty to undo what Alex's father did. A duty to envelop him with the love of the Levys. The family may have been extinguished, but the love lives on. Riva is here to see to it.

It's past nine by the time we pull up to the farm, pitch dark. Alex's car is here. He's back. Oh God, I hope Marley is with him. I imagine Marley hearing my car, running out, *woof, woof, woof.*

I long for the sound of his *woof*s.

I open the door.

Alex looks saggy, sweaty, bedraggled, like he just took a fourteen-hour transatlantic flight.

Riva notices. She looks at me. Looks at me as if to say, "Have you been feeding this man?"

"Alinka!" she says. "Alinka! Oh, my Got! Alinka, what has happened? Rivka must know!"

"Welcome!" he says to her, and gives her a kiss. "Oh, Rivka, I am so happy to see you."

"But Alushinka, something is the matter. You must say me. Because I know. You cannot hide your health from Rivka. Is it your bottom again? Is your bottom okay?"

He cracks up, takes a moment to compose himself. "Just a rough evening," he says. "I had to take Marley to the doctor."

I am staring at him. I am demanding, with my eyes, to know where the hell Marley is.

"In the bedroom," he says. "No broken bones. They think he didn't get run over, that somehow the fender came down on him. He's badly bruised. And they had to put a drain in."

"A drain?"

"Into his gut. Some fluid in there. They said he doesn't have any internal injuries. Just this . . . fluid."

"So he has a drain?" I am saying, as I head back to the bedroom, and Riva follows.

I fling open the door, and there he is, on the floor:

A hairless poodle, covered in mange scabs, with a white plastic valve sticking out of his gut, leaking pink liquid.

"Oh, my Got!" Riva shouts. *"What? What? What is the matter with this animal!"* She looks at Alex, me. She rushes over to Marley, a grandmother with a mission, a calling.

"Um," I am saying, "I think it's actually not as bad as it looks."

"Riva," Alex says. "Rivka, he's fine. You're tired. You should rest. Come on, we'll get you some dinner and put you to bed."

"Rest?" she says. *"Rest!* How can you think to *rest*?" She is bending over Marley, stroking his face gently.

Just then, Bob walks in the room.

Oh, dear.

Skinny, sorrowful Bob.

Oh, dear.

"Remember I wrote to you about Bob?" I say to Riva.

"Bop?" she says. This is how she pronounces *Bob*. She knows Bob, remembers him from her last trip to America, back before Bob got sick, when Bob was still Ram-Bob, defender of the free world.

"This is my Ram-Bop?" she says. "Oh, Mammala, Bop! Oh, Mammala!" I have no idea what *Mammala* refers to, but it's what Riva says when she is worried about you. "Mammala!"

She looks at Marley, Bob. She looks at Alex, me. She looks at Alex and me as if to say, "What is the *matter* with you people?"

"Oh, my Got," she says. "Rivka is here to take care of you, my little Bop. My Mammala Marley. . . ."

I head into the kitchen, put some ravioli on.

But when I call her in, Riva refuses to eat. She insists that both Marley and Bob sleep with her in her room, so she can look after them. So this is what we do. We put them all to bed and close the door.

We sit together and sigh.

"It's going to be an interesting summer," Alex says.

"Interesting," I say.

EIGHTEEN

OBVIOUSLY, THE THING TO DO NOW IS TO GET A gazebo instead of a mule. That's what I'm thinking. A gazebo would probably mean a lot to Alex. A gazebo wouldn't get mange, or get hit by a truck, or leak pink fluid. A gazebo would just stand there. A gazebo can't break your heart.

I'm sitting at my desk. It's mid-June, a few weeks after Marley got hit. He's walking again. Well, limping. And they finally took the drain out. Tim came over a few times with bacon strips for him. A peace offering.

Bob is here, sleeping on the scanner. I don't know how much longer he'll be here. I have this notion that I want him to hang on until the wedding, but that is my wish for me, not him. I mean, he won't even know it's a wedding. Probably the greatest gift I could give him now would be to let him let go, let him die, take him to the vet and have them do whatever it is they do.

It's a pretty day, a Tuesday afternoon. From my desk I can see the pond, now bursting with water lilies. I can see the birch tree, with all different birds flying around it than the birds that were here before. Were the winter birds more colorful? Or do these birds look brown only when set against the green and blue and yellow and red of summer? A lot of hummingbirds stop by, standing tall and straight in the air, their wings a fuzzy flutter, a buzz. At the moment, a hummingbird is inspecting the red needle on the thermometer I have stuck on the window. Hummingbirds are drawn to the color red. It is eighty-three degrees.

I can see the sky in the window above. A sky that hardly moves at all anymore. A sky that is blue and flat, as if someone took a big brush and a can of latex and slapped it on.

This is exactly the sky I imagine will be here on September 13.

I imagine dancing, here in the big room. This would be such a great place to twirl and stomp.

I imagine flowers everywhere in the yard. I imagine a circle of zinnias, a swirl of snapdragons, a stately row of dahlias. I imagine long rows of cosmos flopping this way and that, leaning onto the porch. I imagine baskets of geraniums hanging off the barn. But, um. When am I supposed to find time to start a garden? How am I going to create an explosion of flowers by September 13? I don't even have a dress yet. Or music. And what about food?

I look out at the fields that need a good mow, the driveway that could use another layer of limestone, and the newly shored-up barn that still has all manner of rubble piled around it.

This place is a little rough for 150 people in fancy clothes. Definitely a little rough. Can we get it in shape by September?

I reach into my folder, a big expanding file labeled "Wedding." I take out the yellow pad of paper and flip past a list now grown fifteen pages long. "CLEAN UP," I write, and, "PLANT STUFF."

The phone rings. Line One.

"Hello?"

It's Billy. "I'm in West Virginia," he says.

"Oh," I say. For some reason, I think this means he is with his Uncle Ophie. Ever since he told me about Uncle Ophie, I've had Uncle Ophie in my head. Like he's some cartoon character I used to watch, and I'm hoping for reruns.

"Well, how is Uncle Ophie?" I ask.

"Oh, he's all right," he says.

Silence.

That's it? God, lately I am having to pull stories out of Billy. What in the world is wrong with him?

"Well, did you spend time with Ophie?" I say, prompting him.

"Yesterday," he says, "I walked up, the cans started clanking. Ophie came out in his long underwear."

I laugh. That's better.

"And I said, 'Ophie,' I said, 'Ophie, I come to tell you my mom passed away.' And Ophie, he didn't say anything. He sat right down in the dirt and cried like a baby."

"Oh," I say.

"But anyway," he says, "I found you a mule."

"Oh?"

"And a horse."

Oh, dear.

"You should have a horse if Alex is going to have a mule. The mule would be lonely."

"Oh."

"The mule is kinda small for a mule," he says. "But she's real gentle. *Real* gentle. She's friends with the horse. A big darn horse. But pretty. And kids ride her down here."

He says the horse is a registered American Saddlebred, which does sound impressive to me, even though I have no idea what it means. Hmm. Maybe I'm more a horse person than a mule person.

"What's the horse's name?" I ask.

"Cricket," he says.

Aw. A good name. I love that name.

"What's the mule's name?" I ask.

"Sassafras," he says. "But they call her Sassy."

Sassafras! A mule named Sassafras. That is the best mule name I have ever heard. Actually, it is the first mule name I have ever heard.

"I rode both," he says. "They ride good."

He says the owner wants just five hundred dollars for the mule and fifteen hundred for the horse, including saddles, other tack, and delivery. He says they're in financial trouble and need money quick. He says it's a great bargain. He says he's buying a horse trailer from the same people, so he could put them in the trailer and bring them up tonight.

"Oh," I say. "Well, wow."

But what about a gazebo instead? Um. Think. Okay, I need to think. I think of our wedding day. I think of myself standing here in some amazing satin wedding gown. I think of a bright and sunny afternoon, the sky painted on like a coat of latex. Flowers everywhere. People are scattered in clumps, chatting, sipping champagne, and enjoying the fresh air. And then suddenly—cue the mule—a big dopey mule comes clippity-clopping up the driveway. The mule has flowers in his hair. Her hair? Or, no. The mule has his or her hair done up in a big topknot, sort of like the way I wore mine when my sisters and I played circus and I got to be the clown.

And there's Alex. He is surprised! He is holding his stomach laughing. People are standing around, laughing and pointing and having a good time. And then Alex looks at me, he has his eyes all scrunched up, like, "What? What is this for? Why is this animal *here*?" And I say, um. Okay, what do I say? Um.

I say: "Don't look a gift mule in the mouth."

Because I don't know what the hell else to say. Because the mule, the mule doesn't mean anything. The mule is a four-legged creature of nonsense. The mule is this entire farm adventure in animal form. Equine form. Ungulate form. An adventure we never planned at all, never understood, walked into without the slightest clue what we were doing. An adventure with existential origins of the most absurd variety. An adventure that began as a dream, a dream born of *Green Acres*.

I'm imagining Alex. Alex with his new mule. He's looking at the mule, and he can't stop laughing. He grabs me, hugs me, and we spin around and go tra-la-la into the future.

Yes, this is it. This is the way it must go. I need a mule.

"But I don't need the mule until September thirteenth," I say to Billy. "Where am I supposed to hide the mule until then?"

"I can keep it," he says. "It can stay at my place with Levi." Levi is Billy's horse, which lives in a small barn in his backyard. "Me and Tom can take care of it," he says. "But I really think you should get the horse, too. The mule would be lonely. The mule wouldn't do good. And you got plenty of room in that new barn of yours. Compared to where these animals is living, that barn of yours looks like a Holiday Inn."

Fine. Play the pathetic orphan card. Billy knows me better than I realized.

"Well . . . ," I say, knowing that my next word is going to be: "Okay!" But really, shouldn't I ask Alex what he thinks about this? I mean, isn't a mule and a horse sort of a family decision? When you are part of a couple, do you get to make pet decisions without consulting your partner? Um. And shouldn't I *try out* these animals? How do you try out a mule and a horse? Um. I look at my folder labeled "Wedding" expanding every day with more and more unmade decisions, more and more things to do. I really don't have time to go mule shopping. And anyway, I trust Billy. Billy hasn't steered me wrong yet.

"Okay," I say to him. "Bring on Sassy and Cricket, too."

"All right," he says. "I'll drive them up tonight."

"Okay," I say. "Thanks."

I hang up. I look at Bob.

"Bob, I just bought a mule and a horse," I say.

He lifts his head, looks my way, and closes his eyes.

Bob never thinks anything is a big deal. Bob gives me permission. This is another thing I love about Bob.

THE NEXT MORNING, LINE ONE AGAIN. "THEY'RE here," Billy says. They got in after midnight. He says they had some . . . mishaps.

"Mishaps?"

"Just the unloading part," he says.

"What happened?"

"Well, it was kind of dark out, so I couldn't see too much. Mostly I heard it."

"Oh?"

He says they opened the trailer door and nudged the mule out. The mule took its first step out of that trailer and got spooked.

"Spooked?" I say.

"Mules are spooky," he says.

"Spooky," I say.

"Nervous like."

"Uh-huh. So how did you know it got spooked?"

" 'Cause it went runnin'. It went runnin' right up to the electric fence. But it didn't stop."

"Didn't stop?"

"It got zapped," he says. "That spooked it more. It started yellin' *hee-haw, hee-haw.* You never heard such a hollerin'. That got the horse's attention."

"What did the horse do?"

"It got spooked," he says.

"Spooked."

"Horses are spooky," he says.

"Uh-huh."

"The horse went running after the mule. That got Levi's attention."

"Oh?"

"Horses stick together. Horses, you know, horses are pack animals. Levi followed the others."

"Where did they go?"

"Well now, we couldn't see too much. It was so dark. But we found them up on the highway."

"The *highway*?"

"Route 40. It was late. There weren't a lot of cars. That was in our favor."

"So you were all running down the highway?"

"Well, Tom got his motorcycle. And Homer, he got his four-wheeler."

"Homer?"

"My neighbor. You never met Homer? Oh, Homer and I go way back. I met Homer when—"

"Let's come back to Homer later. What about the horses?"

"Well, we had some other neighbors helping, too. You know, a couple of other motorcycles. And we was hopin' the horses would keep on the hard road, because some of them cycles aren't made for off-road."

"Uh-huh."

"Well, we couldn't see much, like I said. You know, there wasn't hardly no moon last night. I got on the back of Tom's motorcycle. He drove. And I got the lasso, and pretty soon we had Levi."

"Had him?"

"Lassoed him."

"Right."

"I calmed him down. Me and Levi, we're a team. I said to him, I said 'Levi, we gotta get the other two.' So I saddled Levi. And Tom went all the way up to Beallsville, you know, where the traffic light is? And Homer, he was aside me on his four-wheeler. And we went one way and Tom came the other, and pretty soon, well, it was in Joe Crowley's yard we finally rounded them up."

"Joe Crowley?"

"The one with the pool?" he says.

"There's a Joe Crowley with a pool?" I say.

"You don't know Joe?"

"I don't think so."

"Well, we rounded them up there. They didn't go in the pool. Because there was a fence around it."

"Of course."

"So anyway, they're here," he says.

"Is everybody okay?"

"A little tired," Billy says. He does not seem upset or even excited by this drama.

"It's all part of life with horses," he says.

Life with horses, I think.

"Well, come on over and see what you bought," he says.

"Oh," I say. "Are you sure they're . . . ready?"

"Ready?" he asks.

Well, I don't know what I mean, either.

"Should I bring anything for them?" (Like maybe a Valium?)

"Carrots would be good," he says.

I hang up and head out to the kitchen.

Alex and Riva are having bagels, reading the paper. Hmm. I
sure would like to tell them all that I have just learned. I feel quite
alone here. And to complicate matters, now I have to figure out
how to get carrots out of the fridge, and what to say as I grab my
keys and head out. Hmm. Well, I don't want to lie.

"Good morning!" I say to them, as I surreptitiously grab a dish
towel. I babble about having a craving for . . . melon, knowing that
we have no melon. I babble and babble as I kneel in front of the
fridge, pretending I'm looking for melon. Smooth as a thief, I grab
a bag of carrots and wrap the dish towel around it.

"No melon!" I say, swinging around, and taking a giant
step toward the door, where we keep a basket for onions and potatoes. I quickly dump the carrots in the onion basket. Whew. One
step done.

"No melon!" I say. It occurs to me that these two have barely
even registered the fact that I am in the room.

"Hello?" I say. *"Good morning!"* They look up from their
newspapers.

"Hi, baby," Alex says. "I have a horrible headache."

I go over and give him a smooch. Riva gets aspirin.

"So I'm going to go out and get some melon," I say. "You guys
need anything?"

"Melon?" Alex says.

"I have a . . . craving," I say. *Thump.* I feel a most horrible thump in my gut. Just like that. A big fat lie. This is terrible.

In one swift motion I turn, grab the carrots, and head out the door.

Whew. Okay. I'm a little disturbed by the fact that I am still good at this. I haven't had to exercise these skills since I was a teenager.

I jump in the car and head over to Billy's. It is not quite registering in my mind or in my heart that I am now the owner of a horse and a mule.

I pull up to Billy's. Wow. Lots more excavation equipment in the yard. He must have gone on a buying spree. I can't even locate the pump that President Lincoln drank out of. It must be hidden behind a bulldozer or something.

I see Levi. I know Levi. A big galoot of a horse. A sweet horse. And then . . .

My first glimpse of her is Cricket at full gallop. My God! She is a movie star horse. Her hair is blowing in the wind. She is slender, with long legs; she is a chestnut mare that could easily pose for the cover of a horse magazine. She is the horse every kid who ever went through a horse stage dreams of. I remember my horse stage. I remember asking my mom for one. I remember her laughing, saying how cute that was, how silly. I wondered how come my brother, the oldest, wasn't laughed at when he wanted bees. He got six hives full.

"Hey," Billy says.

"Well, wow!" I say.

"Yeah, she's a looker."

"And the mule?" I ask.

"Probably hiding in the barn. Wait here. Oh, and here's Cricket's papers."

He hands me a blue certificate, very official-looking, from the American Saddlebred Horse Association. It details Cricket's entire family tree. Her real name is Santana's Premier Starlet, and she is the daughter of Star's Red Flower, the granddaughter of Go Red Flower, the great-granddaughter of Flower of The Sea. Wow. That is some impressive-sounding lineage. I reach into my bag of carrots, pull one out, and hand it to her.

Cricket sniffs. She's a little wary. She sniffs again. Finally, her lips open, rubber lips, nimble as fingers. The lips grab the carrot. She chews, a deep, low crunching rumble echoing through her big horse mouth. I reach out and touch her nose. A velvet nose. A most wonderful nose. Okay, I am definitely becoming a horse person.

Tom comes out of the house, limping. "So how do you like your damn mule," he says.

"Sorry about that," I say. "Actually I haven't met the mule yet—"

Heeee-haaawwww heeee-haawww!!!!!

My God! The noise is coming from the barn on the other side of the driveway.

"You're about to meet your damn mule," Tom says.

"Giddy-ya!" Billy yells. "Hyaaa!"

The creature emerges.

Oh, dear.

Okay, not a movie star. Definitely not a movie star mule. This is more, well, a daytime talk-show mule, a guest with bad hair. Her bangs are cut short, way short. She has bulging brown eyes. I mean, really sticking-out eyes. She looks like a crazy child just let out of the asylum. She is short. And fat. Is a mule supposed to be this fat?

"Hello . . . Sassafras," I say, as she waddles toward me.

I am standing here with my arm extended, holding a carrot for her. She is not impressed. She turns away. She plods over to a tree and stands there, her backside facing me.

"Well, then," I say.

"She's upset," Billy says. He says she's a little miffed about the events of last night. Plus, the six long hours she spent in the horse trailer to get here from West Virginia.

"Of course," I say.

He approaches Sassy slowly, slowly, and eventually catches her by her halter. "Easy, girl," he says, and in one gentle leap he climbs on her bare back.

Sassy goes down on her front knees.

We all get a good laugh out of that one. "That is some mule!" Billy says, climbing off and walking away.

Tom gets a saddle out of the barn, and a blanket, and all kinds of strappy leather horse things. God, it looks complicated. But Tom saddles Cricket up in no time. He climbs on her, nudges her with his feet, makes a kissing noise. "Let's go, girl." He rides her down the driveway. She is obedient and calm, and her gait is smooth and breezy like a runway model's.

Sassy watches. Sassy seems upset to see Cricket heading off.

Heeee-haaawwww heeee-haawww!!!!!

Oh, dear. Sassy keeps hee-hawing and hee-hawing, like, "Where in the hee-haw are you going without me, Cricket!" She runs toward Cricket. She does not run through the electric fence this time. No, she learned that lesson last night. This time she gets on her knees and tries to slither under it.

Billy cracks up. Oh, Billy has never seen anything this funny in his entire life. He runs and retrieves her. "That is some mule!" he calls back to me. The mule seems to have brightened Billy's mood considerably. "Oh, Alex is going to love this mule!" he says.

"Right-o," I say.

NINETEEN

AND SO THIS IS THE WAY THE SUMMER PROGRESSES.
I step out on Alex a few times a week to go give carrots to my tall,
stately, incredibly beautiful chestnut mare, which he does not know
I own, and his goofy, bug-eyed hee-hawing fat little mule, which he
does not yet know he owns.

I have a sneaking suspicion that I am not doing this bride
thing right.

But the big news is, I found a wedding dress. An ivory satin ball
gown with a basque waist, tulip sleeves, a Sabrina neckline, and a
triple crinoline—all of which I point out by way of showing off
that I am becoming quite fluent in bride lingo.

Nancy was with me when I found the dress—on our second
trip to Wedding World. I didn't actually intend ever to go back to
Wedding World, after that first clumsy visit, but Nancy and I were
driving by, and somehow that aqua blue building and that extreme
pink WEDDING WORLD sucked us back in. Nancy found her dress—
long-sleeve satin bodice, basque waist, tulle skirt, pearl brocade—
right after I found mine. We stood in that dressing room, looking at

each other, cracking up. "Brides!" We high-fived each other. We unzipped each other. We helped each other figure out how to get those giant dresses back on their hangers. We went out to the register and clicked our MasterCards on the counter, waiting for the big-haired lady to complete our orders. It was weird to stand there and pay your entry fee into the bridal kingdom. Nancy said she never imagined it this way; she imagined her mother with her; she imagined herself doing this at twenty-five, not forty. I said that I never allowed myself to imagine this at all.

It's late August. The wedding is only a few weeks away. The fields still need to be mowed. There's still a ton of ex-barn rubble all over the yard. Alex and I have agreed that, yes, the farm is a bit rough for a satin ball gown and 150 gussied-up people. We've decided to have the first part of the wedding, the fancy ceremony and a reception, up at the Century Inn, in their beautiful backyard gazebo. And then we'll have another party back here at the farm. *Cue the mule.*

I took Riva over to Billy's to meet the mule one night. She let out a lot of heavy sighs. She believes, first of all, that I should scale back considerably on my animal parenting. She does not quite see the appeal of the mule, especially since the mule has the habit of turning her backside to people. Only in my most private moments am I able to admit that I am far more in love with the *idea* of this mule than with this mule. And really, if the mule were for me, I wouldn't mind. I can probably fall in love with any animal. But this is supposed to be Alex's mule. And I have to admit that I wish it were, well, a better mule. Only I don't know what a better mule would be.

I found a violinist who does an awesome bluesy "Amazing Grace." I found a priest to officiate at the ceremony. I have decided on an actual wedding party: my two sisters, my sister-in-law, and Amy. My brother, Peter, and Amy's husband, Andy. It's a way of blending the family. A symbolic merging that feels right. Alex and I are starting to choose prayers and poems. We have chosen flowers, and flowers, and more flowers to cover the gazebo up at the inn. We have chosen a spread of hors d'oeuvres and bottomless bottles of champagne. I've ordered 150 butterfly larvae in little white boxes that are due to hatch on September 13 at precisely noon. (Uh-huh.) Everybody will get a box, and open it, and the butterfly will fly out, symbolizing, um, well, symbolizing that I am going a little hog-wild with these wedding plans. I have ordered a horse and wagon to take Alex and me from the Century Inn back to the farm.

Cue the mule.

I am embracing the complications of this wedding. I wonder if I am making it complicated enough. Complexity, in my mind, has come to equate with joy. The wedding is becoming a way of communicating. A way of shouting to the world: I am happy! And the more complicated I make it, the more happy you'll see I am.

Some of the complications are not of my own making. All of Washington County is now in an official drought emergency, putting a real dent in my gardening plans, such as they are. The tractor broke, some big piston problem, and UPS went on strike, so the parts are not getting delivered to the tractor store. We need the parts. We need the tractor. We need to mow this place, which looks hairy, shaggy brown.

And what about a garden? It kills me that I am going to host this party at our new farm and there won't be any flowerbeds. I'm a gardener! I used to be such a gardener. But when in the world was I supposed to start a garden? And to tell you the truth, I am a little garden-shy at this point. I think about the South Side garden, which is not really a garden anymore at all. How can I keep up with that place when I've got fifty acres to care for here? I think back to the hours and hours I spent hoeing and tilling and weeding and worrying and obsessing over that one-quarter-acre plot. In that garden, I knew what to do. In that garden, I had a plan. The space was defined by a fence, and the flowers all had rooms they belonged in.

In that garden, I had order. So much damn order, finally, that I couldn't stand it anymore.

Now, this garden, well, I don't even know *where* this garden really is. You can't have a fifty-acre garden, that's the first thing I've discovered. But I can't seem to really make that point stick in my head. I think of the pond project, the new five-acre pond we'll someday have, as part of the garden. I think of the hills Billy has cleared as part of the garden. I think of the barn, now standing straight and tall, as part of the garden. I think I can walk outside and just hoe and till and pick at this picture and make everything look good.

And so every day I walk outside and get that puny feeling again. I become exhausted before I even reach for my garden gloves. It takes an enormous amount of energy to grab hold, to really begin to control chaos.

That's one thing I'm discovering in a whole new way.

This whole year I've been in a free fall. Or more accurately, a free float. Buying the farm, moving to the farm, it's all been about chaos. About being lured into chaos. About abandoning the rigid equation that my life had become. I was frightened of chaos. Of course I was. Because when you think about chaos, you think it's going to be scary. You think it's going to hurt. You think it's going to be a tornado swirling that will suck you up and spit you out into some unknown place.

But that isn't what chaos is like at all. Chaos is like wind, that's for sure, and sometimes the wind picks up. But chaos doesn't hurt, at least not when you allow yourself to fall into it. Because the wind picks you up, as if you are a balloon, or a seed, or a tiny speck of pollen. The wind takes you places. The wind carries you, and you really have very little to say about it. There's no sense fighting it. You'll just make yourself tired and cranky. The wind will always win. The wind will place you firmly on the ground, when the trip is over.

I don't want the trip to be over. I really don't want to stop floating. I want a life of adventure every bit as vital as the one I'm in. I'm no longer fearful of chaos. I'm fearful of the calm. I'm afraid that yes, once Alex and I get married, that will be it. I will have landed. In a few weeks, I will have landed. I am a balloon about to go *thud,* hit the ground, and maybe drag along the fields for a few miles.

I really don't want to land.

Because when you land, that's when responsibility starts.

Chaos, I think, is youth. Youth at any age. Because as long as you have chaos, you are free of responsibility. When you are in chaos, when you don't know what's going on, when you are an ignorant dreamer falling into the unknown, buying a farm, entering a relationship, when you are floating through space like that, you aren't supposed to get anything right, you aren't supposed to make sense, you're supposed to be befuddled and amused and tender and aware.

It can't go on. Not unless you choose that life. A life of never settling down, never making a claim on who you are, who you love, where you love to sit. Once you make those claims, you become accountable. You have to get to work. You have to step into the chaos and grab hold and land.

Dreams end.

That's one thing I'm discovering.

But that doesn't have to be a depressing thing, a sad thing.

Only when dreams end do you get to have a garden. A fifty-acre garden—why not? A garden that includes a giant pond and a beautiful old barn and rolling hills of green—why not? A lifetime project. A lifetime of commitment I am tiptoeing toward.

WHAT ABOUT BOB?" ALEX ASKS ME.

"I don't know," I say.

He's waiting for me to know. To realize. To see.

We're in the kitchen. Riva is frying up some liver for Bob. Riva has been the best thing that ever happened to Bob's life since me. Riva has made nursing Bob, as well as Marley, her life's work. Thanks to Riva's care, Marley is walking without much trouble now, and his poodle fur is coming in. And Bob is, well, comfortable. Riva is Bob's angel, Bob's hospice nurse. She spoons the liver onto a plate, blows on it, gets down on her knees, and feeds it to him by hand.

"Eat, my Mammala Bop," she says. "Eat for Rivka."

"Oh, Rivka," Alex says. "I don't think—"

Bob takes one piece of the liver, chews it. Riva looks at Alex. "See? Rivka knows how to make Bop happy."

Bob is having the happiest end to his life that you can ever hope a best friend to have. That's what I'm thinking, sitting at this kitchen table. I have so much to do. I have this huge wedding file that keeps getting more and more huge. It's strange the way the wedding file grows as Bob shrinks. He's down to seven pounds. He is losing his hair. His shoulder blades are bald.

Somehow it makes a sad sort of sense that Bob should make his exit just as I approach my wedding day.

Cue the mule.

Cue the . . . mule?

I am having more mule doubts. Major mule doubts. Mule nightmares. Really bad feelings about the mule. It would help if the mule would let me pet her—once. If that mule would at least take a carrot from me. But so far, all summer, I have not been able to so much as touch that mule. This is supposed to be Alex's mule. This is supposed to be his new friend. Shouldn't he have a friend that he can actually relate to? I should give Alex Cricket instead. I mean, anyway, how's it going to look when the His and Hers ungulates walk up the driveway? Here's my present to Alex: a goofy, bug-eyed hee-hawing fat little untouchable mule. A joke. And then here's my present to me: a tall, stately, incredibly beautiful chestnut mare, the daughter, on her father's side, of MountJoy's Tasty Tart, the granddaughter of A Perfect Mate To A Perfect Jewel, the great-granddaughter of Light O'Love.

This isn't right. I really need to edit this plan. It is probably a good thing that I have not formed an emotional bond with that mule, because I don't think that mule is right for Alex at all.

"Eat, Mammala Bop," Riva is saying. But Bob doesn't want any more liver.

I open my wedding folder, get to work. Check. Check. I check off things that are done. I have ordered flowers for Sassy's hair and flowers for Cricket's hair. The same arrangements that my bridesmaids will carry.

I have solved, or sort of solved, the garden problem by ordering mums, hundreds and hundreds of mums to put around the farm, and give this place a splash of color. I know, ho hum, mums. But you have to figure mums will be in season in September, and if I get tons and tons and tons of them, all different colors, and group them all over the place, that could really liven this place up. I've contacted a few nurseries. The mums are growing even as we speak. In about a week I'll start collecting them, bring them here, stoke them up with Miracle-Gro, and get them blooming big and pretty for September 13.

I have to buy a few boxes of Miracle-Gro. I have to find a mule halter that matches the lilac color of the bridesmaids' dresses. I am spending a lot of time shopping for this stupid mule halter. I already found a lilac halter for Cricket, a perfect match.

This is stupid. This is so damn obvious. You have to be flexible. A bride has to be flexible.

Sitting here in this kitchen, sifting through this giant file, I make my decision: I'll give Alex Cricket as his wedding present, instead of the mule.

The mule just isn't working.

Cue the horse.

Dump the mule. The mule should go to someone who knows how to work with it, bring it out of its shell. The mule wouldn't be happy here.

I have to tell Billy immediately. We are moving to Plan B. Not that we ever discussed a Plan B.

"You know what," I say to Alex. "I'm going to go . . . to the flower store. I have to check something out with Ernie, the flower guy." This is getting pathetic, my lying ways.

"You want me to come with you?" he asks.

"No!" I say. "I have to deal with a . . . surprise for you." Well, that wasn't a lie.

"All right."

Riva looks at me, throws her shoulders back, sits up straight. She moves her hands across her mouth, as if closing a zipper.

"Thanks, Riva," I say.

I hop in the car, head over to Billy's, head over to pull the plug. I'll give Alex the horse instead of the mule. I'll put all the flowers in Cricket's hair. She will be so beautiful standing there. And I already have the lilac horse halter.

I pull up to Billy's. God, I'm getting so used to this place. I am feeling so at home here. I wonder how Patty's cantaloupes are coming along. And I wonder where Billy's new backhoe is. I've spent a lot of time here this summer. It's like suddenly I have another brother to visit.

Billy lost two dogs this summer. Sam and Ralph were both hit by cars. I think I was more upset than Billy or Tom or Patty or anybody, but maybe it's just my citified way. When I told them about Marley's injury, Billy wondered why we went to the expense of going to a vet. "If he gets too bad, I can shoot him for you," he said.

"Oh," I said. "No thank you."

He has offered to shoot Bob. It is an offer of kindness. I have come to understand this. I have come to understand that he has an entirely different relationship with death.

"Hey there!" Billy says, stepping out of the house. "Why the glum face?"

"A lot to do," I say. "Stress."

"You need me to do something?"

"Yeah."

"Name it."

"Sell the mule," I say. "Give the mule away," I say. "Donate the mule to charity."

"Oh," he says. He seems to take this as a personal rejection. "But Alex would love the mule."

"I don't think so, Billy. I really don't."

He looks at me. He says wait. He goes into the barn, comes out with a handful of grain. He approaches Sassy, slowly, slowly, he gets near to her. Sassy looks at him. Sassy does not turn her backside to him. That's the first remarkable thing. Soon Sassy takes the grain from Billy's hand. Sassy is eating out of Billy's hand.

"What the hell?" I say.

"I've been working with her. She's coming around. She's a good mule. She's just spooky. Mules are spooky."

"I heard."

He retrieves her saddle from the barn, drapes it over her. "Easy, girl." Gently, he climbs on her back. "Giddy up!" he says.

Sassy walks backward.

"Um," he says. "Forward, Sassy!" He nudges her sides and slides his hips up, as if to communicate which way forward is.

Sassy walks sideways, knocking over a bucket of water.

"She did it earlier," he says. "I swear she did."

"Uh-huh."

He climbs off of her. He pulls her toward me. I reach out my arm, offer her a carrot. She leans in. She sniffs. Her lips, smaller than Cricket's lips, reach into the air and find the carrot. She takes it. She chews, a sound higher in pitch than Cricket's chewing. *Clinkity clinkity clink.* It sounds like she's got dentures in there. I put my hand out. I touch her nose. I touch her thick, luxurious mane.

"Aw," I say. "Hello there, Sassafras," I say.

She looks at me. She chews and chews, looking at me with those bulging eyeballs. She is such a goofy thing. And so short! I can put my arm around her like a girlfriend, like a pal. "Sassafras," I say. "Hey, buddy."

Cricket comes bounding over. CARROTS! Cricket scares Sassy away with her big fat horse sense of entitlement. "Back off, Cricket!" I say.

But Sassy is gone. Sassy is like, "Forget it. Whatever." Her backside is back again.

Well, I certainly understand that one. "Forget it. Whatever. Never mind." You don't grow up the youngest in the family without knowing those sentiments. Maybe by turning her backside to the world, the mule is doing what I did. Retreating. Going inward. God, I can't blame her. I note other traits I have in common with this mule. Those bangs. Why did I always have to have such short bangs? And how was it that I was the comic-relief sister, the one who would dance in front of my sisters' boyfriends going tra la la, refusing to let those boys get too close?

How was it that I spent my entire adulthood up to this point living alone?

No matter. Now I am turning into someone else. Now I am getting married. But does that mean abandoning entirely the person I used to be? Does that mean dumping the mule?

Cue the mule.

I imagine holding a contest. A contest with all the animals on our farm. I imagine the mule surprising everyone, winning Wittiest and Peppiest in the Eighth Grade.

Slowly, I approach Sassy again. Billy holds Cricket back. Sassy lets me pet her. She lets me rub her nose. She lets me pull her lip up. What is it with horses and people and lips? We always want to pull their lips up. I look at Sassy with her lips pulled up. I look the gift mule in the mouth. She has the most enormous, beautiful teeth.

"She has the most enormous, beautiful teeth," I say to Billy.

He smiles. Billy has a way of calming me down. Nothing is ever a big deal to Billy. Sort of like Bob. Billy and Bob are so much alike. I wonder why I have this compulsion to pair animals with humans in my life. Humans with animals. I wonder if this has anything to do with my animal soul rescue service.

I am having such a nice time here at Billy's. I'm glad I'm here, with this horse and this mule, standing in the shadow of all this excavation equipment, in a valley created by mountains of limestone and mulch and sand and other things people might need. Who knew this would be such a safe place?

"Well, I got my cancer back," Billy says, while he's combing Cricket's mane. It's hard to tell if he's talking to me or to Cricket.

"Oh," I say. "When?"

"Maybe a couple of months ago," he says.

Well, that would explain his change in mood.

"Is it bad?"

He shrugs.

"How are you feeling?" I ask.

"I got pain in my back. But I always got pain in my back. I sit in the hot tub, and it goes away." He tells me he's not bothering with treatment this time. He did that already. He can't afford the time off. So that is that.

"But—" I say. I don't know where to begin. "Well, what does your doctor have to say about that?" I ask.

"He thinks I'm crazy," he says. And then he laughs. "But I walked away. I said, 'Doc, if I'm dying, I'd rather just go off and die.'"

Sassy is leaning in to me. Wow. Suddenly she's like a cat, rubbing her head into my hand. I can't believe this is the same mule.

"You still want me to get rid of her?" Billy asks.

"We'll keep her," I say.

"Alex is going to love this mule," he says.

"Yeah, but let's make Cricket be his, too. Just in case."

"All right."

"But, well," I say, "Billy, I really think you should go back to the doctor. There's a lot they can do."

"I'm fixing to get myself into the horse business," he says. He leans over and spits a stream of tobacco juice. "I love having these horses here. I always wanted to be in the horse business."

TWENTY

I WISH I WERE LIKE BILLY. A PERSON WITH SOME EX-
perience with death. Some calluses built up. I wish I were a person
who could casually go out back with a .22 and put an animal out of
its misery. A person who used to fly dead people home from distant
car accidents. A person who can talk about death as a part of life. A
person who can stare death in the face and start a horse business.

I am not that person. I am here on the couch with Bob. He's on
my stomach. He's not purring. He hardly ever purrs anymore.
We're watching reruns of *The Bob Newhart Show*.

Tomorrow Alex is taking him. Because this is what
we've decided.

Alex will take Bob to the vet to be put to sleep, and then he and
I will bury Bob.

"Under the chestnut grove," Alex suggested.

"No," I said, "the magic tree."

"The magic tree," he said. "Of course." The magic tree is the
apple tree Alex worked on last spring, spent the whole weekend clearing, while we waited to hear the truth about whatever it

was that was growing inside him. We've called it "the magic tree" ever since.

Alex said I should spend time with Bob, share stories with Bob, remember me and remember him in my fancy single-girl-on-the-town days.

But lying here on this couch, I can't remember anything.

I'm blank.

On the TV, Bob Newhart is having an argument with Jerry, the dentist. Something about tickets to a basketball game. Bob stomps off, pushes the elevator button, and when the doors open, there's Mr. Carlin, his patient with the funny toupee.

Come to think of it, Bob, you do kind of look like Bob Newhart. But that isn't who you're named after. In fact, your name didn't start out as Bob. Did you know that? I named you Katukas. That's the Lithuanian word for kitten. Katukas. But I didn't feel like saying Katukas. It was too big a word for a little kitten. And then one day I said, "Bob Katukas." I laughed. I thought it sounded like the name of a used-car salesman. I thought it was funny to have a cat with a career as a used-car salesman. Ever since, I called you Bob.

Bob has fallen asleep. He's riding my stomach as it rises and falls with my breath. We used to do this, outside on the chaise longue, in the South Side yard. I would stretch out with a good book under the mulberry tree, and Bob would join me. I would argue with Bob. Because he would always want to lie on my stomach. And I wanted to have my book there. You couldn't read and have Bob on your stomach at the same time. I think Bob knew this. I think he wanted my undivided attention. Eventually, I would put my book down, Bob would climb up, and so I would read Bob. I would marvel at his whiskers. I would tell him how proud I was of his mighty tail. I would ask him to please do something about his long nails. Sometimes mulberries would plop, splat right on us. We'd go inside with purple blotches all over, laughing, but not really laughing, because cats don't laugh out loud.

I can picture Bob. I can picture him rolling, scratching his back on the red brick patio. I can see him sitting on the roof and waiting for pigeons to land, and I can hear people saying what they always said: "That cat has a good life." That cat was the embodiment of a good life. Looking at that cat snoozing in the sun, you felt hope for your own retirement.

You did a good job, Bob. Thank you. Thank you for giving me the courage to love. Thank you, Bob, for ushering me into married life.

He looks peaceful. He's breathing short, quick breaths, as cats do. He is so thin. But his whiskers are still strong. I think of those whiskers as swords. Swords of a fighter, a champion. He has a tear on his ear, a jagged edge. *Oh, God, Bob. Remember that fight?* Bob came inside a beaten-up Ram-Bob, torn up. *But we patched you back up.*

Bob has freckles on his lips. Bob has freckles around his eyelids. I think Bob is Irish on his mother's side. Bob has a bone on the top of his head, a little nub that sticks up. It's his sweet spot. It's the spot he loves me to touch the best. I take my index finger and gently scratch.

I can feel a purr, the tiniest purr from him, resonating into me, my ribs, my lungs, my core.

I love you, Bob.

The truth is sometimes so simple, it sounds stupid. Sometimes it's embarrassing to speak the truth.

"I love you, Bob."

But love doesn't mean you're strong. You can be a weakling and still love. I am a weakling. If I were strong, I would go with Bob. I would be with Bob, hold him, cradle him when they put the needle in him and he falls asleep for the last time. If I were strong, I would be there with him. This is the act of love that should be my final gift.

And I can't do it.

I am sorry, Bob. I am truly sorry. But I'm not going to go.

Instead, Alex will do it. Alex will be with Bob, hold Bob while life leaves him. Talk about an act of love.

You'll never get a chance to meet Sassy, Bob. Or Cricket either. I wish you could have made it until the wedding, Bob. At least until the wedding. Or maybe until my thirty-ninth birthday. But that is just my wish for me.

I look around this room, the big room, the room where the dancing will be. This room will be so full. I'll twirl and stomp and be a bride, and I wonder if I'll think of Bob. I wonder if I'll forgive myself for not holding him as he dies.

I am not strong enough.

Instead I lie here, doing all I know to do. I scratch his sweet spot. I talk to him, but not technically. Because I never say the words out loud. And Bob does not talk back with any cat telepathy or anything. We're normal, me and Bob. We are not the kind of overinvolved cat and cat owner you see in photographs on bags of premium cat food or anything. But we are a unit, me and Bob. Soon, a sleeping unit. I'm drifting. He's letting out a little snore, a gentle jiggle in his throat. I scratch his sweet spot. *I am a crusader for the eternal life of all animals, Bob. In the name of the Father and of the Son and of the Holy Spirit.*

MORNING IS A BLUR. ONE OF THOSE DAYS YOU can't wear your contacts because of the tears that won't stop. I feel like a delirious toddler, waking up from a bad dream, but not waking up at all.

Amy is here. Other family members will start to arrive tomorrow to help with the wedding. Amy says she'll go with her dad. She'll hold Bob in the car so he doesn't have to be in some uncomfortable cat carrier.

Amy picks Bob up, cradles him.

Riva is in the kitchen, her arms crossed tight, crying. "Bye-bye, Mammala Bop. I love you, Bop." She kisses him. She reaches out and strokes him with her thick, muscular hands, hands of power, hands of mercy.

The dogs have gathered. I don't know how they know, what they know. But they're here. Amy kneels, and one by one those dogs go up to Bob. First Betty. She sniffs. Then Wilma. She licks Bob on the head. Then Marley. He sits, looks, cocks his head. The three of them now, sitting here lined up, gazing at Bob. They look as if they might soon break into a mournful three-part harmony of "Amazing Grace." How do you account for sorrow on the part of two mutts and a poodle?

Riva, Alex, Amy, the three dogs, and me. All of us standing here, forming a good-bye circle around Bob. For so long, I was all the love Bob had, all the love he needed. And now look. Now he is surrounded.

"Good-bye, Bob," I say. I touch him one last time, a gentle scratch on the sweet spot.

Alex and Amy get in the car, and they take Bob away. The car goes slowly down the driveway, making that crunching sound, the crunching sound of leaving. The worst sound in the world.

I head down to the barn. It's hot. It's so hot. And I can't see anything. And I'm sweating. And I wish it would rain. It's so hot. I get a shovel and a pick and some other tools that look like they might do the job.

I trudge up the hill. The hill I fell in love with. The hill that today just feels like hard work to climb. I go to the magic tree. It's a most beautiful tree, standing here alone and free. I guess you could call it a mournful tree, the way the branches hang so low, the way the whole thing droops. But in the spring, the blooms are white and hopeful. And everyone visits this tree. Everyone who ever hikes up this hill visits this tree. It's our most popular tree.

I take the pick, hold it over my shoulder with two hands, and with all my oomph pitch it forward, over my head and down, *thud,* on the ground. The hardest ground. Thank God. I am grateful for this packed earth that barely moves, barely budges, even with the piercing of this pick. This is dry ground. This is dried clay. This is the worst kind of dirt to dig. So I will be here for hours, it seems, digging this grave. Is this how digging graves started? Is this how the first humans got the idea to bury the dead? Because they needed to pound . . . some . . . thing. Really hard. Just . . . pound . . . and . . . poke . . . and . . . jab . . . over and over again . . . sweating . . . and . . . sob . . . bing . . . and expelling and howling in the thick summer air.

I wish I would faint. I wish I would keel over with sunstroke. There must be some way out of my steaming hot head.

It feels like a century passes before I have the hole deep enough. Well, I guess this is deep enough. I mean, I don't know how deep to dig. How big to make this hole. How am I supposed to know? I'm thirsty. I'm done. I am doing everything in my power to erase the picture of Bob in my head, the picture of a needle, the picture of life leaving him without me there.

I go down to the house to wait for Alex and Amy. I open the door and see Riva sitting on the couch, watching a soap opera with Marley. Riva has been escorting Marley into a full-blown soap opera stage. It suits him. He's happy. He's relaxed. Riva is twirling his poodle curls, which have grown back so rich and full.

"Did you finish?" she asks.

"Yeah. When they come back, we'll take him up. Will you join us?"

"I cannot," she says. "I am sorry but I cannot." Something about her family. Something about all those graves that never got dug.

"I understand," I say, even though I know I can't.

Roo roo roo roo. Betty announces the return of the car. I look out the window. I see Amy get out with the box.

I go outside and meet them. It's hot. It's so hot out.

"Hi, baby," Alex says, reaching for my shoulder. "It was really peaceful."

"It was," Amy says. I'm looking into her blue eyes, focusing on her eyes, because I don't want to look at the box.

"Let's bury him," I say. "I really need to get this over with."

Alex carries the box. We head up the hill. I mean, I guess we do. I don't know where we're going. I'm looking down. All I see is ground. Blurry ground. Like a kid in a baseball game who just missed the ball and lost the game and everyone is yelling, berating, saying you're no good.

Soon we are at the hole in the ground. Alex puts the box in. That's it. Just a shoebox in the ground. Size seven and a half. Pink lettering. Something about cushioned soles. He covers the box with a shovelful of dirt. It lands, *clunk*. He shovels more in. And more. He pats the earth.

"You want to say something about Bob?" he asks.

I shake my head back and forth fast, sort of like I did in seventh grade when my home ec teacher asked me if I meant to start that fire, which I truly did not.

"I'll say something," he says. "Thank you, Bob," he says. He tells how Bob welcomed him into the South Side yard, at a time he didn't feel welcomed much of anywhere. He tells us Bob made a difference in his life.

We put a big rock to mark the spot where Bob is. I plant a purple mum.

I sob the whole way back down the hill, apologizing to Amy, saying I know this is so stupid.

"It's not stupid," she says, grabbing a handful of Queen Anne's lace, offering it to me. "It's not stupid at all."

"Let me cancel the appointment for you," Alex says as we head into the house.

"No, I'll be fine by then," I say. The appointment is for tonight. My God, of all nights. Wedding World. My final bridal gown fitting. Oh, God, if I have to face that lady with those knots in her hair. Oh, Lord.

"Just go to bed and eat bonbons," Alex says, leading me into the bedroom. "Don't even think of doing anything today."

"I'm taking this kind of hard, don't you think?" I say.

"No," he says. "I think you're taking it soft. I think your heart is very, very soft."

"Mush," I say.

"I think a soft heart is the strongest kind." He pulls back the covers, fluffs the pillow. I get in.

"But I'm afraid I'll never get over it," I say. "A cat! Isn't that stupid?"

"Loss is loss," he says.

"And grief is grief," I say, remembering the lesson.

"And a friend is a friend," he says. "Bob was your friend." He puts his hand on my cheek, because he knows this is what my father did when I was a kid, a crying kid, this was what he always did.

"And I don't think anybody ever gets over loss," he says. "I think you get through it. You let it get through you."

He knows. He has experience with death. But he doesn't have calluses built up. Instead, I think his heart has become elastic. His heart can hold a lot.

He steps out of the room. I can hear the screen door open. "Come on, girl," he says. Betty. He brings Betty in. God, I feel like a crazy lady heading into a coma, and he's bringing in the loved ones. "Up here, girl," he says, patting the bed. Betty is never allowed in the bed. Betty can't believe this is happening. Betty seizes the opportunity, jumps up, curls beside me.

I scratch her head. She has a bone on the top, a little nub that sticks up. It's her sweet spot. I scratch the sweet spot.

She stays with me all day, snoozes, lies on her back, and sticks her right foot up high in the air like a TV antenna. Which I don't actually need. I have five hundred million thousand TV channels. I have a satellite dish. There is nothing on the five hundred million thousand TV channels. I fall asleep. I awaken. I fall back asleep.

I awaken. I think how I had to pick today of all days for a wedding gown fitting. Good Lord. What a stupid day to have a wedding gown fitting. But if I don't go, the gown won't be done in time. I wonder if they'll be able to tell I've been crying. I wonder when the hell I'm going to stop crying.

I emerge from the bedroom, feeling like Bette Davis or one of those old lady actresses who could really do loony.

"You're okay?" Riva says as I enter the kitchen.

"I'm okay," I say. "You?"

"Terrible. I am missing Bop so terrible."

"I know. You were his angel, Riva. Thank you."

"My little Bop. He is feeling no more pain, no more weakness."

"I have to go," I say. "I have to go to the stupid wedding gown store."

"I know this," she says. "Alinka say me. Alinka and Aminka,

they went to buy food. They will prepare for us a very nice meal. They will take care of us."

I love that Riva is sharing in my sorrow. I love her for this.

I grab my keys, tell her good-bye, head out.

It feels good to drive up Wilson Road. It feels good to get away. Not as good as a tranquilizer, probably, but definitely in the right direction.

I go zooming. I zoom down Daniel's Run Road, my official favorite tar and chip road. I blast the radio, blast it big, feel the roar of sound bouncing in my pores. I pass cows and chickens and pigs. I pass pretty little barns and a stately old farmhouse with a pool. I'm late. I should have left a half hour ago. But hey, a bride's gotta go on her own clock. A bride! Here comes the bride! I am in my bride stage. Big-time. A bride should not have to . . . A bride! A bride should not . . .

My God! These tears. Why can't I stop crying? I am eight years old, trying to make it through one day of school without crying. One stinkin' day.

I don't have crying brakes. How do you get crying brakes? A bride! A bride should not be this miserable.

I am zooming. I see cows and sheep and a few horses passing by my window, and I see—whoa! A chipmunk darts in front of the car. *Screeeeeech!* I jam on my brakes, narrowly missing it. I inch toward it, to confirm that I missed it. I roll down my window, turn down the radio. I look out my window and see—wait a second, it's not a chipmunk at all. It's a little gray kitten.

Kitten?

That is one tiny kitten. I hop out of the car, look around for a house, a barn, a cat. A mother. But there is nothing here. Nothing but cornfields. This kitten is too little to be away from the litter. This kitten would fit in the palm of my hand. I pick the kitten up.

A kitten.

I look up at the sky.

You have got to be kidding, Bob. You-have-got-to-be-kidding.

I look at the kitten. Does the kitten have . . . a message or something?

Oh, this is ridiculous.

I must have let you watch way too many made-for-TV movies, Bob.

I look everywhere for the source of the kitten. But everywhere is corn. There is no way this kitten will survive if I leave him here. A bird will come. A dog will come. Or the kitten will starve.

A kitten.

I put the kitten in the car, make a U-turn.

Okay, I am not going to talk to you, Kitten. I am not going to start talking to you. Bob, if this is your idea of a joke, I don't know. . . .

I head back to the farm, pull up the driveway, go running inside. It's not been ten minutes since I left. Riva is sitting in the kitchen. She looks at me. I am speechless. I hold my arms out, presenting her with the gift from the sky. Or the road.

Her eyes widen. Her mouth drops. She holds her hands in the air. "It's a miracle!" she says.

I am so glad she said that, because there is no way I could say it.

"Can you believe it?" I say, and burst back into tears.

She bursts into tears.

This is really getting ridiculous.

We go into fits of laughter, bending over, folding over, tears and laughter all jumbled up. The kitten is on the kitchen table, chasing its tail.

"We can't call him Bob, though," I say. "We really can't."

"Of course, of course, of course," she says.

She asks me to tell her how it happened that I found him, exactly how it happened. And so I do. I tell her I was zooming, I saw a chipmunk—*screeeech!*—I got out, saw that it wasn't a chipmunk. She listens carefully, as only a person fluent in eight languages can listen.

"Screech," she says, looking at the kitten, stroking his tiny head, barely bigger than her thumb. "Rivka has named the miracle cat Screech."

TWENTY-ONE

BOB IS GONE. SCREECH IS HERE. SASSY IS ACCEPT-
ing carrots. Marley is mange-free, is walking normally, is enjoying
The Young and the Restless every day at noon. My dress fits. The
wedding is a week away. On the one hand, you could say things are
really coming together.

Well, one little slip. Marley caught a groundhog the other day.
This put a damper on things.

"You're regressing, Marley boy," I said to him when he showed
up with the floppy thing hanging from his mouth. *"Regressing."*

I am standing on the roof of the garage, watering mums. I put
the mums here, temporarily, to keep them away from the dogs. It's a
flat roof. A red roof. I like it here. I am at peace here. On top of the
farm, on top of the people I love, on top of the world I have come
to call my own. Watering mums. Very thirsty mums. Because still
we have no rain. And still the tractor is not fixed. Still the grass is
brown and long.

I should call Nancy. I should verify that a bride should not, repeat *not* have to worry about these things.

A bride. I am the bride. My inner princess is fully present. I like my inner princess, I like her just fine. Although I have to say, she and I don't have a lot to talk about. Well, you don't expect intellectual stimulation from your inner princess, any more than you expect it from sheep. Basically, my inner princess and I, we shop. We buy fancy toiletries, and we primp for long hours in the tub. We discovered exfoliating the other day. Oh, she thought that was a blast. "Party time!" my inner princess said when I opened the jar of Aloe 'N Peach body scrub, scooped out some of the scratchy gook, wiped it on my leg, and started sloughing. "Excellent!" she said. It was a whole new way of relating to dead skin.

I go along with this. Because I am the bride.

One thing I am finding is that farms and brides are not the most natural match. When you are a bride, your need for perfection is heightened. Perfect hair, perfect nails, perfect groom, perfect mother, perfect sister, perfect . . . farm?

I am so, so far away from the ordered life I once had.

The farm is still not ready for 150 guests and lots of cameras. It really is not. We need to mow. We need the tractor parts to come in. We need those UPS workers to get back to work. We need rain. We need to put these mums around.

It has taken me a long time to accumulate all these mums. I had some setbacks. I drove around for days in the Elly May Clampett pickup with bullet holes in it, buying mums. I spent six hundred dollars on mums. I placed them carefully in a sunny spot behind the barn and watered them. Wilma chewed about two hundred dollars' worth. She did this one morning, while we were all up at the Century Inn making plans. I came back, saw all the chewed mums, and yelled, "Willl-maaa!" I taught Wilma to stay away from the mums, and while I was at it, I lectured Betty and Marley, too.

More family started to roll in. My sister Kristin, from New York, and Katie, her six-year-old daughter, my flower girl. They brought their dog, Nala. Nala is Wilma's sister; they were born in the same barn in Philly.

Nala chewed about a hundred dollars' worth of mums. She did

this at night, while we were all asleep. I woke up, saw all those chewed mums, and yelled at Nala, taught her to stay away from the mums, and while I was at it, I lectured Betty and Marley and Wilma again, too.

Peter arrived with his dog, Quentin. Quentin is no relation to Wilma or Nala. Quentin chewed fifty dollars' worth of mums. He did this while we were all up at Tradesmen's, having wings. I came home, saw all those chewed mums. I considered yelling at Quentin, I considered howling into the night air at all the dogs that ever lived.

Instead, I put the surviving mums on the roof of the garage.

The next day I climbed the ladder to check on those mums. Oh, dear. Half of those mums had baked in the sun. I watered the survivors, about ten measly mums. I headed out in the pickup and bought six hundred dollars' worth of more mums. Now I water them religiously, two and three times a day.

There will be flowers on this farm on my wedding day, if I have to kill someone.

I like taking care of these mums. I like it up here on this roof. Away from all those dogs and all those people and all that noise. It's a way of focusing. A bride needs to focus. There are purple mums and yellow mums and white mums and pink mums with yellow centers.

The water shuts off.

"Hey!" I shout, and walk over to see who's down there at the spigot. No one. "Hey!" I yell.

Riva pokes her head out the kitchen window. "Hey!" she shouts. "I haff no water!"

Water.

I climb down the ladder and find Alex in the barn. "What happened to the water?" I ask.

"Water?"

We go into the basement. He primes the pump a few times. Riva comes down. We stand here, waiting for the news. "It's dry," Alex says. "We are out of water."

Oh.

Apparently, the well went dry from all the water I used on the mums.

"Whoops," I say, wondering how I can separate myself, how I can step out of myself, how I can stand here and put the blame on my stupid inner princess. She ain't no rocket scientist. She knew there was a drought emergency.

"Whoops," I say, hearing a little chirp in my head. A peep. An inner princess in crisis over her next shampoo.

"Hey!" Peter says, coming down to the basement. He has a towel wrapped around his waist, his hair is covered in suds. He's holding the cordless phone. "The phone is dead, too." The phone? Water? Drought? Shampoo? Is there a connection?

I go out to the car, get the cell phone, call the phone company. "Hello?"

"Is this the phone company?"

"Speaking."

"Well, our phone is dead."

"All right. When Tom comes in, I'll tell him."

Tom? The same Tom who was on the pole the last time this happened? I am beginning to suspect that there is no Tom, there is no pole. When did Tom plan on coming in?

"He's in a ditch, so I don't know."

The phone lady says no, she doesn't know of any connection between phones and water and shampoo. "I'll send Tom out," she says.

No phone. No water. No usable toilet. No shower. Seven people here. Four more arriving tomorrow. Five dogs here. A wedding in a week. No tractor. Long grass. Brown grass. Place looks like hell. Mums need water. Inner princess needs to exfoliate again. "Shut up, inner princess. Take a nap."

I am glad Screech is here. There is nothing like a new baby in the house to get people's minds off death and drought and sewage problems.

Riva and Amy have been fawning all over Screech, and so has Katie, my niece. Oh, Katie loves that little kitten. That little kitten has given her life meaning. She has drawn pictures of Screech. She has them hung up on the basement walls surrounding his little kitten bed. She has asked me if she could please take Screech home with her. She has begged me. I haven't quite known how to handle this question. I want to explain to her the symbolic nature of Screech, want to explain to her who Screech is to me, where Screech really came from, but I don't know where to begin.

"Why don't we go to the Humane Society and get you a little kitten of your own?" I said to her this morning.

She gazed up at me with her intelligent green eyes. She just as quickly looked away. Her hair was in braids, with purple barrettes at the end of each, and she had a loose tooth in front. She held the kitten up to her cheek. "My baby Screech," she said. "Come on, Screechie, let's go outside. You're the only one that understands."

I looked at Katie and saw myself, and not for the first time. I wondered if she had a place she went to, a secret place to separate, to differentiate herself from the world. I wondered what God has ever said to her, and if she believes in animal souls.

And now I am back up here on the roof of this garage. It is easier to be here than deal with the water situation, the tractor, the drought, the phone, the toilet that won't flush. Because I need to think. A bride needs to think. Well, no she doesn't. But a bride does need to *bathe*. I can only hope that I get an actual bath on the morning of my wedding.

I like it here on this roof. I have a clear head here. I wonder how Sassy and Cricket are. I wonder how Billy is. I wish he would go back to his doctor. I wonder how he will fix Sassy's hair for the wedding. He did find a lilac mule halter, right? Yes, he did. So that's good. And on the morning of the wedding, Nancy is going to deliver the flowers to him for their hair. Nancy is a trouper. Nancy is having a normal wedding. A nighttime service in a beautiful old mansion, with a deejay and dancing and no worries about drought or phones or tractor parts.

It seems so simple, her life.

It's hot up here on this roof. It's hot, but I don't mind. The roof is red. Tin. I am standing on a hot tin roof. I am a person on a hot tin roof. So naturally, I mean, of course I think about Bob. In my quietest moments, I think he sent Screech to me because he couldn't make it to the wedding, couldn't last. He tried, but his little body would not hold on. He sent Screech as his lieutenant. Or no, he sent Screech because he knew my grief was too much for me to bear. In my quietest moments, I think he sent Screech to help get me through.

My quietest moments. Up on the roof of this garage, I have my quietest moments. The roof is red. The garage is next to the barn. The roof is red just like the shed was red. The shed at the farm behind our house on Lorraine Drive. The shed I would escape to as a kid. The place I would go to cry, to think, to form opinions, to draw pictures and write letters to God.

I am back at the shed. Back at that place of solace, of solitude.

Only now I am on top of the shed instead of inside it. That's how far I've come.

That may not sound like very far. But I'm telling you, it is. Because I am learning something about sheds. About solitude. About inward and outward. The self is like a shed, a thing you enter and exit. At first that's about all you can do, like a turtle going in and out of a shell. And maybe that's enough. Maybe you can go your whole life only knowing inward and outward, inward and outward.

But I have discovered above. And above has led me to suspect that maybe there is a below, too. A beside and an in front of. The self is like a shed. A thing you enter and exit. But a thing with many other dimensions, too. I am just beginning. I am on top of the shed. Knowing the self is knowing how to climb and dig. And maybe how to do a headstand, too. I am on top of the shed. Someday maybe I'll do a headstand behind it. Someday maybe I'll bounce a ball on it, paint a picture of it, train a morning glory vine to grow all over it.

The self is like a shed. There may be infinite ways of relating to it, infinite perspectives, but I don't know. I am just beginning. I am on top of the shed.

Alex comes out of the basement. He has his overalls on again, and his cute little tool belt. I know; men don't like to hear that their tool belts are cute, but this one is. He sees me sitting up on the garage roof. "You up there again?" he says. "Why don't you come down here with me?"

"I have to watch the mums," I say.

"I know," he says. "But just take a break with me, and we'll come back and watch the mums together."

I consider this. "You promise?"

"I promise."

This is one of the good things about marrying a shrink. He doesn't ever regard you as crazy, not even if you are sitting for hours and hours on a garage roof, baby-sitting mums. He can talk you down.

I climb down the ladder. "Let's get out of here," he says. "Let's go to the mailbox."

A wonderful idea. Let's run away from drought and tractor parts and sewage problems. I could use a walk. I could use some time alone with him.

We sneak away so even the dogs don't see us.

There are all new weeds on the side of Wilson Road. This week's feature: purple. The brightest purple. They're like feathers sticking up, lacy feathers set against the deepest, bluest green. And because Mother Nature has an eye for flower arranging, there are orange speckles reaching out of the green, adding dimension. I wonder what these orange things are, what these purple things are.

I have to get a weed book.

I have to get a wildflower book.

I have to get a mule book and a horse book, too.

Alex and I hold hands and wander without purpose into the late summer sun. Our feet make a crackling sound on the bed of red dog. Red dog. What a funny name for a road surface.

"One week," Alex says. "In one week we will be married. You scared?"

"Not about marrying you," I say. "Are you?"

"No," he says. "The hard part is over."

"Well, the hard part will be over in a week," I say. "My inner princess is, like, totally exhausted."

He smiles. "She's been through a lot," he says.

"She still hasn't even figured out which shade of self-tanner to use."

"Poor thing."

"And your inner prince?" I ask.

"Um," he says. I can tell he hasn't even thought about his inner prince.

"My inner prince has one request," he says.

"Oh?"

"A waltz," he says. "On our wedding day."

"All right," I say, thinking: Oh God, I have to get a waltz book.

"You promise?" he says.

"I promise."

"But you have to learn how to waltz," he says.

"One more thing to do," I say. "Do, do, do."

"I'll teach you right now," he says.

"Here?"

"Right here in front of George's sheep."

"Baaa," I say, to no one sheep in particular, to the scenery, to the view. The view. The beautiful postcard view we first fell in love with a year ago. The place where I met the hunters. The place where we saw the dead deer hanging off the tree.

"Baa," I say. The sheep are separated from a cornfield by an electric fence. The corn is planted in a wave pattern; I wonder if that's to make it look prettier, but I doubt it.

Baa, the sheep say back. Only it's more like *mehh.*

Alex gets a rock. He carves a line in the red dog, draws a square. "Waltzing starts with a box," he says. He draws little ovals in the box. "Feet," he says. "These are your feet."

"All right," I say. "But I take a size seven and a half."

He makes the ovals bigger. He begins a somewhat lengthy explanation of the movement of one's feet when one does a waltz.

"It sounds kind of science-y," I say. I'm more of a do-your-own-thing dancer.

He stands in the box and holds his arms in the air, as if holding on to me. In this moment, he looks exactly like I imagine Arthur Murray to look. Except in overalls. And with sheep behind him.

Mehhh. Mehhhh.

"It's okay, sheep," I say. "He's okay. But thank you for your concern."

"*Rut* ta ta," Alex says. "*Rut* ta ta. *Rut* ta ta." He dances with the air. "Do you see the pattern?"

"Sort of," I say. "I think I need to feel it more. Let me in, coach."

He takes my waist in his right hand. No, left. No, how do we do this?

"Let go," he says. "I'm in charge. You follow."

Oh, dear. But I am a train. I am a train who is used to chugging on her own power.

"Let go!" he says, holding my wrist, shaking it, wobbling it. "Let your muscles relax. I'm in charge."

"Gotcha," I say.

Mehh, the sheep say.

"Quiet, girls," I say to them. "This is important."

He holds me close, so close that he can whisper in my ear. "Just follow," he says. "*One* two three, *one* two three." *One* two three, *one* two three. Our feet crackle on the red dog. The sheep watch. The hills stretch out onto the horizon, as if cuddled beneath quilts of corn, quilts with a pretty swirling pattern.

One two three, *one* two three. He holds me. He moves me. I step on his toes.

One two three, *one* two three. He holds me. He moves me. He sings gently in my ear. "Can I have this dance," he sings. "*Rut* ta ta . . . for the rest of my life . . ."

"You can have this dance," I sing, as I watch my feet, work on the box pattern. "And I'll be your wife."

"*Rut* ta ta," he sings. "And we'll eat steak with a knife."